Studies in Celtic History XVI

GRUFFUDD AP CYNAN

The reign of the North Welsh king Gruffudd ap Cynan (1075–1135) marked the culmination of a century of rapid social and political change. A product of three cultures (Welsh, Irish and Scandinavian), Gruffudd faced a Wales divided by Norman incursion and dynastic rivalry, and demonstrated a unique adaptability. His re-creation of his North Welsh kingdom saw him acting on the wider (and often deadly) stage of Anglo-Norman politics, and surviving where more 'traditional' Welsh rulers failed. His reign encouraged a new growth in Welsh literature and creativity, and is often looked upon as a literary 'golden age'. This collaborative biography analyses key aspects of the career and context of this remarkable king.
Dr K. L. MAUND teaches in the School of History and Archaeology, University of Wales, Cardiff.

STUDIES IN CELTIC HISTORY
ISSN 0261–9865

Already published

GRUFFUDD AP CYNAN
A COLLABORATIVE BIOGRAPHY

edited by

K. L. MAUND

THE BOYDELL PRESS

First published 1996
The Boydell Press, Woodbridge

ISBN 0 85115 389 5

The Boydell Press is an imprint of Boydell & Brewer Ltd
PO Box 9, Woodbridge, Suffolk IP12 3DF, UK
and of Boydell & Brewer Inc.
PO Box 41026, Rochester, NY 14604–4126, USA

British Library Cataloguing in Publication Data
Gruffudd ap Cynan : a collaborative biography. – (Studies
in Celtic history ; 16)
1. Gruffudd ap Cynan, ca. 1055–1137   2. Wales – Kings and
rulers – Biography   3. Wales – History – 1063–1284
I. Maund, K. L., 1962–
942.9'02'092

Library of Congress Cataloging-in-Publication Data
Gruffudd ap Cynan : a collaborative biography / edited by K.L. Maund.
     p.   cm. – (Studies in Celtic history, ISSN 0261–9865 ; 16)
Includes bibliographical references (p.   ) and index.
ISBN 0–85115–389–5 (acid-free paper)
  1. Gruffydd ab Cynan, King of Gwynedd, 1055?–1137.   2. Wales –
Civilization – Scandinavian influences.   3. Gwynedd (Wales) – Kings
and rulers – Biography.   4. Wales, North – Kings and rulers –
Biography.   5. Wales – Civilization – Irish influences.
6. Civilization, Medieval – 12th century.   7. Wales – History –
1063–1284.   8. Normans – Wales – History.   I. Maund, K. L., 1962–   .
II. Series.
DA716.G77G78   1996
942.902–DC20   96–24757

This publication is printed on acid-free paper

Printed in Great Britain by
St Edmundsbury Press Ltd, Bury St Edmunds, Suffolk

CONTENTS

GENERAL EDITOR'S FOREWORD

In this volume Dr Maund has gathered a sheaf of varied, interesting, and often provocative studies which offer various views of that enigmatic king of Gwynedd, Gruffudd ap Cynan. Gruffudd would be an extraordinary figure of the political life of the Cambro-Norman era even without the existence of his mediaeval biography. That searching questions about the origin, date, and reliability of *Historia Gruffud vab Kenan* are now being asked is a tribute to her imagination and tenacity: she began the process in an earlier volume of *Studies in Celtic History* and in various periodicals, and it is carried in several new directions by the authors of this 'collaborative biography'. But there is much more here: significant contributions to our understanding of the context of Gruffudd's rule, a major re-assessment of Meilyr Brydydd's elegy for Gruffudd and its place in the literature of the period, and the first study devoted specially to the Neo-Latin translation of the *Historia* from Welsh. It is a pleasure to welcome these scholars to *Studies in Celtic History* and to commend their contributions to all students of eleventh- and twelfth-century history and culture.

David N. Dumville
Girton College,
Cambridge

EDITOR'S PREFACE

Gruffudd ap Cynan, king of Gwynedd 1095–1137, occupies a unique place in Welsh history. His long and chequered career was the culmination of a century of rapid social and political change, and combined Scandinavian free-booting with the legacy of expansion and exploitation left by his predecessors Gruffudd ap Llywelyn (1039–1063) and Bleddyn ap Cynfyn (1063–1075). A product of three cultures (Welsh, Irish, and Scandinavian), Gruffudd faced a Wales divided by Norman incursion and dynastic rivalry, and he demonstrated a unique adaptability. In re-establishing the kingdom of Gwynedd, he acted on the wider stage of Anglo-Norman politics, and survived where more traditional Welsh rulers failed. In doing this, he also refounded the hegemony of the dynasty of Rhodri Mawr in Gwynedd, giving rise both to a direct line of succession, which included Llywelyn ab Iorwerth and Llywelyn ap Gruffudd, and to a new ideology of dynastic legitimacy. From his beginnings as a Hiberno-Scandinavian-style raider operating throughout the Irish-Sea province, Gruffudd proved himself an able practical politician, possessed of the skills necessary for success in a rapidly changing environment. He made use of his Irish and Scandinavian connexions to build valuable military relationships with Irish and Hiberno-Scandinavian rulers. He avoided the internal dynastic strife which weakened his contemporaries within Wales itself, and, arguably, he remade his kingship in Gwynedd on a recognisable Norman model. The thirty years of comparative stability with which his reign ended seem also to have encouraged a new growth in Welsh literature and creativity; and his reign is often looked upon as a literary 'golden age'. His achievements were commemorated in *Historia Gruffud vab Kenan*, the first extant biography of any Welsh king, and a valuable, though controversial, source for the history of mediaeval Wales.

The present volume brings together a variety of scholars in a collection of essays concerned with the various aspects of the life and context of this remarkable king. Dr David Moore discusses the Welsh background to Gruffudd's activities, analysing the personalities, events, and institutions which allowed Gruffudd to establish and maintain the stable kingdom from which his heirs were to benefit. Dr C. P. Lewis analyses the Norman impact upon Gwynedd and the complexities of their changing relations with, and reactions to, North Wales in the turbulent years at the end of the eleventh century. Dr David Thornton places Gruffudd in his ideological and dynastic framework – Welsh, Irish and Scandinavian – in a detailed discussion of the

pedigrees preserved in the *Historia*. In my own contribution I have discussed the ideology of legitimacy in the same text. Dr Judith Jesch provides
a valuable insight into a little-explored area of Gruffudd's career, in her
analysis of the Scandinavian aspects of the *Historia*. Dr Nerys Ann Jones
draws attention to the construction of the biography itself, and raises new
and exciting questions concerning its date, form, and purpose. The later
history and context of the *Historia* are explored in Mr Ceri Davies's
discussion of its sixteenth-century translation into Latin. Finally, Professor
J. E. Caerwyn Williams contributes a much-needed new text and translation
of, and commentary on, Meilyr Brydydd's Elegy for Gruffudd, focussing
attention on the literary activity associated with his reign.

Gruffudd ap Cynan lived in interesting times: it is hoped that this
interdisciplinary collection of papers will illuminate our understanding of
the man, the period in which he lived, and the legacy which he left.

K. L. Maund
School of History and Archaeology,
University of Wales, Cardiff

ABBREVIATIONS

ABT	The Welsh genealogical tract *Achau Brenhinoedd a Thywysogion Cymru*
AC (B)	The B-text of *Annales Cambriae*
AC (C)	The C-text of *Annales Cambriae*
AI	The Annals of Inisfallen
ALC	The Annals of Loch Cé
ASC (C)	The C-text of the Anglo-Saxon Chronicle
ASC (D)	The D-text of the Anglo-Saxon Chronicle
ASC (E)	The E-text of the Anglo-Saxon Chronicle
AT	The Annals of Tigernach
AU	The Annals of Ulster
ByS	*Brenhinedd y Saesson*
ByT (Pen. 20)	*Brut y Tywysogion*, Peniarth MS. 20 version
ByT (RB)	*Brut y Tywysogion*, Red Book of Hergest version
JC	The Welsh genealogies in Oxford, Jesus College, MS. 20

I

GRUFFUDD AP CYNAN AND
THE MEDIAEVAL WELSH POLITY

David Moore

Gruffudd ap Cynan's direct descendants ruled Gwynedd without interruption for almost 150 years after his death. By the time that Llywelyn ap Gruffudd was killed in 1282, the princes of Gwynedd had made far-reaching claims, and had in many ways almost accomplished a revolution in the structure of the mediaeval Welsh polity. They styled themselves princes of Wales, claiming the homage of other native rulers, and in trying to give permanence to their hegemony they went out of their way to seek the king of England's recognition of this new status. In creating a new '*principatus*', the thirteenth-century princes asserted that there was such a thing as a political Welsh nation, and they went to great pains to ensure that their dominions were inherited in their entirety by a single heir of the prince's body.[1]

In contrast, Gruffudd ap Cynan's Gwynedd was torn by dynastic rivalry and even partially conquered by Norman invaders in the 1080s and 1090s. Such problems were not unique to the eleventh century, but the similarities between the Gwynedd of 1098 and that of 1267 are not obvious. Any search for the roots of the later principality are further hindered by the lack of source material. Apart from the native Welsh chronicles, only three sources – the *Historia Gruffud vab Kenan*, the *Historia Ecclesiastica* of Orderic Vitalis, and *Domesday Book* – reveal anything of substance about the events of the crucial period before 1100. Of these, the only native Welsh source is a unique biography,[2] highly eulogistic of its subject, frustratingly reticent about many important happenings and confusingly vague in its chronology.[3] The *Historia* is almost certainly a twelfth-century source,[4] and, although its

---

[1] See Smith, *Llywelyn ap Gruffudd*.
[2] The only comparable sources are lost *bucheddau* of Llywelyn ab Iorwerth, and Dafydd ap Llywelyn. *Ibid.*, pp. 394–5.
[3] *Historia*, ed. Evans, pp. ccxxxiii–ccxxxiv.
[4] *Ibid.*, pp. ccxliii–ccxlix.

author claims to have received his information from Gruffudd's '*kedem-deitheon*',[5] its treatment of some important aspects of Gruffudd's career leaves much to be desired. It has been criticised as misleading in its treatment of dynastic politics,[6] and the fact that much of its detail is not supported by other sources raises the possibility that there is a certain amount of padding to make up for a lack of real facts about Gruffudd's early life:[7] the story of a long imprisonment, for example, may be a mere device brought in to obscure further his obscurity in the years after 1081.[8] What is clear is that, whereas Llywelyn ab Iorwerth fought his way to supremacy in Gwynedd in his twenties, Gruffudd ap Cynan appears to have spent at least fifty years achieving little of lasting value, and it seems that it was only in the last third of his life that his rule was undisputed.

Yet there are indications that Gruffudd contributed to the later strength of Gwynedd. Such was to be expected of the ruler of a kingdom which had been a major power since the sub-Roman period,[9] and the hegemony which had existed under Gruffudd ap Llywelyn was a recent reminder of Venedotian potential. Despite his difficulties, and despite the lack of evidence, it is possible to trace in Gruffudd ap Cynan's rule the themes which were to become characteristic of the later twelfth and thirteenth centuries. Restriction of inheritance, resistance to Norman incursions and closer – yet not more subservient – dealings with the king, some assertion of more effective and demanding kingship within Gwynedd, a certain amount of territorial expansion, a developing concept of overlordship over other native kingdoms, and a growing sense of Welsh nationality were all at work under Gruffudd. Despite the apparently all-consuming nature of the Norman occupation, the Welsh polity remained essentially self-sufficient: outsiders eventually found that they could not but be subsumed into the traditional Welsh patterns of power. While there was no deliberate move towards a radical new principality in this period, such a development was made possible by a sea change in Welsh politics away from the ill-defined supremacy of Gruffudd ap Llywelyn. Yet at the same time, Gruffudd's career reveals the essential weaknesses of the native polity which were to lead to the destruction of Venedotian independence by Edward I.

Gruffudd's legacy to his sons was more tangible, if perhaps not more important, than that left by Gruffudd ap Llywelyn. At his death in 1137, Gwynedd was strong. Gruffudd ap Cynan and his family were successfully married into the aristocratic nexus of Gwynedd and Powys, and he had a string of military victories behind him. The *Historia* boasts that Gruffudd

5   Maund, *Ireland, Wales and England*, p. 173; *Historia*, ed. Evans, p. 17.
6   Maund, *Ireland, Wales and England*, p. 172 (but compare Lloyd, *A History*, ii.379).
7   Maund, 'Trahaearn', p. 472.
8   *Historia*, ed. Evans, p. ccxl.
9   Davies, *Wales in the Early Middle Ages*, p. 104.

successfully repulsed the men of Chester, Powys and Arwystli,[10] and he also conducted two successful campaigns against Henry I in 1114 and 1121. After Henry's second campaign, the *Historia* reports that there was peace for many years. Gwynedd was prosperous, and Gruffudd was well known far and wide. He built churches, orchards and gardens all over his kingdom, so that Gwynedd sparkled with churches like stars in the firmament.[11] He ruled with a rod of iron,[12] and the respect in which he was held even by his enemies is indicated by his reported neighbourly relations with Henry I, king *Mwrchath* of Ireland, and the king of the Isles and Denmark, and by the presence of archdeacon Simeon, the prior of St. Werburg's, Chester, at his deathbed.[13] The hopeful adventurer of the 1070s was now 'head and king and defender and pacifier of all Wales'.[14] Equally importantly, having emerged triumphant from the *mêlée* of opponents, he was able to pass on his kingdom to his eldest surviving son, Owain. To appreciate the significance of this feat, it is necessary first to examine the means by which Gruffudd asserted his claim to Gwynedd.

Gruffudd was born and bred in and around Dublin.[15] Nevertheless, his biography stresses that he was reared with a strong sense that Gwynedd was his 'true inheritance' ('*wir dreftat*'), since his father, Cynan, had been king there.[16] While he was young, Gruffudd's mother allegedly reminded him of his patrimony in Wales, and of the oppressors who now inhabited it. This is said to have saddened him for many days, until finally he resolved to recover his inheritance, inspired by the prophecy of his kinswoman, Tangwystl, that he would one day be king.[17] Thus, according to the *Historia*, began his career in Gwynedd. The *Historia* is at great pains to emphasise Gruffudd's right to rule: its opening sections are dominated by an account of his genealogy, and those who later turned against him are denounced as traitors to their rightful lord.[18] Historians have seen the *Historia*'s function primarily as a justification of a man seen as a legitimate heir against non-legitimate usurpers,[19] and some have themselves tended to accept this portrayal of

---

[10] *Historia*, ed. Evans, pp. 29–30; *A Mediaeval Prince*, ed. & transl. Evans, pp. 80–1.

[11] *Historia*, ed. Evans, pp. 30–1; *A Mediaeval Prince*, ed. & transl. Evans, pp. 81–2.

[12] *Historia*, ed. Evans, pp. 9, 30; *A Mediaeval Prince*, ed. & transl. Evans, pp. 61, 82.

[13] *Historia*, ed. Evans, pp. 30, 32; *A Mediaeval Prince*, ed. & transl. Evans, pp. 81, 83. For the possible identity of *Mwrchath*, see Maund, *Ireland, Wales and England*, pp. 180–1.

[14] *ByT* (Pen. 20) [1136=1137].

[15] *Historia*, ed. Evans, p. 1; *A Mediaeval Prince*, ed. & transl. Evans, p. 53. For further details of Gruffudd's claim to Gwynedd, see Evans, in *Historia*, ed. Evans, p. ccxl.

[16] *Historia*, ed. Evans, pp. 1, 7; *A Mediaeval Prince*, ed. & transl. Evans, pp. 53, 58.

[17] *Historia*, ed. Evans, pp. 6, 7; *A Mediaeval Prince*, ed. & transl. Evans, pp. 58, 60.

[18] *Historia*, ed. Evans, pp. 1–5, 10–11; *A Mediaeval Prince*, ed. & transl. Evans, pp. 53–7, 62–3.

[19] Maund, *Ireland, Wales and England*, p. 173.

Gruffudd's life.[20] Yet it is far from obvious that contemporaries accepted Gruffudd's right to rule as any better than that of his opponents.

It is doubtful whether Cynan was ever king of Gwynedd. It has been suggested that he may have had rule there for a few months – perhaps May to August – in 1064, around the period of the death of Gruffudd ap Llywelyn, but there is no direct evidence to support this.[21] Welsh sources do not mention Cynan, and on his first appearance in the Welsh annals, in Môn in 1075, Gruffudd is described as 'wyr Iago' and 'nepos Iacob'. The same appellation is applied in Brut y Tywysogion's account of the battle of Mynydd Carn in 1081, with the implication that Gruffudd's grandfather, Iago, was better known in Wales than Cynan.[22] Iago had certainly been king of Gwynedd, and had died in 1039, to be succeeded by Gruffudd ap Llywelyn.[23] It will be seen that this in itself was enough to qualify Gruffudd to challenge for the kingship, but the Historia's insistence on his legitimacy to rule suggests that it was far from being sufficiently convincing to guarantee success. Gruffudd had not been a contender to succeed Gruffudd ap Llywelyn in 1063/1064, presumably because of his age – the Historia says that he was eighty two in 1137, which means he would have been a child of eight in 1063.[24] Bleddyn ap Cynfyn had ruled strongly since Gruffudd ap Llywelyn's death, and had fought and killed Maredudd and Idwal, his predecessor's sons, in 1069.[25] Gruffudd ap Cynan's chance to press his claims came in 1075, when Bleddyn himself died and Trahaearn ap Caradog assumed rule in Gwynedd.[26]

It is possible that Gruffudd's family asserted a claim to the kingship after 1039. Irish sources state that a certain 'son of "Iacoib" ' was responsible for the death of Gruffudd ap Llywelyn,[27] and an Armagh MS., probably dating from the twelfth century, names this man more specifically as 'Chanan mac Iacco'.[28] Was this Cynan ab Iago ab Idwal, the father of Gruffudd ap Cynan? Cynan's kin held sensitive positions in Gruffudd ap Llywelyn's household: a certain Llywarch Olbwch, known to the Historia as the husband of Gruffudd ap Cynan's kinswoman Tangwystl, was the king's 'guas ystavell a thrysoryer', and Tangwystl was able to lay hands on Gruffudd's personal effects.[29] Moreover, seventeenth-century Irish evi-

20 The History, ed. Jones, p. 33.
21 Hudson, 'The destruction', pp. 348, 332–6.
22 ByT (Pen. 20) [1073=1075]; AC [1075]; ByT (RB) [1081].
23 ByT (Pen. 20) [1037=1039].
24 Historia, ed. Evans, p. 33; A Mediaeval Prince, ed. & transl. Evans, p. 83.
25 AC [1069]; ByT (Pen. 20) [1068=1069].
26 ByT (Pen. 20) [1073=1075].
27 ALC 1063; AU 1063; for Gruffudd's fall, see Lloyd, A History, ii.369–71.
28 London, British Library, MS. Add. 30512; Hudson, 'The destruction', p. 340.
29 Historia, ed. Evans, p. 7; A Mediaeval Prince, ed. & transl. Evans, p. 60. It has even been suggested that Tangwystl killed Gruffudd in his bath. (Hudson, 'The destruction', p. 341.)

dence suggests that Cynan attacked Gruffudd with help from Dublin in 1039x1050 and 1050, and that he was in league with Gruffudd's enemies in the south in 1063x1064.[30] Yet there is no conclusive evidence that this was the father of Gruffudd ap Cynan. The 'son of Iago' mentioned in contemporary sources need not have been related to Gruffudd ap Cynan and Iago ab Idwal,[31] and the notion that Cynan ab Iago held a grudge against Gruffudd ap Llywelyn for the killing of his father in 1039 is dubious.[32] Welsh sources ascribe the death of Gruffudd ap Llywelyn merely to treachery, not to any individual.[33] It could be argued that the story of Gruffudd's downfall was censored by the twelfth-century princes, who found it embarrassing rather than useful: Gruffudd's part in the rise of Venedotian supremacy now meant more than the overthrow of a 'usurper', whilst the interests of dynastic security might lessen the appeal of an episode which seemed to condone plotting against the incumbent. Nevertheless, the overriding impression given by the sources is that, far from being hailed as the rightful heir to Gwynedd, Gruffudd ap Cynan was in fact the least well known of the combatants at Mynydd Carn in 1081.[34] His success is therefore all the more intriguing.

The *Historia* makes it plain that Gruffudd's apologists, at least, shared the Welsh obsession, noted by Gerald of Wales, of tracing ancestry back some six or seven generations.[35] The reason for this was simple: in practice, royal lineage was the only prerequisite for candidates for kingship in mediaeval Wales.[36] Gruffudd ap Cynan made his claim to Gwynedd on the grounds of hereditary right, since succession was dynastic; genealogical descent was the chief means of legitimising a man's right to kingship, as witnessed by the numerous conflicts between brothers, cousins, and more distant relations in the aristocratic élite. Possession of an impressive genealogy, however, was anything but a guarantee of success. Welsh kingship

---

[30] *Ibid.*, pp. 342, 345–8; Cynan's Dublin connexion seems plausible in the light of Gruffudd ap Cynan's early life. Harold Godwinesson's possible presence in Dublin in 1051 may have brought him into contact with Cynan and formed the basis of concerted action against Gruffudd ap Llywelyn in 1063/4. (Maund, 'Cynan ab Iago', p. 61.)

[31] *Ibid.*, p. 64.

[32] Only *ByS* involves Gruffudd in Iago's death. The other Welsh sources do not mention the killer, and the AU say that he was killed '*a suis*' (*ByS* [1037=1039], *ByT* (Pen. 20) [1037=1039], *AC* [1039]; AU *s.a.* 1039). *ByS* is generally a less reliable source than the others. (Maund, 'Cynan ab Iago', p. 63.)

[33] *ByT* (Pen. 20) [1061=1063].

[34] *ByT* (Pen. 20) [1079=1081]; *AC* [1081]; Gruffudd is portrayed in an auxiliary rôle, under the leadership of Rhys ap Tewdwr.

[35] *Giraldi Cambrensis Opera* (edd. Brewer *et al.*, vi.200); *Historia*, ed. Evans, pp. 1–5; *A Mediaeval Prince*, ed. & transl. Evans, pp. 53–7.

[36] This is comparable with ninth-century Anglo-Saxon England. (Dumville, 'The Ætheling', pp. 17–18.)

had been heritable from an early period,[37] and there was a clear rule that there should be one kingship and one heir, but neither custom nor the laws were precise in specifying who was eligible.[38] The dynasty, rather than any individual, was heir, and this multiplicity of eligibility was a source of considerable instability.[39] According to the laws, those entitled to claim kingship were regarded as *aelodau'r brenin* or *membra regis* – a group which might include the sons, nephews and cousins of an incumbent or recently deceased king.[40] It is not clear how many generations comprised such a kin-group. Most of the extant evidence for succession and inheritance is possibly compromised by the fact that it dates from the late twelfth and thirteenth centuries, when Llywelyn ab Iorwerth of Gwynedd and Rhys ap Gruffudd of Deheubarth are known to have tampered with the rules for their own purposes; from what is known of the tenth century, it seems that the idea of restriction of succession within a four-generation kin group (along with that of the nomination of successors) was not applicable.[41] In comparison, the laws for land and *galanas* – which are admittedly in a different category from the laws of kingship – specify a kin group of four and seven generations respectively.[42] It seems likely that, in the time of Gruffudd ap Cynan, eligibility tended towards inclusivity rather than exclusivity.

As generations passed, the natural concomitant of multiple eligibility was dynastic segmentation. These segments were prolific after the tenth century,[43] not least in Gwynedd. In the tenth and eleventh centuries, Venedotian segments held rule in most parts of Wales, and inter-segmentary rivalry led to hostilities between the sons of Idwal and the sons of Hywel (great-grandsons of Rhodri Mawr) in 951–961, whilst the sons of Idwal fought each other in the 970s, and Idwal's grandsons followed suit in the years before 985.[44] It was often the case that no segment could keep grip on power for long,[45] and candidates on the fringe of a kin-group – no doubt motivated by a sense of desperation – could often challenge extremely effectively.[46] The lengthy genealogies cited by the *Historia* were therefore probably sufficient to enable Gruffudd to make a claim on Gwynedd. How good that claim was, and whether it was better than those of other candidates, was another matter.

---

37 Powys was a *hereditas* in the ninth century. (Davies, *Wales in the Early Middle Ages*, pp. 122–3.)
38 Smith, 'Dynastic succession', pp. 203–5.
39 Smith, 'The succession', p. 67.
40 *Llyfr Iorwerth* (ed. Wiliam, pp. 4–5).
41 Davies, *Patterns of Power*, p. 45.
42 *Llyfr Iorwerth* (ed. Wiliam, pp. 55–6, 70–1).
43 Davies, *Wales in the Early Middle Ages*, pp. 124–5.
44 Davies, *Patterns of Power*, pp. 44, 45.
45 The Uí Chennselaig dynasty of Leinster, where succession procedures were similar, provides an excellent example of this. (Ó Corráin, 'Irish regnal succession', p. 31.)
46 For examples of this in Ireland, see Binchy, *Celtic and Anglo-Saxon Kingship*, pp. 26–7.

Some candidates had a better chance than others. A ruling segment naturally did its best to remain in power, with the result that Wales shared in the European tendency to concentrate power in the hands of a single segment of a single dynasty; customary practice became the product of years of dynastic self interest.[47] Consequently, the kingship of Gwynedd passed directly from father to son for four generations from Rhodri Mawr to Anarawd to Idwal to Iago (the grandfather of Gruffudd ap Cynan) and Idwal ab Idwal, and, from the ninth century to the eleventh, its incumbents remained within five generations of Idwal Foel ab Anarawd ap Rhodri Mawr, and those of the kingship of Deheubarth within four of Owain ap Hywel Dda.[48] Indeed, the line of Rhodri Mawr included all but four of the rulers in north and south-west Wales between the last quarter of the ninth century and the third quarter of the eleventh century,[49] and the need for some kind of identification with this nexus is clear in the poet Meilyr's description of Gruffudd as '*nerth rodri*'.[50]

Any impression of closely controlled inheritance is illusory, however. Linear succession was exceptional: there were only two instances in Gwynedd between the early eleventh century and 1282,[51] although sons' sons sometimes inherited, leading to the succession of cousins, and further segmentation.[52] The *Historia*'s ambiguity in its treatment of Gruffudd ap Llywelyn is symptomatic of the lack of definition of who the *membra regis* were, and what constituted legitimate rule. He is portrayed as a usurper,[53] perhaps because, in replacing Iago ab Idwal in 1039,[54] he had interrupted a tradition of succession from father to son which stretched back to Rhodri Mawr; this was a tradition from which Gruffudd ap Cynan might have hoped to benefit. Yet, at the same time, Gruffudd ap Cynan's kinswoman, Tangwystl, is said to have given him a shirt and cloak which had once belonged to Gruffudd ap Llywelyn.[55] Whether Gruffudd did receive such gifts, and whether linear succession was a recognised goal, are less important than the point that Gruffudd ap Llywelyn could both be vilified and used as a legitimising association in the same cause. Succession was clearly

---

[47] The Capetian kings of France, for instance, insisted upon their legitimacy to rule, unitary succession, and linear succession. This led ultimately to primogeniture. (Smith, 'Dynastic succession', pp. 206–7.)

[48] Davies, *Wales in the Early Middle Ages*, pp. 123, 124.

[49] Davies, *Patterns of Power*, p. 45.

[50] Williams, 'Meilyr Brydydd', below, pp. 00–00.

[51] Gruffudd ap Cynan was succeeded by his son, Owain, in 1137, and Llywelyn ap Seisyll (1018–1023) was succeeded by his son, Gruffudd. (Lloyd, 'Wales and the coming', p. 125.)

[52] Davies, *Wales in the Early Middle Ages*, p. 124.

[53] *Historia*, ed. Evans, p. 6; *A Mediaeval Prince*, ed. & transl. Evans, p. 58.

[54] *ByT* (Pen. 20) [1037=1039].

[55] *Historia*, ed. Evans, p. 7; *A Mediaeval Prince*, ed. & transl. Evans, p. 60.

dependent on a range of factors more complicated than can be explained merely in terms of a dynastic segmentary clique.

The *Historia*'s dislike of usurpers and its insistence on the importance of descent are unique amongst eleventh-century Welsh sources, and this has brought into question the idea that kinship with Rhodri Mawr was an essential legitimising factor in this period. Whilst this dynasty was clearly important, very little is known about it in the ninth and tenth centuries, and it is difficult even to establish precisely where its members ruled in the tenth century. Other dynasties appear just as prominent in the period before *ca* 950, and many rulers in the eleventh century were either from uncertain backgrounds or linked only indirectly to Rhodri. Indeed, every part of Wales except Morgannwg came under 'intrusive' rulers from other dynasties in the eleventh century. These 'intruders' were not mere aberrations: some of them, such as Bleddyn ap Cynfyn, established powerful dynasties. Thus, whilst Rhodri's heirs held substantial power, there is no indication that descent from Rhodri was ever a mark of inherent legitimacy or a prerequisite for kingship.[56] Nor is there any sign that a man from one area was not entitled to rule in another. Whilst this was not necessarily popular,[57] it was accepted. Gruffudd ap Llywelyn probably originated from Dyfed,[58] whilst genealogies link Trahaearn ap Caradog with Arwystli,[59] and there is no evidence for any king of Powys in the eleventh century who did not also have rule in Gwynedd. Bleddyn ap Cynfyn began his career as king of Gwynedd but was seen by posterity as the head of the Powys dynasty.[60]

It seems that all the kings of Gwynedd in the eleventh century could claim some form of legitimacy. That the chronicles do not tend to identify 'intruders' suggests that such a concept was either unknown or of little consequence to them.[61] The Venedotian succession was far from smooth in this period: between 1075 and 1098, none of the claimants to Gwynedd were sons or grandsons of the previous incumbent. Yet no comment is passed by the *Annales Cambriae* or *Brut y Tywysogion* about the suitability or other-

---

56 Maund, 'Trahaearn', p. 475; Maund, *Ireland, Wales and England*, pp. 7–10.
57 Gerald of Wales accused Gruffudd ap Llywelyn of oppressing all of Wales. *Giraldi Cambrensis Opera* (edd. Brewer *et al.*, vi.28–9).
58 Davies, *Wales in the Early Middle Ages*, p. 106.
59 Bartrum, *Welsh Genealogies*, i.04.
60 Lloyd, *A History*, ii.769; this is because he was the elder of the sons of Cynfyn, and the male descendants of his brother, Rhiwallon, were shortlived and produced no heirs.
61 This was not unusual in the Celtic world. Of the Uí Chennselaig kings of Leinster from the seventh century to 1171, 54% were sons of the previous incumbent, 16% grandsons, 3% great grandsons, 20% great great grandsons and further removes (of which 8.5% were from outside any royal kin group), and 7% were of unknown origin. On average, a successor was more likely to be the son of recent segmentary predecessor than an incumbent's own son. (Ó Corráin, 'Irish regnal sccession', pp. 8, 10–27, 28, 29, 38; Binchy, *Celtic and Anglo-Saxon Kingship*, p. 25.)

wise of candidates. A closer examination of the genealogical claims reveals that, although there is no descent in the male line, there is what has been called 'collateral cohesion', in that all the incumbents were related more or less distantly. Llywelyn ap Seisyll was the son of (the perhaps fictional) Prawst, the daughter of Elise ab Anarawd ap Rhodri Mawr; Gruffudd ap Llywelyn, his son, inherited his father's claim, and also had one through his mother, Angharad ferch Maredudd ab Owain ap Hywel Dda ap Cadell ap Rhodri Mawr; Bleddyn ap Cynfyn was the son of the same Angharad and was Gruffudd ap Llywelyn's half-brother; Cynan ap Hywel, Iago ab Idwal and Gruffudd ap Cynan were all descendants of Idwal Foel ab Anarawd ap Rhodri Mawr (through Iago's father, Idwal ap Meurig ab Idwal Foel ab Anarawd ap Rhodri Mawr), and were possibly cousins of the segment which included Llywelyn ap Seisyll, including Gruffudd ap Llywelyn. Llywelyn ap Seisyll was possibly a distant cousin of Iago ab Idwal; Iago a distant cousin of Gruffudd ap Llywelyn; Gruffudd ap Llywelyn, Bleddyn and Rhiwallon ap Cynfyn were maternal half-brothers; and Bleddyn and Trahaearn ap Caradog possibly first cousins. There was no blood relationship between Trahaearn and Gruffudd ap Cynan, but the latter was a grandson of Iago ab Idwal, who was a distant cousin of both Gruffudd ap Llywelyn and the sons of Cynfyn. Owain ab Edwin, who appears to have challenged for the kingship and possibly held it in the 1090s, was the son of Iwerydd ferch Cynfyn, and therefore a nephew of Bleddyn ap Cynfyn.[62] He and his brother Uchdryd, who also took part in campaigns against Gruffudd ap Cynan in the 1090s, may have been sons of Edwin ap Goronwy ab Einion ab Owain ap Hywel Dda, who may have held lands in Tegeingl in 1086.[63] Thus, despite the apparent incohesion, there was arguably a 'network of staggered kingship', in which links through the female line were very important.[64]

In this light, Gruffudd ap Cynan's claim to Gwynedd does not seem particularly tenuous, and this impression is strengthened when an examination is made of the degree of kinship between each incumbent and his predecessor, based on descent from a common ancestor who had rule in Gwynedd.[65] Iago ab Idwal and Llywelyn ap Seisyll had a common ancestor in Anarawd ap Rhodri Mawr – a gap of four generations on Iago's side, and three on Llywelyn's; Gruffudd ap Llywelyn and Iago also shared Anarawd – four generations on each side; Bleddyn ap Cynfyn and Gruffudd ap Cynan had to go back to Rhodri Mawr to find a common ancestor – six generations

[62] Iwerydd was the half-sister of Bleddyn and Rhiwallon. (Lloyd, *A History*, ii.406–7; Maund, *Ireland, Wales and England*, p. 101.)
[63] Lloyd, *A History*, ii.407; *Domesday Book* I, fo. 268b.
[64] Maund, *Ireland, Wales and England*, pp. 98, 100–1, 116.
[65] This is drawn in part from the genealogical table given by Maund, *Ireland, Wales and England*, p. 101.

on Bleddyn's side and five on Gruffudd's; whilst Trahaearn ap Caradog and Bleddyn had no common ancestor who ruled Gwynedd, although they may have been first cousins.[66] Indeed, since it seems that Bleddyn and Trahaearn were probably not first cousins,[67] Trahaearn's claim was very likely not founded on the narrow rule of legitimacy from which the *Historia* condemns his lack of right to rule. Whilst the *Historia* is perhaps exposed as a work of anachronistic special pleading in this respect, since Trahaearn was clearly accepted as a rightful king by every one else, the tenuousness of his claim when compared with that of Gruffudd ap Cynan is illuminating.[68] By the standards of the eleventh century, Gruffudd was anything but an outsider.

Ultimately, right to rule depended not upon blood relationships but upon practical considerations. A claimant relied on his access to resources: his succession to and retention of authority was primarily a reflection of the balance of power.[69] It was on these grounds that Trahaearn won and lost his kingdom. Gruffudd ap Rhys may have been recognised as king of Brycheiniog by the wildfowl on Llangors lake,[70] but he nevertheless failed utterly in his attempts to control the area: his success in gaining a foothold in Ystrad Tywi, and his sons' rise to pre-eminence in Ceredigion, Ystrad Tywi and Dyfed in the 1150s, was due to armed violence. This reality, neatly encapsulated by the Irish expression '*feabta la flaith*',[71] explains the success of numerous Welsh claimants, including Dafydd ab Owain Gwynedd and Llywelyn ap Gruffudd, against better qualified opposition. Even those such as Owain Gwynedd and Llywelyn ab Iorwerth, who might have had as good a theoretical case as their rivals, had to fight their way to power. Bleddyn and Rhiwallon ap Cynfyn fought against the sons of Gruffudd ap Llywelyn in 1069, and the death of Cynwrig ap Rhiwallon at the hands of the men of Gwynedd in 1075 after the death of Bleddyn was probably the result of an attempt by Trahaearn ap Caradog (or perhaps Gruffudd ap Cynan) to remove contenders for the kingship.[72] A measure of the significance of economic and military power is the fact that some Irish kingships passed remarkably

---

66 *ByT* (Pen. 20) [1073=1075]; *AC* [1075].
67 The only link between them in the genealogies is through a remote ancestor, Tegonwy ap Teon, and Bleddyn's relationship to Tegonwy is not securely established. (Bartrum, *Welsh Genealogies*, I.96–7; Maund, *Ireland, Wales and England*, p. 80.)
68 *Ibid.*, 476–7; Bartrum, *Welsh Genealogies* I.14 and n.1. Trahaearn possibly married a sister of Gruffudd ap Llywelyn, who was Bleddyn's half-brother; Bartrum, *Welsh Genealogies* I.41, 198.
69 This was as true of Ireland as it was of Wales. (Ó Corráin, 'Irish Regnal Succession', pp. 8–9, 30.)
70 *Giraldi Cambrensis Opera* (edd. Brewer *et al.*, vi.34).
71 Simms, *From Kings to Warlords*, pp. 48–9, 59.
72 *ByT* (Pen. 20) [1068=1069], [1073=1075]; it is also possible that Bleddyn was involved in the death of Gruffudd ap Llywelyn.

often to people outside the four-generation kin group.[73] It is not for nothing that the *Historia* boasts of Gruffudd ap Cynan's military qualities.[74] Yet it cannot be assumed that military victories always had significant political consequences.[75] If Gruffudd depended as much on force as on genealogy for his success, he also had a good deal of luck, and it seems that it was many years before his hold on the whole of Gwynedd was secure.

Gruffudd's first foray into Gwynedd from Ireland appears to have been in 1075, probably in an attempt to take advantage of the confusion created by the death of Bleddyn ap Cynfyn.[76] According to the *Historia*, it was an unqualified success. He defeated Cynwrig ap Rhiwallon in Llŷn and took possession of Gwynedd, going on to overcome Trahaearn ap Caradog at Gwaed Erw in Meirionnydd. From that day on, we are told, Gruffudd was called king.[77] Yet there is no mention of his becoming king at this time in any other source. *Brut y Tywysogion* and the *Annales Cambriae* both say that Trahaearn ap Caradog now ruled Gwynedd, and neither mentions Gruffudd.[78] Even when they record Gruffudd's successful rôle at Mynydd Carn in 1081, the *Brutiau* do not say that he became king.[79]

The *Historia* is probably overstating its case. In the other sources, Gruffudd's rôle in the events of 1075 is hardly mentioned. The *Brutiau*, having stated that Trahaearn was king, merely record a battle at Bron yr Erw between him and Gruffudd;[80] the *Historia* testifies that this was a victory for Trahaearn, who was king afterwards.[81] Even before Bron yr Erw, there is very little evidence that Gruffudd held much land: the note in *Brut y Tywysogion, MS Peniarth 20 version* that he held Môn after the death of Bleddyn, while Trahaearn was king, is less reliable than the accounts of *Brut y Tywysogion, Red Book of Hergest version* and the *Annales Cambriae*, which merely say that he besieged it.[82] Similarly, Gruffudd is not mentioned by any source as being responsible for the death of Cynwrig ap Rhiwallon, which is attributed to the men of Gwynedd,[83] although the *Historia* implies

---

73 O Corráin, 'Irish regnal succession', pp. 32–3.
74 *Historia*, ed. Evans, pp. ccxxv–ccxxvi.
75 Davies, *Patterns of Power*, p. 2.
76 *ByT* (Pen. 20) [1073=1075]; *ByT* (RB) [1075]; *ByS* [1073=1075].
77 *Historia*, ed. Evans, pp. 8–9; *A Mediaeval Prince*, ed. & transl. Evans, p. 60. The battle at Gwaed Erw is also referred to by Meilyr in his elegy for Gruffudd; Williams. 'Meilyr Brydydd', below, pp. 181, 185.
78 *ByT* (Pen. 20) [1073=1075]; *ByT* (RB) [1075]; *ByS* [1073=1075]; *AC* [1075].
79 *ByT* (Pen. 20) [1079=1081]; *Byt* (RB) [1081]; *ByS* [1079=1081].
80 *ByT* (Pen. 20) [1073=1075].
81 *Historia*, ed. Evans, pp. 10–12; *A Mediaeval Prince*, ed. & transl. Evans, pp. 62–4.
82 *ByT* (Pen. 20) [1073=1075]; *ByT* (RB) [1075]; *AC* [1075]; see Jones, ed. *ByT* (Pen. 20), p. 153.
83 *ByT* [1073=1075] *ByT* (RB) [1075]; *ByS* [1073=1075]. Gruffudd is known to have fought Cynwrig. *Historia*, ed. Evans, p. 8; *A Mediaeval Prince*, ed. & transl. Evans, p. 60.

some responsibility when it says that Trahaearn asked the men of Powys for help against Gruffudd in order to avenge Cynwrig.[84]

The rôle of Powys is intriguing. Its dynasty had a long-standing dynastic interest in Gwynedd, especially since Bleddyn ap Cynfyn became king there in 1063x1064.[85] Cynwrig's involvement in the fight for Gwynedd suggests an attempt to preserve Powysian control, as does the fact that Gwrgeneu ap Seisyll fought with Trahaearn against Gruffudd in 1075, returning again in the company of a Norman expedition some time during the six years between Bron yr Erw and Mynydd Carn.[86] In 1081, after his victory, Gruffudd went out of his way to punish the men of Powys and Arwystli for supporting Trahaearn.[87] It is also possible that the 1094 rebellion, led by Cadwgan ap Bleddyn ap Cynfyn against the Normans,[88] was in part another attempt to assert a Powysian claim against Gruffudd ap Cynan, who may recently have escaped from prison. That Cadwgan and Maredudd ap Bleddyn joined forces with Gruffudd in 1098 was perhaps only because of common opposition to Owain and Uchdryd ab Edwin, who in turn represented another challenge to Gruffudd's hold on Gwynedd. On this occasion, it is again Cadwgan, not Gruffudd, who is given prominence as leader of the Welsh, and all the leaders except Gruffudd were from Powys dynasties.[89] It may be that Gruffudd's escape was shortly before this rebellion (he may either have caused it or joined in). Whatever the case, it is clear that, despite the protestations of the *Historia*, Gruffudd had not rid Gwynedd of lords from 'other places'; since he had been in prison for many years, this is not surprising.[90]

Nor can it be accepted without question that Gruffudd's rule was 'undisputed' in the period after 1100,[91] despite the *Historia*'s insistence that he took the whole of Gwynedd fairly quickly.[92] In 1099, he is not said to have held more than Môn,[93] and the *Annales Cambriae* do not even credit him

84 *Historia*, ed. Evans, p. 10; *A Mediaeval Prince*, ed. & transl. Evans, p. 62.
85 John of Worcester, *Chronicon* 1064; ASC (D) 1063.
86 *Historia*, ed. Evans, pp. 10, 13; *A Mediaeval Prince*, ed. & transl. Evans, pp. 62, 65.
87 *Historia*, ed. Evans, p. 16; *A Mediaeval Prince*, ed. & transl. Evans, p. 69. Trahaearn had the support of the men of Arwystli at Mynydd Carn; *Historia*, ed. Evans, p. 14; *A Mediaeval Prince*, ed. & transl. Evans, p. 66.
88 *ByT* (Pen. 20) [1092=1094]; *ByT* (RB) [1094]; *ByS* [1092=1094].
89 *Historia*, ed. Evans, p. 23; *A Mediaeval Prince*, ed. & transl. Evans, p. 76; *ByT* (Pen. 20) [1096=1098]; *ByT* (RB) [1098]; *ByS* [1096=1098]; see Maund, *Ireland, Wales and England*, p. 151.
90 *Historia*, ed. Evans, pp. 9, 17, 18; *A Mediaeval Prince*, ed. & transl. Evans, pp. 61, 69, 70.
91 Maund, *Ireland, Wales and England*, p. 171.
92 *Historia*, ed. Evans, p. 28; *A Mediaeval Prince*, ed. & transl. Evans, pp. 79–80.
93 *ByT* (Pen. 20) [1097=1099]; *ByT* (RB) [1095=1099]; *ByS* [1097=1099].

with this, saying only that he besieged it.[94] Gruffudd's military weakness is shown by the *Historia*'s admission that, after winning victories in the period 1094x1098, he sailed away with only one ship.[95] After 1098, he was given '*teir tref*' by Hugh of Chester, and Henry I gave him Llŷn, Eifionydd, Ardudwy and Arllechwedd before 1114.[96] Little is known of Owain ab Edwin at this time, but it is significant that, although Owain died in 1105, his son, Goronwy, was a prominent Venedotian leader in 1114: the *Brutiau* imply that he and Gruffudd were of similar importance, and, as late as 1121, Gruffudd is not mentioned as holding more than Môn.[97] It remains unclear why neither the *Historia* nor Meilyr – both of which can be assumed to be propagandist – give much information about Gruffudd after 1100. Is this because he had overcome all his greatest problems? Or was he forced to accept some compromise which later eulogists thought it best not to mention?[98]

Gruffudd's influence probably depended a great deal on the strength of a few local power bases. The *cantrefi* with which he is most usually associated are Môn, Arfon and Llŷn. On his first visit, he landed at Abermenai in Arfon, and gathered the support of the men of Môn and Arfon, as well as Asser, Meirion and Gwgon (the sons of Merwydd) and other *guyrda* in Llŷn.[99] Cynwrig ap Rhiwallon was defeated in Llŷn, where Gruffudd's supporters included sixty Tegeingl men and eighty from Môn. Gruffudd then took possession of Môn, Arfon and Llŷn. On his second visit, he took Llŷn and Arfon as far as Môn, which he ravaged (probably only in order to provide spoils to keep his dissatisfied Hiberno-Scandinavian allies happy), and, in 1081, Cynddelw ap *Conus* brought 160 men from Môn to help him at Mynydd Carn. Môn seems to have been loyal to Gruffudd most of the time: seventy of its men died on his side at Bron yr Erw, and it was straight to Môn that Gruffudd went on his way to Ireland after his escape from prison. It was there that he returned to lay his claim to Gwynedd soon

---

94 *AC* [1099]; see Jones, transl., *ByT* (Pen. 20), p. 160. The *Historia* mentions that Gruffudd successfully besieged a castle in Môn around this time, and goes on to say that he took the whole of Môn. (*Historia*, ed. Evans, pp. 20–1; *A Mediaeval Prince*, ed. & transl. Evans, pp. 72–3).

95 *Historia*, ed. Evans, pp. 19–20; *A Mediaeval Prince*, ed. & transl. Evans, pp. 72–3.

96 *ByT* (Pen. 20) [1097=1099]; *Historia*, ed. Evans, pp. 27, 28; *A Mediaeval Prince*, ed. & transl. Evans, pp. 79, 80.

97 *ByT* (Pen. 20) [1102=1105], [1111=1114], [1118=1121]; *ByT* (RB) [1102=1105], [1111=1114], [1118=1121]; *ByS* [1102=1105], [1111=1114], [1118=1121].

98 Another explanation is that the *Historia* may be an account of Gruffudd as a young adventurer, rather than as king; see Maund, *Ireland, Wales and England*, p. 173.

99 *Historia*, ed. Evans, pp. 6, 7; *A Mediaeval Prince*, ed. & transl. Evans, p. 59. Gruffudd also used Abermenai as a port on other occasions, and he gave it to his wife when he died. (*Historia*, ed. Evans, pp. 11, 12, 32; *A Mediaeval Prince*, ed. & transl. Evans, pp. 63, 64, 83.)

afterwards, going on to Llŷn. He was now joined by the men of Llŷn, Eifionydd, Ardudwy, Arfon, Rhos and Dyffryn Clwyd.[100] Yet he could not depend on support anywhere in Gwynedd. Some of the Môn men defected to the Normans in 1098,[101] reminding Gruffudd that Welsh *uchelwyr* were not prone to blind obedience: those of Ystrad Tywi killed Bleddyn ap Cynfyn in 1075,[102] and Gruffudd suffered similar treachery at the hands of the three sons of Merwydd, the men of Llŷn, and Tudur and Gollwyn (two brothers from Môn).[103] Significantly, Gruffudd always made for his homeland, Ireland, when he needed support. Taking control of the whole of Gwynedd was not easy.

Nor was Gruffudd easily rid of his dynastic rivals. As late as 1125, his marriage with Angharad, the daughter of Owain ab Edwin, was reportedly arranged because he was sometimes in difficulties; this is no doubt the *Historia*'s euphemism for the fact that the support of Owain's segment was vitally important for Gruffudd's success. Angharad became the mother of three of Gruffudd's most prominent sons, Owain, Cadwaladr and Cadwallon.[104] The importance of links with this segment is underlined by the marriage of Owain with Cristin, the daughter of Goronwy ab Owain.[105]

That Gruffudd co-existed with rivals for many years, and that he was unable to control substantial portions of Gwynedd, raises the possibility that the kingship was split. Partition of lands was not unusual – it took place in Powys in the 1160s, Gwynedd in the 1170s, and Deheubarth in 1197 – but kingship was only partible under exceptional circumstances, the most striking instance occurring in Powys in the 1190s.[106] It is possible that this is what happened in Gwynedd in both 1075 and 1098. In 1075, Trahaearn ap Caradog and Cynwrig ap Rhiwallon are said to have split Gwynedd between them;[107] this mirrors the situation in Deheubarth in the same year, when 'the South' was held by both Rhys ab Owain and Rhydderch ap

---

100 *Historia*, ed. Evans, pp. 8, 12, 14, 11, 18, 20–1; *A Mediaeval Prince*, ed. & transl. Evans, pp. 60, 62–3, 65, 67, 70–1, 72–3. Gruffudd was hidden by the sons of Gollwyn (Eginir, Gellan and Merwydd) after his escape. *Historia*, ed. Evans, p. 19; *A Mediaeval Prince*, ed. & transl. Evans, p. 71.

101 *ByT* (Pen. 20) [1096=1098]; *ByT* (RB) [1094=1098]; *ByS* [1096=1098].

102 *ByT* (Pen. 20) [1073=1075]; *ByT* (RB) [1075]; *ByS* [1073=1075].

103 *Historia*, ed. Evans, p. 10; *A Mediaeval Prince*, ed. & transl. Evans, p. 62.

104 *Historia*, ed. Evans, p. 21; *A Mediaeval Prince*, ed. & transl. Evans, p. 74; *ByT* (Pen. 20) [1122=1125]; *ByT* (RB) [1122=1125]; *ByS* [1122=1125]; Maund, *Ireland, Wales and England*, p. 101.

105 Lloyd, *A History*, ii.522.

106 Smith, 'Dynastic succession', pp. 203–5; divided kingship also occurred in Ireland (see Ó Corráin, 'Irish Regnal Succession', p. 7). Gerald of Wales says that inheritance to Welsh kingdoms was inherently divisive and destructive (*Giraldi Cambrensis Opera* edd. Brewer *et al.*, vi.134, 211, 225) but he did not distinguish between inheritance of land and of kingdoms, or between contested and partible succession.

107 *Historia*, ed. Evans, pp. 6–7; *A Mediaeval Prince*, ed. & transl. Evans, p. 59.

Caradog.[108] Since these were from rival dynasties (as were Trahaearn and Cynwrig), it is possible that these are two examples of split kingship; alternatively, each incumbent may have been akin to an Irish *tánaise*, or heir designate.[109] Such an explanation might also cover the obscure relationship of Gruffudd ap Cynan and Goronwy ab Owain after 1098. These concepts were not alien to the *Historia*, which alleges that Rhys ap Tewdwr promised Gruffudd ap Cynan half his *cyfoeth*.[110] Such an arrangement would probably be only temporary in intention; this was the case in Ystrad Tywi in the thirteenth century,[111] although the experience of Powys proved permanent. It is possible that Gruffudd ap Cynan shared his kingdom with Goronwy ab Owain until the 1120s: only when Goronwy was killed by Gruffudd's son, Cadwallon, was Gruffudd able to rule freely and perhaps restore a unified kingship.

In 1137, Gruffudd passed his kingship to his son, an achievement unparalleled since the accession of Gruffudd ap Llywelyn. Indeed, no other eldest surviving legitimate son would succeed to Gwynedd until after the Edwardian conquest. A measure of Gruffudd's dynastic success is the large number of claims of descent from him (not all genuine) in the twelfth and thirteenth centuries: he was a high-status progenitor.[112] The key to this was partly force and partly luck. Hence the *Historia* boasts that Gruffudd ruled with a '*guyalen haearnaul/ gwialen haearnawl*', and that he repulsed the men of Chester, Powys and Arwystli,[113] whilst the killing of Goronwy, Rhiryd and Meilyr, the sons of Owain ab Edwin, by Cadwallon in 1125 was a great dynastic *coup*.[114] Marriage alliances were also important: Gruffudd's daughter, Susanna, helped to improve relations with Powys by marrying Madog ap Maredudd ap Bleddyn,[115] and his son, Owain Gwynedd, married a daughter of Llywarch ap Trahaearn.[116]

The rôle of luck, however, was not insignificant. The sons of Bleddyn ap Cynfyn chose not to press their claims in Gwynedd after Cadwgan's failure in 1098,[117] and Llywarch ap Trahaearn similarly neglected his father's claim

---

108 *ByT* (Pen. 20) [1073=1075]; *ByT* (RB) [1075]; *ByS* [1073=1075].
109 Maund, 'Trahaearn', p. 473.
110 *Historia*, ed. Evans, p. 14; *A Mediaeval Prince*, ed. & transl. Evans, p. 67.
111 Smith, 'The *Cronica de Wallia*', pp. 266–8; for an alternative view, see Hughes, 'The Welsh Latin Chronicles', p. 18.
112 Bartrum, *Welsh Genealogies* I.40, 47, 96–7, 115, 118.
113 *Historia*, ed. Evans, pp. 9, 29–30; *A Mediaeval Prince*, ed. & transl. Evans, pp. 31, 61, 80–1.
114 *ByT* (Pen. 20) [1122=1125]; *ByT* (RB) [1122=1125]; *ByS* [1122=1125].
115 Lloyd, *A History*, ii.566; for dynastic marriages, see Roderick, 'Marriage and Politics'.
116 *Giraldi Cambrensis Opera* (edd. Brewer *et al.*, vi.134); Lloyd, *A History*, ii.549.
117 *ByT* (Pen. 20) [1096=1098]; *ByT* (RB) [1094=1098]; *ByS* [1096=1098]. Cadwgan received lands in Powys and Ceredigion in 1099; *ByT* (Pen. 20) [1097=1099]; *ByT* (RB) [1095=1099]; *ByS* [1097=1099].

to Gwynedd, preferring instead to involve himself with the Powys dynasty,[118] as did Uchdryd ab Edwin.[119] It cannot be assumed that this was because of Gruffudd's strength. Equally fortunate for Gruffudd were the deaths of Meurig and Griffri ap Trahaearn at the hands of Owain ap Cadwgan in 1106.[120] That the succession to Gwynedd in 1137 and 1170 was contested only by the previous incumbents' sons and grandsons was due not least to factors beyond Venedotian control.

It is also possible that the restriction of inheritance was due to a greater insistence on 'legitimacy' in the twelfth century: it has been argued that 'legitimacy and dynastic connexions cannot be shown to have been as important in the eleventh century as they were to become in the twelfth century and later'.[121] However, the twelfth century was primarily distinctive, not for its greater emphasis on theoretical legitimacy, but rather for the increasing attempts to deal with the same multiplicity of eligibility which had caused problems before 1098. Certainly, the theory of legitimacy was modified in some quarters in the twelfth and thirteenth centuries, under the pressures of dynastic self-preservation and ecclesiastical censure, but the practical difficulties faced by Rhys ap Gruffudd and Llywelyn ab Iorwerth as a result were enormous. Rather than change the rules to deny the rights of dissatisfied *membra regis*, it was much less trouble simply to develop more sophisticated methods of disposing of them physically. Killing was gradually superseded by mutilation, enforced *clericatus*, mediatisation, designation of heirs, and the adoption of the continental European practices of appanage and parage. There is no evidence for most of these under Gruffudd ap Cynan, but it does seem that his rule saw some extension of the king's control over the succession. The inactivity of some of Gruffudd's opponents may be connected to a possible reduction of their status; however, firm evidence for such a process of mediatisation is only found towards the end of the twelfth century, and the same is true of imprisonment and enforced *clericatus*.[122]

There is no unequivocal indication that Gruffudd chose his heir. The first recorded designation of an heir in Wales is that of Rhun by his father, Owain Gwynedd. After his death, Owain designated another son, Hywel, but Gruffudd's exemplary influence in this is unclear.[123] Even in the thirteenth

---

118 *ByT* (Pen. 20) [1103=1106], [1106=1109], [1108=1111], [1110=1113]; *ByT* (RB) [1106], [1105=1109], [1107=1111], [1110=1113]; *ByS* [1103=1106], [1106=1109], [1108=1111], [1110=1113].

119 *ByT* (Pen. 20) [1094=1096], [1106=1109], [1113=1116], [1115=1118]; *ByT* (RB) [1092=1096], [1105=1109], [1113=1116], [1115=1118]; *ByS* [1094=1096], [1106=1109], [1113=1116], [1115=1118].

120 *ByT* (Pen. 20) [1103=1106]; *ByT* (RB) [1106]; *ByS* [1103=1106].

121 Maund, *Ireland, Wales and England*, p. 172.

122 Smith, 'Dynastic succession', p. 208.

123 *ByT* (Pen. 20) [1145=1146]; *ByT* (RB) [1144=1146]; *ByS* [1145=1146]; see Lloyd, *A*

century, jurists disagreed about whether there could be more than one *gwrthrych*, or acknowledged heir, and it was not even clear with whom the right of designation should lie.[124] Owain had to withstand the challenge of the younger brother, Cadwaladr, in the 1140s, but his succession does nevertheless represent primogeniture, controlled or not.[125] The *Historia's* failure to mention Gruffudd's children by concubines perhaps indicates that there was indeed some concept that some children were more eligible than others – despite Owain's rejection of ecclesiastical censure on the issue of consanguineous marriage in the 1160s. Whether Owain's relatively easy succession was due to Gruffudd's careful planning or to chance is impossible to say.

That Gruffudd may have practised some form of designation is suggested by the fact that he was the first Welsh ruler to introduce appanage, but this may be an indication of the weakness of his position, rather than its strength. It was usual in Wales for lands to be divided amongst a man's sons, but Gruffudd's appanages were almost unique in twelfth-century Wales.[126] In France, where the Capetians and Valois designated one son and gave the rest appanages, the purpose was to strengthen central authority against challenges by dissatisfied *membra regis*.[127] When Gruffudd gave his 'furthest *cantrefi*' to his young sons as a defensive measure against neighbouring powers,[128] there would be little point in creating appanages, except as a recognition of the limits of royal power.[129] Indeed, appanages could provide power bases for potential rivals.[130] Gruffudd may have intended to groom his sons for the time when they would take over – in 1136, when he was an old man, Owain and Cadwaladr are described as 'the splendour of all Britain and her defence and her freedom'[131] – but it can only be speculated whether this increasingly important rôle was assumed with or without Gruffudd's consent. In comparison, Owain Gwynedd gave appanages to his brother and sons apparently in order to divert their attentions away from Gwynedd: Cadwaladr received Ceredigion Uwch Aeron and Meirionnydd; Dafydd the Perfeddwlad; and Hywel Ceredigion Is Aeron,[132] and it was perhaps this attempt by Owain to confine Cadwaladr to Ceredigion which caused the

---

  History, ii.466; Smith, 'Castell Gwyddgrug', pp. 76–7; Smith, 'Dynastic succession', p. 215.
[124] *Llyfr Iorwerth* (ed. Wiliam, pp. 4–5.)
[125] *ByT* (Pen. 20) [1143=11444]; *ByT* (RB) [1142=1144]; *ByS* [1143=1144].
[126] Davies, *Wales in the Early Middle Ages*, p. 123.
[127] Wood, *The French appanages*, chapter 1.
[128] *Historia*, ed. Evans, p. 30; *A Mediaeval Prince*, ed. & transl. Evans, p. 82.
[129] Davies, *Conquest, Co-existence and Change*, p. 245.
[130] Smith, 'Dynastic succession', p. 216.
[131] *ByT* (Pen. 20) [1135=1136]; *ByT* (RB) [1135=1136].
[132] *ByT* (Pen. 20) [1142=1143], [1146=1147]; *ByT* (RB) [1141=1143], [1145=147]; *ByS* [1142=1143], [1146=1147]; Smith, 'Dynastic succession', pp. 214, 217.

final rift between them.[133] The introduction of appanage, whilst it later became useful in consolidating the kingdom, did not in itself guarantee stability; it may rather reflect dynastic tensions.

Gruffudd's rule might appear to give weight to the view that mediaeval Wales was characterised by what has been called 'chronic instability',[134] and that Gruffudd did little to stabilise Gwynedd. The absence of a unitary rule of succession certainly contributed to these problems, but succession practices reflected instability as much as they caused it.[135] It is true that Gruffudd's son, Owain, failed to ensure a smooth succession after 1170, and also that dynastic conflicts dogged Gwynedd until the end of native Welsh independence, but it is also true that Gruffudd passed on his kingdom in one piece to his eldest surviving son, and that he achieved this by traditional means. Early twelfth-century Powys provides another example of the inherent stability of the Welsh polity: despite extreme dynastic problems, Maredudd ap Bleddyn passed the kingship to his son, Madog, without difficulty in 1132.[136] Gruffudd ap Cynan's lack of innovation needs to be seen in the context of his success in ridding himself of his rivals. Nowhere was the resilience and stability of his polity demonstrated more clearly than in his relations with the Normans and the Hiberno-Norse.

For much of the 1080s and 1090s, Gwynedd was controlled by Normans, who forced the Welsh to submit '*multis modis*'.[137] The death of Gruffudd ap Llywelyn had thrown Wales into confusion. Indeed, the twelfth-century poet, Geoffrey Gaimar, says that there was no more heed paid to the Welsh after 1063x1064.[138] The date of the first Norman incursions in Gwynedd is difficult to tell, but there was a week-long raid on Llŷn in the period 1075x1081, when the land was allegedly laid waste for eight years and many men of Llŷn fled into a long exile. Hugh of Chester and his accomplices are said to have done great slaughter amongst the Welsh, and Robert of Rhuddlan took the lands of Welsh lords, made them submit, and kept them in chains: he defeated *Trehellum* (Trahaearn ap Caradog?) and captured a certain Hywel (ab Ithel?).[139] The *Historia* relates that, shortly after his victory at Mynydd Carn in 1081, Gruffudd ap Cynan was tricked by one of his own men into meeting Hugh of Chester and Hugh of Shrewsbury, who

133 Lloyd, *A History*, ii.476; *ByT* (Pen. 20) [1143=1144]; *ByT* (RB) [1142=1144]; *ByS* [1143=1144].
134 Stephenson, *Governance*, p. xvii.
135 Davies, *Conquest, Co-existence and Change*, p. 267; Davies, *The British Isles*, p. 4.
136 Davies, *Conquest, Co-existence and Change*, p. 60.
137 Orderic Vitalis, *Historia Ecclesiastica* (ed. Chibnall, iv.138).
138 Geoffrey Gaimar, *L'Estoire des Engleis* (ed. Bell, v.5084); and see discussion by Lewis, below, pp. 61–76.
139 *Historia*, ed. Evans, pp. 12–13; *A Mediaeval Prince*, ed. & transl. Evans, p. 65; Orderic Vitalis, *Historia Ecclesiastica* (ed. Chibnall, ii.260, iv.138, 144); Lloyd, *A History*, ii.384.

promptly imprisoned him at Chester. The earl of Chester then made himself 'lord of the land', erecting castles in Môn, Arfon (on the site of Constantine's old castle at Caernarfon), Meirionnydd, and at Bangor. His soldiers perpetrated terrible crimes, while Gruffudd is said to have remained in prison for twelve or sixteen years.[140] As a result of all this, *Domesday Book* records Hugh of Chester in possession of Rhuddlan, whilst Robert of Rhuddlan acquired Rhos, Rhufoniog and *Nortwales* by 1086, and the Breton Hervé was imposed as bishop of Bangor in 1092.[141] Gruffudd ap Cynan had great difficulty in attempting to re-assert himself. After his escape from prison, he was worried for his safety until he reached Ireland, and did not dare to come straight back to Gwynedd. When he arrived in Ardudwy, he was forced to hide in caves for months, and, despite harrassing Hugh of Chester with 160 men, eventually had to flee again; a further expedition was brief and similarly unsuccessful.[142] Between 1081 and 1094, the only reference to any challenge to this Norman supremacy is when Robert of Rhuddlan was killed by a certain *Grithfridus*.[143]

Norman power remained considerable even after the Welsh revolts of 1094 and 1098. The earls of Chester and Shrewsbury ravaged Môn in 1098,[144] and Hywel ab Ithel was forced to flee from the Perfeddwlad in 1099.[145] Despite the Norman defeat in Môn in 1098 at the hands of a Scandinavian force, Gruffudd ap Cynan depended upon Hugh of Chester for his position when he returned in 1099. He and Cadwgan ap Bleddyn were given lands only after making peace with 'the French',[146] and even the *Historia* implies that Hugh expected to give permission for any extension of Gruffudd's power.[147] The persistence of Norman influence in Gwynedd after 1100 is shown by Henry I's gift to Gruffudd of Llŷn, Eifionydd, Ardudwy and Arllechwedd.[148]

Yet Norman power was not invincible. In 1075, one of Gruffudd ap Cynan's first acts after defeating Cynwrig ap Rhiwallon was to take the

---

[140] *Historia*, ed. Evans, pp. 17–18; *A Mediaeval Prince*, ed. & transl. Evans, pp. 69–70.

[141] *Domesday Book* I fo. 269a–b; Haddan and Stubbs, *Councils and ecclesiastical documents* i.299. Pope Paschal II called Hervé's election 'barbarous'. Haddan and Stubbs (*Councils and ecclesiastical documents* i.303–6). See also Lewis, below, pp. 74–5.

[142] *Historia*, ed. Evans, pp. 18–19; *A Mediaeval Prince*, ed. & transl. Evans, pp. 70–2.

[143] Orderic Vitalis, *Historia Ecclesiastica* (ed. Chibnall, iv.140).

[144] *ByT* (Pen. 20) [1096=1098]; *ByT* (RB) [1098]; *ByS* [1096=1098].

[145] *ByT* (Pen. 20) [1097=1099]; *ByT* (RB) [1095=1099]; *ByS* [1097=1099]; *AC* [1099].

[146] *ByT* (Pen. 20) [1097=1099]; *ByT* (RB) [1095=1099]; *ByS* [1097=1099]; *Historia*, ed. Evans, p. 27; *A Mediaeval Prince*, ed. & transl. Evans, p. 79.

[147] *Historia*, ed. Evans, pp. 28, 29; *A Mediaeval Prince*, ed. & transl. Evans, p. 80. Gruffudd received the support of the men of Rhos and captured some lands '*hep gannyat yarll Kaer*'.

[148] *Historia*, ed. Evans, p. 28; *A Mediaeval Prince*, ed. & transl. Evans, p. 79.

cantrefi bordering England, and he then destroyed Rhuddlan castle.[149] The great raid on Llŷn does not seem to have shaken the authority of Trahaearn ap Caradog, and Robert's death indicates the fragility of the Norman position in Gwynedd, as does the ease of Gruffudd's escape from Chester. It is interesting that his rescuer, one Cynwrig Hir, hailed from Edeirnion, where Gruffudd had been captured; although Reginald the sheriff is said to have held this *cwmwd* in 1086, Cynwrig's action may reflect an increasing Welsh dissatisfaction with Norman rule.[150] In 1094, the conditions for revolt were ideal. There were no major Norman leaders in north Wales – Robert of Rhuddlan was dead, and Hugh of Chester and the king, William Rufus, were in Normandy[151] – and it may be that Gruffudd ap Cynan was only recently returned to Gwynedd from prison.[152] The Welsh of Gwynedd, unable to bear the 'tyranny and injustice of the French', rose up and destroyed their castles, and a Norman relief expedition was subsequently defeated by Cadwgan ap Bleddyn at Coed Ysbwys.[153]

Although they seem to have restored some control, in 1098 the earls of Chester and Shrewsbury were again forced to bring in troops to relieve castles which were being attacked, presumably by the Welsh. It is apparently in the period 1094x1098 that the *Historia* reports that, despite his earlier failures, Gruffudd ap Cynan returned to Môn, where he defeated the Normans, destroyed their castles, and despoiled a ship from Chester before returning to take a castle in Môn for the second time. Other castles, including Aberlleiniog, were also seized, and, following a further victory in Môn, the Normans were driven out. The earls returned, intent on avenging these losses. However, although Gruffudd and his allies, Cadwgan and Maredudd ap Bleddyn were compelled to retire to Môn, a Scandinavian force appeared and routed the Normans, so that they 'fell from their horses like the fruit of figs from their trees'. This induced another Welsh revolt, in which Owain ab Edwin led the opposition to French laws and injustice.[154] Whether or not Gruffudd ap Cynan acquired Môn permanently in 1099,[155] Hugh of

---

149 *Historia*, ed. Evans, pp. 8, 9–10; *A Mediaeval Prince*, ed. & transl. Evans, pp. 61, 62; Meilyr also refers to Gruffudd's attacks on the march. (Williams, 'Meilyr Brydydd', below, pp. 00–00.)

150 *Historia*, ed. Evans, pp. 17, 18; *A Mediaeval Prince*, ed. & transl. Evans, pp. 70–1; *Domesday Book* i. fo. 255a.

151 Barlow, *William Rufus*, p. 357; ASC (E) 1094; John of Worcester, *Chronicon* 1094; William of Malmesbury, *De gestis regum Anglorum*, ed. Stubbs, ii.376).

152 Lloyd, *A History*, ii.404.

153 *ByT* (RB) [1094].

154 *Historia*, ed. Evans, pp. 20–1, 23, 26; *A Mediaeval Prince*, ed. & transl. Evans, pp. 72–3, 75, 78; *ByT* (Pen. 20) [1096=1098]; *ByT* (RB) [1098]. *ByS* says that the French built Aberlleiniog in 1098. (*ByS* [1096=1098].)

155 *ByT* (Pen. 20) [1097=1099]; *ByT* (RB) [1095=1099]; *AC* (B) [1099]; see Jones, transl., *ByT* (Pen. 20) p. 160.

Chester's power in Gwynedd was damaged to the extent that he removed all his goods to Rhos, and even there, more and more of the inhabitants offered their services to Gruffudd ap Cynan every day.[156] That the security of Gruffudd's position had improved considerably is suggested by the fact that he is not known to have fled to Ireland again after 1098–1099. Hugh's death in 1101, to be succeeded by his son, Richard, a minor,[157] further undermined Norman authority, and in 1102, Pope Paschal II arranged for Bishop Hervé to be removed to England. In 1109, Hervé was translated to Ely,[158] and the bishopric was kept vacant for eleven years. As a result, a Welshman, Dafydd, was elected as bishop of Bangor in 1120 'by king Gruffudd and the clergy and people of Wales',[159] and Gruffudd's prestige was such that he was consulted about the translation of the teeth of Saint Dyfrig from Bardsey to Llandaff.[160] Although there were royal expeditions, he was not troubled by the Norman marcher lords again during his lifetime. Gruffudd's kingdom remained unconquered, and in 1136, Owain and Cadwaladr defeated the Normans of Chester and Deheubarth.[161] The marcher hold on Gwynedd may be compared with that in Deheubarth, which was conquered in 1093. Ceredigion, Dyfed and other areas were taken, but it seems that the invaders' foothold was not secure. The sources hardly mention the Norman seizure of power, and by 1094 all their castles in Deheubarth except Pembroke and Rhyd y Gors were razed or deserted, whilst Pembroke town was ravaged by the Welsh, the Normans in Gwent and Brycheiniog were annihilated, and Montgomery itself was captured.[162] Having wrested control, the Normans found difficulty in retaining it in Powys and Deheubarth in the 1130s and 1140s, and strong native resistance persisted even in the most comprehensively Normanised parts of Wales.[163] In Gwynedd, Gruffudd ap Cynan ejected the Normans completely.

In assessing the impact of the Normans on Gwynedd, it is important to consider the nature of their military rôle. There was an element of avarice – Orderic Vitalis describes Hugh 'the Fat' of Chester as greedy, lustful and

156 *Historia*, ed. Evans, pp. 26–8; *A Mediaeval Prince*, ed. & transl. Evans, pp. 78–80.
157 *Annales Cestriensis* 1101.
158 Haddan and Stubbs, *Councils and Ecclesiastical Documents* i.304; William of Malmesbury, *De gestis regum Anglorum* (ed. Stubbs, ii.329).
159 Haddan and Stubbs, *Councils and Ecclesiastical Documents* i.314; John of Worcester, *Chronicon* 1120.
160 *The Text of the Book of Llan Dâv*, edd. Rhys and Evans, pp. 5, 84–5; and see Lewis, below, p. 76.
161 Cronne, 'Ranulf de Gernons', p. 111; *ByT* (Pen. 20) [1135=1136]; *ByT* (RB) [1135=1136]; *ByS* [1135=1136].
162 *ByT* (Pen. 20) [1092=1094], [1093=1095], [1094=1096]; *ByT* (RB) [1094], [1091=1095], [1092=1096]; *ByS* [1092=1094], [1093=1095], [1094=1096]; ASC (E) 1095.
163 For the situation in Morgannwg, see Crouch, 'The slow death', pp. 20–41.

violent, and native sources refer to Norman tyranny[164] – but, according to Orderic, the Normans' primary aim was to defend their lands in England.[165] It was the turbulence of the native polity which drew them in. When there was a strong ruler, the Normans kept their distance. Robert of Rhuddlan merely skirmished with Bleddyn ap Cynfyn, apparently in retaliation for a raid,[166] and, when Bleddyn died, Norman intervention was not immediate: it was only when there was '*llawer o drwc a govut yg Gwyned*' that a raid was launched on Llŷn.[167] Stability was a crucial factor: if it was not at stake, marcher lords often did not bother to intervene. Roger of Montgomery, for instance, stayed out of Deheubarth after 1075 despite the deaths of Bleddyn ap Cynfyn, Goronwy and Llywelyn ap Cadwgan ap Meurig, Rhys ab Owain, Trahaearn ap Caradog and Caradog ap Gruffudd, who all contended for the kingship in the period 1075–1081.[168] Hugh of Chester's retreat in 1098 may have been due to his satisfaction at the establishment of Owain ab Edwin as a stable ruler as much as it was caused by his lack of seapower.

The weakness of native inheritance rules was undoubtedly the catalyst of Norman intervention, but the Welsh polity did not simply collapse, either before or after the Norman onslaught. The Normans usually acted as part of the native polity, not against it. They were invited in. Gruffudd ap Cynan sought the support of Robert of Rhuddlan in 1075, and it was Meirion Goch, not the Norman earls, whose idea it was to lure Gruffudd to be captured. Caradog ap Gruffudd also had Norman military support at Mynydd Carn, first having used it in 1072,[169] and in 1098 it was Owain ab Edwin who brought the Normans into Gwynedd, possibly merely to further his own dynastic claims – he was very quick to turn against them.[170] As in Deheubarth in the 1130s and 1140s, Normans and Welsh were brought together in mutually beneficial arrangements: the experience of Hugh of Chester showed that direct Norman control of Gwynedd was never a realistic proposition. Thus, when Gervase of Canterbury says that the Welsh went back to their old ways in 1136, it must be asked to what extent they had ever

164 Orderic Vitalis, *Historia Ecclesiastica* (ed. Chibnall, ii.260); *ByT* (Pen. 20) [1092= 1094]; *ByT* (RB) [1094]; *ByS* [1092=1094].
165 Orderic Vitalis, *Historia Ecclesiastica* (ed. Chibnall, iv.138). See also Lewis, below, pp. 61–76.
166 Orderic Vitalis, *Historia Ecclesiastica* (ed. Chibnall, iv.144); this interpretation is based on the fact that Bleddyn had large quantities of booty with him.
167 *Historia*, ed. Evans, pp. 12–13; *A Mediaeval Prince*, ed. & transl. Evans, p. 65.
168 *ByT* (Pen. 20) [1073=1075], [1075=1077], [1076=1078], [1079=1081]; *ByT* (RB) [1075], [1077], [1078], [1081]; *ByS* [1073=1075], [1075=1077], [1076=1078], [1079=1081].
169 *Historia*, ed. Evans, pp. 7, 16, 14; *A Mediaeval Prince*, ed. & transl. Evans, pp. 59, 66, 69; *ByT* (Pen. 20) [1070=1072]; *ByT* (RB) [1072]; *ByS* [1070=1072].
170 *ByT* (Pen. 20) [1096=1098]; *ByT* (RB) [1094=1098]; *ByS* [1096=1098].

left them.[171] Nevertheless, it was worth forging links with the Norman world. Gruffudd ap Cynan gave patronage to churches at Chester and Shrewsbury, and, whilst sometimes condemning the 'foreigners', the *Historia* is keen to point out Gruffudd's links with them: it is claimed that his alleged ancestor, Harold Harfagr, had a brother, *Rodulf*, who conquered Normandy, and a clear connection is made between this man and William I, William II, Henry I and Stephen, Gruffudd's '*gytoeswyr*'.[172] Yet, although there is no doubt that the Normans were an important new influence, it is significant that, unlike the thirteenth-century princes of Gwynedd, Gruffudd did not marry into Anglo-Norman aristocratic society. His world was still primarily that of the Irish Sea polity.

Having been born and raised in Ireland, Gruffudd's connexions with Ireland were naturally strong. His mother's name, *Ragnell verch Avloed*, was distinctively Scandinavian, and according to the *Historia*, his maternal grandfather, *Avloed* (Olaf Sihtricsson), was a Hiberno-Norse king of Dublin, a fifth of Ireland and '*lawer o enyssed ereill, Denmarc, a Galwei, a Renneu, a Mon, a Gwynedd*'. Gruffudd consequently possessed extensive genealogical links in Ireland and the Scandinavian world. Although many of the *Historia*'s statements are incorrect, it is clear that great pride was taken in the claim of descent from Harald Harfagr and Brian Bóroimhe, and the assertion that Gruffudd's two uterine brothers were kings of Ulster. The *Historia* also takes a great interest in Irish and Hiberno-Norse politics, and, whilst the account of Gruffudd's connexions with Munster, Meath and Ulster is inaccurate,[173] the claims that he was on good terms with both king *Mwrchath* of Ireland and the king of the Isles and Denmark, and that the Irish and Danes mourned his death, are convincing.[174] Certainly, Gruffudd gave 20s. to the church of Christ in Dublin in his will.[175]

Gruffudd relied heavily on Ireland as a place of refuge and as a source of military support: it was usually his first destination when he met difficulties in Wales. His first expedition was launched from Ireland, and after Bron yr Erw he returned to Wexford, where the king of Leinster heard his complaints and urged him to return quickly to Wales. Betrayed by his Welsh allies, Gruffudd was soon back with a king *Diermit* in Wexford. He made

---

[171] Gervase of Canterbury, *Historical Works* (ed. Stubbs, i.95); but see also Lewis, below, pp. 61–76.

[172] *Historia*, ed. Evans, pp. 4, 30; *A Mediaeval Prince*, ed. & transl. Evans, pp. 56, 81; and see also Maund, below, pp. 109–16.

[173] *Historia*, ed. Evans, pp. clxxii–clxxix, 1, 3–4, 5, 6; *A Mediaeval Prince*, ed. & transl. Evans, pp. 53, 55–6, 57, 58; Charles, *Old Norse Relations with Wales*, pp. 56–8. But see also Thornton, below, pp. 79–108.

[174] *Historia*, ed. Evans, pp. 30, 32; *A Mediaeval Prince*, ed. & transl. Evans, pp. 81, 83. 'Mwrchath' may have been either Murchad mac Diarmait or Muirchertach hUa Briain. (Maund, *Ireland, Wales and England*, pp. 180–1).

[175] *Historia*, ed. Evans, p. 31; *A Mediaeval Prince*, ed. & transl. Evans, p. 82.

straight for Ireland again after his escape from prison, and rowed from
Aberdaron after his abortive attempt to wrest control of Gwynedd from the
Normans. Yet another transfretation between Gwynedd and Ireland after a
brief visit to Wales was followed by a visit to his *'gyueillt'*, *Gothrei*, in the
'islands of Denmark'. Gruffudd returned there again before 1098, when he
and Cadwgan ap Bleddyn fled to Ireland.[176] The core of Gruffudd's expeditions was essentially Hiberno-Scandinavian. Danes and Irish, including
his foster-father *Cerit* and *Varudri*, the lord of Cruach Breandain in Munster,
fought with him at Bron yr Erw, and he was given thirty ships by the king
of Leinster. He was fitted out again with a Danish, Irish and Welsh fleet for
the Mynydd Carn campaign, when the Irishman *Gucharki* killed Trahaearn
ap Caradog. Gruffudd was also given a fleet of sixty ships by *Gothrei*, and
he received a further sixteen from Ireland in 1098.[177] He is also said to have
been involved in a raid by Norsemen from the northern isles on Barry and
Newport in the reign of William I,[178] and the rôle of the Norwegian fleet,
although unexpected and unsolicited, in defeating the Normans in 1098 was
crucial in allowing Gruffudd a vital foothold in Gwynedd.[179]

Clearly, the Hiberno-Scandinavian world was of vital importance to
Gruffudd, but how influential was it in the Welsh polity generally? That
Gruffudd had such strong personal connexions with Ireland would seem to
make him an exception in this respect: the *Historia*, for instance, is the only
Welsh source with sufficient knowledge or interest to distinguish between
Irish and Danes.[180] Since other Welsh sources rarely mention the Hiberno-
Scandinavians, the fact that the *Historia* portrays Gruffudd so often in their

---

176 *Historia*, ed. Evans, pp. 11, 12, 13, 18, 19, 20, 24; *A Mediaeval Prince*, ed. & transl.
Evans, pp. 63, 64, 65, 71, 72, 76. The *Historia*'s reference to king *'Diermit'* in 1081 is
confused. It apparently refers to Diarmaid mac Máel na mBó, who died in 1072. (Maund,
'Trahaearn', pp. 468–9) It is possible that *'Gothrei'* or *'Guthrie'* may be identified with
Godfrey Meranach, king of Dublin and the Isles in the early 1090s. Alternatively, he
may be Godred Crovan of Man. Maund, *Ireland, Wales and England*, p. 181; Orderic
Vitalis, *Historia Ecclesiastica* (ed. Chibnall, iv.140) In either case, this could be the same
person as the *'Grithfridus rex Guallanorum'* who killed Robert of Rhuddlan. Orderic
says that Hugh of Shrewsbury was concerned to defend Degannwy against Welsh and
Norse raiders in 1098; were these Gruffudd ap Cynan and *'Gothrei'*? (Orderic Vitalis,
Historia Ecclesiastica, ed. Chibnall, v.224.)
177 *Historia*, ed. Evans, pp. 10, 11, 12, 13, 14, 15, 19, 23–4; *A Mediaeval Prince*, ed. &
transl. Evans, pp. 62, 63, 64, 65, 66, 67, 68, 72, 76. The name *'Varudri'* may represent
'mac Ruaidhrí', possibly Cathal mac Ruaidhrí O Conchobhair of Connacht. (Fitzgerald,
The Contacts between Britain and Ireland, pp. 256–7.)
178 *Vitae sanctorum Britanniae*, ed. Wade-Evans, pp. 182–4.
179 *Historia*, ed. Evans, pp. 25–6; *A Mediaeval Prince*, ed. & transl. Evans, pp. 77, 78.
Magnus Berfœtts appeared without warning and did not appear to know where he was
or what was happening in Môn. When told, he sympathised with the Welsh and brought
in three ships.
180 *Historia*, ed. Evans, pp. 14, 15; *A Mediaeval Prince*, ed. & transl. Evans, pp. 66, 67.

company creates an impression that he was by far the most significant user of their help in Wales. This is reinforced by the resurgence of viking raids on Wales during the 1070s and 1080s after a lull of twenty years, coinciding with Gruffudd's struggle for power.[181] However, other than the *Historia*, the Welsh sources (which are admittedly laconic) mention Gruffudd's Hiberno-Scandinavian forces only twice,[182] and there is no reference at all to his Irish background. Even Meilyr makes very little of the Irish dimension in Gruffudd's career. Furthermore, there is no mention of him in Irish annals, although they do note Llywelyn ap Seisyll, Iago ab Idwal, Gruffudd ap Llywelyn and Rhys ap Tewdwr in the eleventh century.[183] Despite Gruffudd's ultimate success, he meant less to the Irish than some of his Welsh contemporaries. Moreover, the Welsh themselves do not seem to have regarded his Irish links as unusual. The implication is that, whilst Gruffudd's personal circumstances make him an exception to a certain degree, contact between Wales and Ireland was considerable.

Welsh contacts with Ireland increased in the eleventh century. *Brut y Tywysogion* records the battle of Clontarf in 1014 in considerable detail, and some Welshmen were present at the battle, possibly concerned to protect trading interests in eastern Ireland.[184] An Irish trade, including the sale of Welsh captives, is mentioned at Aberdyfi in the early twelfth century,[185] and there were also ecclesiastical links: in 1120, Gruffudd ap Cynan threatened to have an Irishman sent over to consecrate the bishop of Bangor.[186] The *Brutiau* give obits for Donnchadh hUa Briain of Munster in 1065, Diarmait mac Máel na mBó of Leinster in 1072, and Toirrdhealbhach hUa Briain of Munster in 1086, and the attention was reciprocated across the Irish Sea: the *Chronicle of the kings of Man and the Isles* gives more attention to the death of Gruffudd ap Llywelyn than it does to that of William the Conqueror.[187] Welsh rulers found Ireland increasingly attractive as a refuge. The only

---

[181] According to the Welsh chronicles, there were apparently no viking raids in Wales between 1055 and 1073. St Davids and Bangor were attacked in 1073, and St Davids again in 1080 and 1089. *ByT* (Pen. 20). [1071=1073]; *ByT* (RB) [1073]; *ByS* [1071=1073]; *AC* (B) [1080], *AC* (C) [1081]; *ByT* (Pen. 20) [1078=1080]; *ByT* (RB) [1080]; *ByS* [1078=1080]; *AC* (B) [1089]; *ByT* (Pen. 20) [1087=1089]; *ByT* (RB) [1089]; *ByS* [1088=1089].

[182] *ByT* (Pen. 20) [1079=1081], [1096=1098]; *ByT* (RB) [1081], [1094=1098]; *ByS* [1079=1081], [1096=1098].

[183] Maund, *Ireland, Wales and England*, p. 163.

[184] *ByT* (Pen. 20) [1014]; *ByT* (RB) [1014]; *ByS* [1013=1014]; ALC 1014; Charles, *Old Norse relations with Wales*, p. 160.

[185] *ByT* (Pen. 20) [1106=1109], [1107=1110]; *ByT* (RB) [1105=1109], [1106=1110]; *ByS* [1106=1109], [1107=1110].

[186] Pryce, 'Church and Society in Wales', p. 28.

[187] *ByT* (Pen. 20) [1064=1065], [1070=1072], [1084=1086]; *ByT* (RB) [1065], [1072]; *ByS* [1064=1065], [1070=1072], [1084=1086]; *Chronicle of the kings of Man and the Isles*, ed. Broderick and Stowell, pp. 5, 7.

one known to have visited Ireland before the eleventh century is Rhodri Mawr,[188] but in the period 1075–1110 he was followed by Rhys ap Tewdwr, Gruffudd ap Cynan, Cadwgan ap Bleddyn, Owain ap Cadwgan, Hywel ab Ithel, Madog ap Rhirid and Gruffudd ap Rhys,[189]and many men of Llŷn may also have fled to Ireland after the Norman raid there.[190]

Ireland was most important as a source of military support. Cynan ab Iago is said to have had help from Dublin in mounting two attacks on Gruffudd ap Llywelyn in 1039x1050 and 1050,[191] which may help to explain Gruffudd's capture by the men of Dublin in 1042, and also the Irish fleet which foundered in south Wales in 1052.[192] Hiberno-Norse mercenaries were also used by Maredudd ab Owain and Hywel ab Edwin, and Gruffudd ap Llywelyn's fleet in 1063 was possibly Norse.[193] Rhys ap Tewdwr is found with Hiberno-Scandinavian forces twice: he paid them a large *census* for fighting the sons of Bleddyn ap Cynfyn in 1088, and in 1093 he was joined by a certain Turcaill mac Éola.[194] Cadwgan ap Bleddyn received support from Muirchertach hUa Briain in 1109, and Gruffudd ap Rhys probably had Irish help as well in 1115. Gruffudd's sons, Anarawd and Cadell, together with Owain and Cadwaladr ap Gruffudd ap Cynan, employed fifteen Hiberno-Norse ships when they attacked Cardigan in 1138, and Cadwaladr was forced to pay his Irish mercenaries two thousand head of cattle under duress for their services in 1144.[195] Cadwaladr's unpleasant experience was not unusual. Gruffudd ap Cynan and Cadwgan ap Bleddyn fled when they feared Hiberno-Norse treachery in 1098, and Gruffudd's fears were realised on other occasions when he failed to reward his followers as promised.[196]

188 AU 877.
189 *AC* (B) [1087], [1098], [1099]; *AC* (C) [1087], [1098], [1099]; *ByT* (Pen. 20) [1086=1088], [1096=1098], [1097=1099], [1106=1109], [1107=1110], [1112= 1115]; *ByT* (RB) [1088], [1094=1098], [1095=1099], [1105=1109], [1106=1110], [1112=1115]; *ByS* [1088], [1096=1098], [1097=1099], [1106=1109], [1107=1110], [1112=1115]. It is possible that Gruffudd ap Llywelyn died in Ireland, Hudson, 'The destruction', p. 349.
190 *Historia*, ed. Evans, p. 13; *A Mediaeval Prince*, ed. & transl. Evans, p. 65.
191 This is from a seventeenth-century Irish source. Hudson, 'The destruction', p. 342.
192 *ByT* (Pen. 20) [1040=1042], [1050=1052]; *ByT* (RB) [1040=1042], [1050=1052]; *ByS* [1040=1042], [1050=1052].
193 *ByT* (Pen. 20) [991=992], [1042=1044]; *ByT* (RB) [990=992], [1044]; *ByS* [1042=1044]; John of Worcester, *Chronicon* 1063.
194 *ByT* (Pen. 20) [1086=1088]; *ByT* [1088]; *ByS* [1088]; *AC* (B) [1087]; *AC* (C) [1087]; AI 1093.
195 *ByT* (Pen. 20) [1106=1109], [1112=1115] [1143=1144]; *ByT* (RB) [1105=1109], [1112=1115], [1142=1144]; *ByS* [1106=1109], [1112=1115], [1143=1144]; *AC* (C) [1138]. Cadwaladr's fleet was probably the '*llu nortmein*' which Owain Gwynedd fought. (*Llawysgrif Hendregadredd* ed. Morris-Jones and Williams, p. 83.)
196 *Historia*, ed. Evans, pp. 11, 12, 24, 25; *A Mediaeval Prince*, ed. & transl. Evans, pp. 62–3, 65, 76, 77; *ByT* (Pen. 20) [1096=1098]; *ByT* (RB) [1094=1098]; *ByS* [1096=1098]. Gruffudd seems to have ravaged Môn in order to collect spoils for them.

Not surprisingly, the Irish were not universally popular. Fifty two of Gruffudd ap Cynan's supporters were killed by the men of Llŷn, and Madog ap Rhirid soon came home from Ireland, 'unable to suffer the evil ways and evil customs of the Irish'.[197]

The picture of interaction between Ireland and Wales is one of a network in which the *Historia* is unexceptional. Although contacts declined in the later twelfth century, nearly all the major Welsh rulers of the late eleventh and early twelfth centuries are known to have used Ireland as a base or a supply of troops. Rhys ap Tewdwr, in particular, emerges in a very similar light to Gruffudd ap Cynan in all the sources except the *Historia*. In the Welsh chronicles, both are found twice with Irish mercenaries, and Rhys, like Gruffudd, had relatives in Ireland: his son, Gruffudd, was sent to Ireland by his kin for protection, probably after Rhys's death in 1093.[198] That this Irish Sea dimension persisted into the twelfth and thirteenth centuries is attested by the composition of the *Historia* – a striking example of cultural assimilation – probably in the 1160s.[199] A certain Godred, 'king of Man', was in Gwynedd in 1241, and Godred Magnusson fled to Wales in 1275. As late as 1276x1282, Edward I feared that Llywelyn ap Gruffudd might receive supplies from Scotland, Norway and Man.[200] There were also dynastic links: Cynan ab Owain Gwynedd may have had an Irish mother, and Hywel ab Owain certainly did, whilst Rhodri ab Owain arranged to marry the daughter of Reginald Godredsson of Man, probably in the period 1190x1195. Llywelyn ab Iorwerth attempted to marry the same woman between 1199 and 1203.[201] Gruffudd ap Cynan's successors also held lands in Ireland. In 1218, an inquisition was held in Dublin into whether Maelgwn ab Owain had ever held certain lands in Dublin, so that seisin could pass to Llywelyn ab Iorwerth,[202] and there are references to the family of a certain *Richerid/ Rericius/ Ritheric/ Righerid* in Dublin in the late twelfth and thirteenth centuries.[203] Their lands at Cloghran, between Dublin and

---

[197] *Historia*, ed. Evans, p. 10; *A Mediaeval Prince*, ed. & transl. Evans, p. 62; *ByT* (Pen. 20) [1107=1110]; *ByT* (RB) [1106=1110]; *ByS* [1107=1110].

[198] *ByT* (Pen. 20) [1079=1081], [1086= 1088], [1096=1098], [1112=1115]; *ByT* (RB) [1081], [1088], [1094=1098], [1112=1115]; *ByS* [1079=1081], [1088], [1096=1098], [1112=1115]; *AC* (B) [1087]; *AC* (C) [1087]; AI 1093; *The Myvyrian archaiology of Wales*, edd. Jones, Williams and Owen, ii.522.

[199] For this date, see *Historia*, ed. Evans, ccxliii–ccxlix; the work includes a description of Gruffudd given from the accounts of his '*kedemdeitheon*' (*Historia*, ed. Evans, p. 17; *A Mediaeval Prince*, ed. & transl. Evans, p. 70), so it presumably dates from the decades after his death.

[200] Smith, *Llywelyn ap Gruffudd*, p. 37; Broderick, 'Irish and Welsh Strands', p. 36; Edwards, *Calendar of Ancient Correspondence*, pp. 45–6.

[201] Lloyd, *A History*, ii.549.

[202] Hardy, ed. *Rotuli Litterarum Clausarum*, i.362b.

[203] Curtis, 'The Fitz Rerys', p. 15.

Gruffudd ap Cynan's childhood home at Swords, may have been a Venedotian tenure since Gruffudd's time or that of Cynan ab Iago.[204] The military rôle of Ireland persisted, even after the Anglo-Norman invasion, although there are no examples for twenty five years before 1169. Maelgwn ab Owain went to Ireland in 1173, Maelgwn ap Rhys employed an Irishman to kill Cydifor ap Gruffudd in 1205, and Rhodri ab Owain and the son of Godred Olafsson of Man (Reginald Godredsson?) campaigned in Môn in 1193.[205]

The Hiberno-Norse involvement in Wales consisted of more than mercenary work.[206] There had been viking raids since the late ninth century,[207] and, although these lessened in the period 1001–1033,[208] they resumed in the 1080s,[209] and Gruffudd ap Cynan had to fight off raids on Venedotian satellites in the twelfth century.[210] Viking raids in the tenth century were generally for tribute,[211] but there is evidence for Scandinavian settlement and rule in Gwynedd from the tenth century.[212] Ingimund founded a settlement at Osfeilion, near Llanfaes, in Môn in 902–903, and Gruffudd ap Cynan's grandfather, Olaf Sihtricsson, is said to have made a castle with a mound and a ditch at Bon y Dom in Gwynedd.[213] Magnus *Berfoetts*, the king of Norway, was believed to have intended to make a settlement in Môn, and his motives in arriving off Môn in 1098, and then returning there and

---

204 This possibility is supported by the seventeenth-century Cardiff MS. 25. (Bartrum, 'Achau brenhinoedd y thywysogion Cymru', p. 207.)
205 *ByT* (Pen. 20) 1173, 1193, 1205; *ByT* (RB) 1173, 1193, 1205; *ByS* 1173, 1193, 1205. See Jones, transl., *ByT* (Pen. 20), p. 189. The Môn episode was known as '*haf y gwydyl*', Lloyd, *A History*, ii.588.
206 For the vikings and Wales, see Davies, *Wales in the Early Middle Ages*, pp. 116–20; Davies, *Patterns of Power*, pp. 48–60; Maund, *Ireland, Wales and England*, pp. 156–82.
207 *ByT* (Pen. 20) [853=855], [876=877], [890=892], [894=896], [900=903], [918], [950=952], [959=961], [961=963], [966=968], [969=971], [970=972], [977=978], [979=980], [986=987], [988=989], [992=993], [1000=1001], [1020=1022], [1031=1033], [1040=1042], [1042=1044], [1050=1052], [1071=1073], [1078=1080], [1087=1089], [1096=1098], [1100=1102]; *ByT* (RB) [855], [877], [892], [896], [900=903], [918], [950=952], [961], [963], [968], [971], [970=972], [980], [987], [989], [993], [1001], [1022], [1030=1033], [1040=1042], [1044], [1050=1052], [1073], [1080], [1089], [1094=1098], [1100=1102]; *ByS* [853=855], [876=877], [890=892], [894=896], [900=903], [914=918], [959=961], [961=963], [966=968], [969=971], [970=972], [979=980], [986=987], [988=989], [992=993], [1000=1001], [1020=1022], [1040=1042], [1042=1044], [1050=1052], [1071=1073], [1078=1080], [1087=1089], [1096=1098], [1100=1102].
208 Maund, *Ireland, Wales and England*, pp. 161–2.
209 *ByT* (Pen. 20) [1071=1073], [1078=1080], [1087=1089]; *ByT* (RB) [1073], [1080], [1089]; *ByS* [1071=1073], [1087=1089]; *AC* (B) [1078], [1089]; *AC* (C) [1078], [1089]. Diarmait hUa Briain also raided in Wales. (AI 1080).
210 *Historia*, ed. Evans, p. 31; *A Mediaeval Prince*, ed. & transl. Evans, p. 82.
211 Davies, *Patterns of Power*, pp. 57–8.
212 *Ibid.*, pp. 51–6 (for Scandinavian settlement), and pp. 56–60 (for rulers).
213 *AC* (A) [902]; Wainwright, 'Ingimund's Invasion', pp. 145–69; *Historia*, ed. Evans, p. 2; *A Mediaeval Prince*, ed. & transl. Evans, p. 55.

collecting timber in 1102, are obscure:[214] he may have been interested in trading links, or concerned about the growing power of the Normans in north Wales. The twelfth-century *Orkneyinga Saga* also mentions a settlement at *Jarlsness* (possibly named after the killing of Hugh of Shrewsbury), which was visited by Swein Asleifarsson and Holdboði in 1139x1148.[215]

Scandinavians may have controlled large parts of Gwynedd between *ca* 960 and *ca* 1025. At that time, native members of the Venedotian dynasty may have paid tribute to the Scandinavians and were not called kings of Gwynedd. A Scandinavian, Sigferth, was present both when the Welsh rowed Eadgar on the Dee in 973 and at Eadred's court in 955, apparently in the rôle of a Welsh ruler, and in the 970s and 980s the sons of Harold – based in Man – seem in effect to have controlled Gwynedd.[216] The memory of kings of Norway exercising lordship in Môn still existed in the twelfth century, and Môn was listed in the *Chronicle of Man and the Sudreys* as their possession. Olaf Sihtricsson is said by the *Historia* to have been king in Gwynedd, and Diarmaid mac Máel na mBó was styled '*rí Breatan*', possibly referring to rule in Wales itself, rather than of Welshmen in Ireland.[217] Such was Scandinavian influence that it was believed in Wales and England in 1098 that Magnus *Berfoetts* had brought Harold, the son of Harold Godwinesson, with him, and that he intended to conquer the whole island of Britain.[218]

Yet an extensive Hiberno-Scandinavian presence and military influence does not mean that the native dynasty was ousted, and there is certainly no evidence for Scandinavian polities – by which is implied large enclaves with a hinterland – in Wales.[219] There was never any possibility of a Scandinavian takeover. The only individuals from the Hiberno-Scandinavian world who came near to achieving kingship were Gruffudd ap Cynan and Rhain, who may have been of mixed Welsh, Irish and Hiberno- Scandinavian descent,[220] and who claimed in 1022 to be the son of Maredudd ab Owain of Deheubarth. He won support and lands, but was ultimately defeated, despite an apparent attempt to revive his fortunes by Olaf Sihtricsson.[221] Both

---

[214] Orderic Vitalis, *Historia Ecclesiastica* (ed. Chibnall, v.224); *ByT* (Pen. 20) [1096=1098], [1100=1102]; *ByT* (RB) [1094=1098], [1100=1102]; *ByS* [1096=1098], [1100=1102].

[215] Pálsson and Edwards, transl., *Orkneyinga Saga* p. 146; Charles, *Old Norse relations with Wales*, p. 115; Jesch, below, pp. 117–47.

[216] Davies, *Patterns of Power*, pp. 58–9.

[217] Pálsson and Edwards, transl., *Orkneyinga Saga* p. 85; *Chronicle of Man and the Sudreys*, ed. Munch, pp. 58, 158; *Historia*, ed. Evans, p. 2; *A Mediaeval Prince*, ed. & transl. Evans, pp. 54–5; AT 1052, 1072.

[218] William of Malmesbury, *De gestis regum Anglorum* (ed. Stubbs, ii.376); *ByT* (Pen. 20) [1096=1098]; *ByT* (RB) [1094=1098]; *ByS* [1096=1098].

[219] Davies, *Patterns of Power*, p. 57.

[220] Maund, *Ireland, Wales and England*, p. 160.

[221] *AC* (B) [1022]; *AC* (C) [1022]; *ByT* (Pen. 20) [1020=1022]; *ByT* (RB) [1022]; *ByS* [1020=1022].

Gruffudd and Rhain achieved what they did through native institutions, not merely by external force. Furthermore, the primary Hiberno-Scandinavian aim was not necessarily conquest. In an attenuated polity of dominions stretching from Scandinavia, through the Faroes, Shetland, Orkney, the Hebrides, the Scottish mainland and Man, Môn was on the periphery. Gwynedd's importance lay in its situation on the Dublin-Chester trade route, as well its ability to provide useful allies, as Magnus *Berfoetts* found in 1058.[222] Contrary to William of Malmesbury and the *Brutiau*, the *Historia* and *Orkneyinga Saga*, which can be assumed to know at least as much about the Scandinavian world, portray Magnus *Berfoetts*'s Norsemen in Môn in 1098 as having arrived accidentally, with no intention of conquering anything – Magnus even had to be told where he was, who held it, and who was attacking it. He reportedly said that he had only come to look at Britain and Ireland, and one of his men, Magnus Erlendsson, said that he had no quarrel with anyone in Môn.[223] This impression is borne out by Irish sources, which do not mention these events at all.

Nevertheless, the Scandinavian military influence was arguably as great if not greater than that of the Normans. For instance, in 1098 it was the Irish upon whom the Welsh called for help, and it was they who, when bribed, brought the Normans to Môn.[224] Although the sources are generally laconic about the Hiberno-Scandinavian connexion, native rulers were as keen to ally themselves with foreigners from Ireland as they were with foreigners from England. The Norman impact was strong, but it remains that many of those Welshmen who brought troops from Ireland never used Norman support. Indeed, such was the relative importance of Ireland and England in Welsh eyes that, as late as 1135, the *Brut y Tywysogions obit* for Muirchertach hUa Briain – 'the man of greatest power and authority and victory of the men of Ireland' – is far more impressive than that for Henry I, who was merely the 'son of William the Bastard'.[225] The importance of the Irish Sea polity was not lost on the Normans. Arnulf of Montgomery married a Leinster princess in 1102,[226] and in 1098 Hugh of Chester enticed Gruffudd ap Cynan's Danish supporters into changing sides, promising them rich rewards.[227] The defeat of the Norman earls by a Scandinavian

---

222 *ByT* (Pen. 20) [1056=1058]; *ByT* (RB) [1058]; *ByS* [1056=1058].
223 *Historia*, ed. Evans, p. 26; *A Mediaeval Prince*, ed. & transl. Evans, p. 78; Pálsson and Edwards, transl., *Orkneyinga Saga* p. 84.
224 *ByT* (Pen. 20) [1096=1098]; *ByT* (RB) [1094=1098]; *ByS* [1096=1098] says that only then did the Welsh retreat, for protection against the Irish and sea pirates.
225 *ByT* (Pen. 20) [1116=1119], [1134=1135]; *ByT* (RB) [1116=1119], [1134=1135]; *ByS* [1116=1119]. It may be argued, of course, that Henry and William needed no introduction.
226 *ByT* (Pen. 20) [1100=1102]; *ByT* (RB) [1100=1102]; *ByS* [1100=1102]; Curtis, 'Muirchertach O'Brien', pp. 116–24; Mason, 'Roger de Montgomery', p. 23.
227 *Historia*, ed. Evans, p. 24; *A Mediaeval Prince*, ed. & transl. Evans, p. 76. They later

fleet in 1098 showed clearly that Venedotian politics were still influenced as much by the Irish Sea as by England.

Moreover, like that of the Normans, the Irish and Scandinavian rôle in Gwynedd stemmed ultimately from the workings of the native polity. Both were to a large extent part of a native Welsh tendency to employ external aid which had begun with the use of Anglo-Saxon help in the tenth century.[228] Both usually came into Gwynedd by invitation. The internecine warfare and external interventions which shook Gwynedd between the 1070s and the 1090s were almost all conducted along the conventions of the native polity, and thus Gruffudd ap Cynan's kingdom emerged in the 1120s and 1130s having survived intact.

The importance of this period lies not only in Gruffudd's eventual success in retaining native control of Gwynedd and asserting strong rule, but also in the contribution he made in the evolution of the later principality of Wales. Less than twenty years after Gruffudd's death, Owain Gwynedd would anticipate Llywelyn ab Iorwerth and Llywelyn ap Gruffudd in heading an alliance of the most prominent native rulers and calling himself '*princeps Walliae*'.[229] At the same time, the king of England came to play an increasingly important rôle, which in the thirteenth century was to culminate in the formal subjection of Gwynedd to the crown, and ultimately the destruction of native autonomy. These developments need to be examined from the point of view of Gruffudd ap Cynan and the native polity.

Gwynedd withstood several royal campaigns in this period,[230] but the extension of the king's influence can not be judged merely in military terms.[231] The tradition of English royal influence was a long one. In 878, the Welsh sought the lordship and protection of Alfred of Wessex, and Anarawd ap Rhodri of Gwynedd similarly asked for an alliance in 893, agreeing to be obedient to the royal will. Another submission was made to Edward the Elder in 918, and in 927 Æthelstan is said to have levied a yearly

---

turned against him when they found they had been deceived; *Historia*, ed. Evans, p. 27; *A Mediaeval Prince*, ed. & transl. Evans, p. 79.

[228] Davies, *Patterns of Power*, p. 77; it is perhaps in this context that such viking activity as the ravaging of Dyfed in 1042, the attack diverted by Gruffudd ap Rhydderch in 1049, and the capture of Meurig ap Hywel in 1039 should be seen. (*ByT* (Pen. 20) [1037=1039], [1040=1042]; *ByT* (RB) [1039], [1040=1042]; *ByS* [1037=1039], [1040=1042]; John of Worcester, *Chronicon* 1049; *AC* (C) [1037].)

[229] *AC* (B) [1165]; *AC* (C) [1165]; Robertson ed. *Materials for the history of Thomas Becket*, v.239.

[230] *ByT* (Pen. 20) [1092=1094], [1095=1097], [1111=1114]; *ByT* (RB) [1094], [1093=1097], [1111=1114]; *ByS* [1092=1094], [1095=1097], [1111=1114].

[231] The isolation of Wales from the rest of Celtic Britain by the Anglo-Saxons was largely the result of peaceful colonisation, rather than warfare. (Davies, *Patterns of Power*, pp. 62–4.) For the development of the relationship between the native Welsh rulers and the king of England, see Roderick, 'The Feudal Relationship', pp. 201–12.

tribute. There were also Welshmen at the West Saxon court in this period, and a further submission was made to Eadgar in 973. Gruffudd ap Rhydderch is alleged to have sworn fealty to Harold Godwinesson in 1042, and in 1056 it is reported that Gruffudd ap Llywelyn become Edward the Confessor's 'loyal and faithful *"undercyning"* '. Gruffudd is said to have met Edward and become his man, but only after Edward recognised his equal status as a king. Nevertheless, in 1063x1064, Bleddyn and Rhiwallon were seen by the English as Harold Godwinesson's *'satellites'*, under the *'imperium'* of King Edward, who entrusted Wales to them on condition that they observed all the duties done by their predecessors, and that they helped the king by land and sea and were obedient.[232] Welsh submissions to the Anglo-Saxons represented a relationship of alliance as much as overlordship, and the eleventh century was characterised more by mutual containment than by intrusive royal authority, but the intensification of English influence is clear.[233] Gruffudd ap Cynan inherited a well-established tradition of Wessex-based Anglocentric monarchal dominance of the British Isles.

This tradition was continued by the Norman kings. William the Conqueror is said to have forced Gruffudd to make peace, and his visit to St. Davids in 1081 seems to have marked some form of assertion of overlordship.[234] He is also reported to have taken tribute from all the Welsh, and English royal superiority is made explicit by the *Brutiau* and other native sources, which call him 'king of the English and of Wales'.[235] There was a long-standing idea in Wales that Britain was a single polity, and that its centre lay in England. In the laws, *'mechteyrn dyled'* was due to the king of London, of whom Welsh lands were held, and in *Pedeir keinc y Mabinogi*, Pryderi submits to Caswallon ap Beli in Oxford. The king of England was therefore like Arthur, who is referred to by the *Historia* as king of the kings of Britain.[236] Henry I was believed by the Welsh to have subdued the whole

232 Asser, *Life of King Alfred* (transl. Keynes and Lapidge, p. 96); Davies, *Wales in the Early Middle Ages*, p. 114; William of Malmesbury, *De gestis regum Anglorum* (ed. Stubbs, i.148, 237, 280); ASC (A) 973; ASC (C) 1055, 1063; John of Worcester, *Chronicon* 973, 1064; Walter Map, *De nugis curialum* (ed. James, p. 192).

233 For Anglo-Saxon overlordship in Wales between the ninth and eleventh centuries, see Davies, *Patterns of Power*, p. 73ff; for English raids on Wales in this period, see *ibid.*, pp. 67–73.

234 *Vitae sanctorum Britanniae*, ed. Wade-Evans, pp. 182–4.

235 *ByT* (Pen. 20) [1079=1081]; *ByT* (RB) [1081]; *ByS* [1079=1081]; ASC (E) 1081; William of Malmesbury, *De gestis regum Anglorum* (ed. Stubbs, i.316); *The Text of the Book of Llan Dâv*, edd. Rhys and Evans, p. 274.

236 *Llyfr Iorwerth* (ed. Wiliam, pp. 67–8); *Pedeir Keinc y Mabinogi*, ed. Williams, pp. 50–1; *Historia*, ed. Evans, p. 11; *A Mediaeval Prince*, ed. & transl. Evans, p. 64. According to Gerald, Wales was not only not a kingdom, it was a part of England: *'Wallia quidem portio est regni Anglicani, et non per se regnum'*. (*Giraldi Cambrensis Opera*, edd. Brewer *et al.*, iii.166).

island of Britain,[237] and moreover intervened in an unprecedented manner, particularly in Powys, where Iorwerth ap Bleddyn is said to have feared the king and his law.[238] In 1109, Cadwgan ap Bleddyn had to plead and pay £100 to recover Ceredigion, and in 1110 Henry took Cadwgan's lands there back again and gave them to a Norman. Although he gave Cadwgan Powys in 1111, the king divided it between Owain ap Cadwgan and the sons of Rhirid in the same year, taking hostages and tribute. Tribute was raised again in 1121.[239] Similarly, Henry gave Powys to Iorwerth ap Bleddyn in 1110, telling him not to conspire with anyone on pain of forfeiture and death. Powys was given to Owain ap Cadwgan in 1114, and the king also distributed lands in Cantref Mawr to Gruffudd ap Rhys.[240] Nor did Gwynedd escape Henry's influence: he gave Gruffudd ap Cynan Llŷn, Eifionydd, Ardudwy and Arllechwedd.[241]

Henry's reign marked not only an increased interest in Wales but also an intensification of royal overlordship, as well as an extension of English ecclesiastical claims over Wales.[242] The king regarded Wales as part of his dominions,[243] and extended the traditional bonds between the king and the Welsh. The first hostages were given by Iorwerth ap Bleddyn in 1110,[244] and the men of Powys were seen as the king's 'vassals' in 1114, when the Anglo-Saxon Chronicle reports that the Welsh swore allegiance.[245] The king was now an important figure in Wales, so that Owain ap Cadwgan and Madog ap Rhirid asked for royal recognition of their acquisition of lands in Powys, and visits to the royal court became more frequent. Gruffudd ap Cynan went before 1114 and again in 1115, and other Welsh visitors

---

[237] *ByT* (Pen. 20) [1113=1116]; *ByT* (RB) [1113=1116]; *ByS* [1113=1116].

[238] *ByT* (Pen. 20) [1107=1110]; *ByT* (RB) [1106=1110]; *ByS* [1107=1110]; for Henry's manipulation of native rulers in Powys, see Davies, 'Henry I and Wales', pp.132–47.

[239] *ByT* (Pen. 20) [1106=1109], [1107=1110], [1108=1111], [1118=1121]; *ByT* (RB) [1105=1109], [1106=1110], [1107=1111], [1118=1121]; *ByS* [1106=1109], [1107=1110], [1108=1111], [1118=1121].

[240] *Giraldi Cambrensis Opera* (edd. Brewer *et al.*, vi.34); *ByT* (Pen. 20) [1107=1110], [1111=1114]; *ByT* (RB) [1106=1110], [1111=1114]; *ByS* [1107=1110], [1111=1114].

[241] *Historia*, ed. Evans, p. 28; *A Mediaeval Prince*, ed. & transl. Evans, p. 79.

[242] Canterbury claimed Wales within its province in 1114x1123, and in 1125 the English clergy proposed the transfer of Bangor from the province of Canterbury to that of York. The translation of saint Dyfrig's relics required the consent of the archbishop of Canterbury, and bishop Dafydd of Bangor was consecrated at Canterbury. (Haddan and Stubbs, *Councils and ecclesiastical documents* i.308, 316; *The Text of the Book of Llan Dâv*, edd. Rhys and Evans, p. 5; Pryce, 'Church and Society in Wales', p. 32.)

[243] Davies, 'Henry I and Wales', p. 135.

[244] *ByT* (Pen. 20) [1107=1110]; *ByT* (RB) [1106=1110]; *ByS* [1107=1110]. Owain ap Cadwgan also gave hostages the following year, as did 'the Welsh' in 1121. (*ByT* (Pen. 20) [1108=1111]; *ByT* (RB) [1107=1111]; *ByS* [1108=1111]; John of Worcester, *Chronicon* 1121.

[245] ASC (E) 1114; ASC (H) 1114.

included Cadwgan ap Bleddyn, Owain ap Cadwgan, Gruffudd ap Rhys and Iorwerth ap Bleddyn. Very often these men were invited (or rather summoned) by Henry – Iorwerth was tricked into appearing before the court for trial in 1103 – so Henry's gift of lands to Gruffudd on his visit may even represent an assertion of feudal overlordship.[246] There was always a blurred line between a medieval agreement or treaty and a feudal contract, and the Norman kings seem to have at least tried to move that line in their favour. It is therefore interesting that John of Worcester claims that 'kings ceased to rule in Wales' after the death of Rhys ap Tewdwr in 1093: this raises some difficult questions about Gruffudd ap Cynan's status when he received 'love and recognition' ('*charyat a chyfatnabot*') as well as lands when he met Henry.[247]

According to the *Historia*, Gruffudd was captured by the Normans in 1081, and remained incarcerated at Chester for either twelve or sixteen years. With Gruffudd out of the way, Hugh of Chester moved into Gwynedd and became 'lord of the land' ('*argluyd ar e tir*').[248] Gruffudd cannot have exercised a direct influence over events from prison, and his status during this period is very difficult to ascertain, especially since Robert of Rhuddlan is found in the 1086 *Domesday* survey holding '*Nortwales*' *de rege* for £40 *per annum*: after his death, the king gave '*Nort Wales*' to Hugh of Chester.[249] The terms of Robert's tenure seem very similar to those agreed with '*Riset de Wales*' (probably Rhys ap Tewdwr of Deheubarth), who is also recorded as paying £40 *per annum* to the king.[250] If Gwynedd was now not only in Norman hands but also in the gift of the king, what had happened to the kingship ('*vrenhinyaeth*') which Gruffudd had been enjoying immediately before his capture?[251]

The reasons for the Norman invasion of Gwynedd can only be guessed at. There may have been an attempt to wrest the kingdom from native control (either by the king or by his barons), or else the marcher lords perhaps acted

246 *Historia*, ed. Evans, p. 28; *A Mediaeval Prince*, ed. & transl. Evans, p. 79; *ByT* (Pen. 20) [1101=1103], [1107=1110], [1108=1111], [1111=1114], [1113=1116]; *ByT* (RB) [1101=1103], [1106=1110], [1107=1111], [1111=1114], [1112=1115], [1113=1116]; *ByS* [1101=1103], [1107=1110], [1108=1111], [1111=1114], [1113=1116]. Owain ap Cadwgan was made a knight ('*marchog*') by the king, and accompanied him on campaign in 1114. (*ByT* (Pen. 20) [1111=1114]; *ByT* (RB) [1111=1114]; *ByS* [1111=1114].)
247 John of Worcester, *Chronicon* 1093; *Historia*, ed. Evans, p. 28; *A Mediaeval Prince*, ed. & transl. Evans, p. 79.
248 *Historia*, ed. Evans, pp. 17, 18; *A Mediaeval Prince*, ed. & transl. Evans, p. 70, and see also Lewis, below, pp. 67–72.
249 *Domesday Book*, i fo. 269b; Geoffrey Gaimar, *L'Estoire des Engleis* (ed. Bell, v.6043); for the *Domesday* issue, see Edwards, 'The Normans and the Welsh March', p. 161.
250 *Domesday Book*, i fo. 179b.
251 *Historia*, ed. Evans, p. 16; *A Mediaeval Prince*, ed. & transl. Evans, p. 69.

as Gruffudd's proxies: Rufus's 1097 campaign might then be seen as an aid to Gruffudd against Cadwgan ap Bleddyn.[252] The evidence is inconclusive. The Normans moved against Gruffudd very promptly after his assumption of kingship in 1081 – the *Historia* says there was an interval of only a few days. It would seem that the Norman earls gave him very little chance to assert himself and achieve stability, which he succeeded in doing.[253] Since it seems unlikely that Gruffudd was in serious difficulties after Mynydd Carn, the explanation for the Norman attack can only be greed. Having acquired Gwynedd, measures were taken to secure a legal right to it. As well as the *Domesday* evidence, there is Geoffrey Gaimar's statement that Hugh of Chester was given Gwynedd by the king, and the *Historia* reports that Henry I attacked Gwynedd because Gruffudd had taken lands without permission.[254] The king clearly took an interest in the conquest of Gwynedd, perhaps even to the extent that William I was party to Gruffudd's capture. If the king had assumed the right to decide who should rule Gwynedd, the implications for native *regalitas* are profound. In 1098, *Brenhinedd y Saeson* says that the Normans brought in Owain ab Edwin (the other sources say the opposite). If this is correct, was Owain being imposed as a client?[255] There was a precedent – Bleddyn and Rhiwallon were apparently selected (according to English sources) in 1063 or 1064[256] – and it may be significant that Owain emerged successfully from the confused events of 1098.[257] The Anglo-Normans certainly imposed kings in Ireland within a short time after their arrival, and Richard fitz Gilbert even claimed Leinster for himself.[258] Whether or not this happened in Gwynedd, Gruffudd ap Cynan's biographer was very keen to furnish him with a Norman pedigree as an aid to the assertion of his legitimacy to rule.[259]

Alternatively, Gruffudd may have been party to the *Domesday* agreement himself. His presence with Rhys ap Tewdwr at St. Davids around the time of William I's visit there in 1081 certainly allows this as a possibility, and

---

[252] *ByT* (Pen. 20) [1095=1097]; *ByT* (RB) [1093=1097]; *ByS* [1095=1097]. But see also Lewis, below, pp. 73, 74.

[253] *Historia*, ed. Evans, p. 16; *A Mediaeval Prince*, ed. & transl. Evans, p. 69.

[254] Geoffrey Gaimar, *L'Estoire des Engleis* (ed. Bell, v p. 6043); *Historia*, ed. Evans, p. 29; *A Mediaeval Prince*, ed. & transl. Evans, p. 80.

[255] *ByS* [1096=1098]; *ByT* (Pen. 20) and (RB), which say that Owain brought the Normans in, are usually more reliable as sources than *ByS*. (*ByT* (Pen. 20) [1096=1098]; *ByT* (RB) [1094=1098]. See also Maund, 'Cynan ab Iago', p. 63).

[256] John of Worcester, *Chronicon* 1064; ASC (D, E)1063. The next instance of royal interference – at the request of the Welsh – in Welsh succession practices is when Gruffudd ap Rhys was 'made heir' to Deheubarth in 1197, *AC* (B) [1197].

[257] That he is said to have rebelled against the Normans suggests either that the plan went awry or that the native chronicler misunderstood Hugh of Chester's failure to oust him. *ByT* (Pen. 20) [1096=1098]; *ByT* (RB) [1094=1098]; *ByS* [1096=1098].

[258] Simms, *From Kings to Warlords*, p. 46; Martin, *No hero in the house*.

[259] *Historia*, ed. Evans, pp. 2–3; *A Mediaeval Prince*, ed. & transl. Evans, p. 55.

Gwynedd is not referred to as a tenancy ('*deillyadaeth*') before this date.[260] It is not necessarily the case, however, that the arrangement was inaugurated in 1081. The Norman raid of 1075x1081, which certainly did not remove Trahaearn ap Caradog, may have been intended to help Trahaearn in the interests of stability, perhaps in return for £40 *per annum* – it was clearly important, since the *Historia* rarely mentions events which did not concern Gruffudd directly. It may have been this which Gruffudd was expecting to discuss with his captors in 1081: significantly, he is said to have held a '*deillyadaeth*' before his capture.[261] This may have been Gwynedd proper, although it may represent Edeirnion or land in the Perfeddwlad which is not recorded under his name in 1086 because he was in prison. Gwynedd was certainly a tenancy after 1086, and it is possible that Gruffudd retained his kingship in prison, while Gwynedd was governed by what were technically Norman proxies. Whilst the Welsh disliked Norman rule, there were no complaints about its legality. Even the *Historia* accepts Hugh of Chester as 'lord of the land',[262] and the lack of Welsh opposition in the period 1081–1094 may have been due to an acceptance of the foreigners as Gruffudd's proxies: Cadwgan ap Bleddyn's revolt in 1094 may therefore have represented a dynastic move against a recently liberated Gruffudd, as much as anti-Norman aggression.[263]

Whether or not Venedotian regality was under threat while Gruffudd was in prison, the *Domesday* agreement did not last long. The death of Robert of Rhuddlan in 1086x1097 was symptomatic of the weakness of the Norman position, and it is possible that his killer, a certain '*Grithfridus rex Guallorum*', who was raiding Rhuddlan and Degannwy, was Gruffudd ap Cynan.[264] An examination of the issues surrounding Robert's death is useful in trying to understand the nature of Gruffudd's return to power and the undoing of the 1086 settlement after his escape: it also throws precious light on Gruffudd's activities between 1081 and 1097.[265]

Gruffudd had good reason to want to kill Robert, since he would naturally wish to recover personal control of Gwynedd. If the *Historia*'s account is correct, he spent at least twelve years in captivity,[266] and so could not have attacked Robert before 1093. There is some evidence that Robert was killed in 1093. The 1094 rebellion would be explained by the recent death of a

---

260 *Historia*, ed. Evans, pp. 14, 17; *A Mediaeval Prince*, ed. & transl. Evans, pp. 66, 69; *ByT* (Pen. 20) [1079=1081]; *ByT* (RB) [1081]; *ByS* [1079=1081].
261 *Historia*, ed. Evans, pp. 12–13, 17; *A Mediaeval Prince*, ed. & transl. Evans, pp. 65, 69.
262 *Historia*, ed. Evans, p. 18; *A Mediaeval Prince*, ed. & transl. Evans, p. 70.
263 *ByT* (Pen. 20) [1092=1094]; *ByT* (RB) [1094]; *ByS* [1092=1094].
264 Orderic Vitalis, *Historia Ecclesiastica* (ed. Chibnall), iv.140.
265 For a discussion of this, see Orderic Vitalis, *Historia Ecclesiastica* (ed. Chibnall, iv.136).
266 *Historia*, ed. Evans, p. 17; *A Mediaeval Prince*, ed. & transl. Evans, p. 69.

Norman leader,[267] and Robert was buried at St. Werburh's, Chester, which did not become a daughter house of Bec until 1092, shortly after its foundation by Hugh of Chester. Orderic's statement that Robert died on the third of July would fit a date of 1093, whilst Robert is not on a list of ecclesiastical benefactors in Chester after 1093, when earl Hugh is found in possession of lands which had been held *in capite* by Robert in 1086.[268] However, that the *Historia* does not mention Gruffudd killing such an important Norman raises doubts about this interpretation. It may be that the Welsh did not realise whom they had killed,[269] but it remains that the *Historia* mentions only one of Rufus's campaigns (presumably that of 1097), whilst Gruffudd does not appear at all in Welsh chronicles until 1098.[270] The dating of Robert's death to 1093 depends upon only one piece of information provided by Orderic, whilst overlooking several of his other statements. He says that Robert died around the same time as William I (1087),[271] and also that he was active in Wales for fifteen years.[272] According to this reckoning, Robert died no later than 1090, since he was at Rhuddlan before Bron yr Erw in 1075.[273] Furthermore, Orderic says specifically that Gruffudd raided Robert's lands around Rhuddlan during the rebellion against Rufus in 1088.[274]

According to the *Historia*'s chronology, if Robert died before 1093, Gruffudd probably did not kill him. Yet it is difficult to find a candidate to fit Orderic's description, especially since the killer is specifically identified

---

[267] *ByT* (Pen. 20) [1092=1094]; *ByT* (RB) [1094]; *ByS* [1092=1094].

[268] Eadmer, *Life of St. Anselm* (ed. Southern, p. 63); Orderic Vitalis, *Historia Ecclesiastica* (ed. Chibnall, iv.136, 140).

[269] There is such a similarity between Orderic's account of Robert's death and the *Historia*'s version of Gruffudd's attack on Aberlleiniog that they might refer to the same event. Any confusion might be explained by the fact that in the former Robert's body was mutilated, whilst in the latter the *pencerdd* Gellan was killed, perhaps depriving the Welsh of a record. (Orderic Vitalis, *Historia Ecclesiastica*, ed. Chibnall, iv.140; *Historia*, ed. Evans, p. 21; *A Mediaeval Prince*, ed. & transl. Evans, p. 73.)

[270] *Historia*, ed. Evans, p. 22; *A Mediaeval Prince*, ed. & transl. Evans, pp. 74–5. It has been argued, however, that the 1094 revolt was partly the result of Gruffudd's escape. (Lloyd, *A History*, ii.404).

[271] Orderic Vitalis, *Historia Ecclesiastica* (ed. Chibnall, iv.112); he took part in the 1088 rebellion against Rufus. (Orderic Vitalis, *Historia Ecclesiastica*, ed. Chibnall, iv.124, 144).

[272] Orderic Vitalis, *Historia Ecclesiastica* (ed. Chibnall, iv.138).

[273] *Historia*, ed. Evans, p. 7; *A Mediaeval Prince*, ed. & transl. Evans, p. 59; *ByT* (Pen. 20) [1073=1075]; *ByT* (RB) [1075]; *ByS* [1073=1075]; this does not contradict the statement that he was not buried until 1093 – he died in an inaccessible area and his head was thrown into the sea. (Orderic Vitalis, *Historia Ecclesiastica* (ed. Chibnall, iv.140).

[274] Orderic Vitalis, *Historia Ecclesiastica* (ed. Chibnall, iv.136); it is possible that there is confusion here with the 1075 raid – unless that was actually in 1081. *Historia*, ed. Evans, p. 9; *A Mediaeval Prince*, ed. & transl. Evans, p. 62; Maund, *Ireland, Wales and England*, pp. 154, 155.

as Welsh.[275] A very unlikely possibility is Gruffudd ap Maredudd, who was associated with Deheubarth. There are no other known significant Welsh Gruffudds at this time, and it may be that *Grithfridus* was in fact Hiberno-Scandinavian.[276] It is equally likely that Gruffudd ap Cynan did kill Robert, and that the *Historia*'s twelve and sixteen years for Gruffudd's incarceration are both wrong. The sixteen years offered gives a date of 1097 for his escape, which fits nicely with the account of Rufus's campaign and Gruffudd's appearance in the chronicles in 1098, and Orderic mentions Welsh and Norse raiders around Degannwy in 1098, who may perhaps be identified with Gruffudd ap Cynan and his ally '*Gothrei*'.[277] However, the *Historia* also mentions two years of peace between Gruffudd's escape and his great attack on Norman power in Gwynedd, during which time he was on the run and looking for support.[278] To calculate the date of his return to prominence in Gwynedd, two years must accordingly be added to the sixteen years: using 1081 as a base, this would give 1099, which is clearly wrong. Is the *Historia*'s chronology reliable at all here? This, together with the fact that Gruffudd's treatment in prison was much worse than that suffered by any other Welsh prince in an English prison in this period, raises the suspicion that the whole story of the imprisonment is a mere fiction, designed to cover up Gruffudd's obscurity. Yet even this will not stand undisputed, since the *Historia* is supported by Orderic in saying that the Normans (in this case Robert of Rhuddlan rather than Hugh of Chester) captured 'Gruffudd'.[279] If Gruffudd was not captured, his obscurity would be hard to explain.

Given that the *Historia* seems thoroughly confused about the period 1081–1097, it is possible that Gruffudd did indeed kill Robert, and that he may therefore have been at liberty for a considerable time before 1097. Did he escape in 1088x1093, attack Rhuddlan and kill Robert, only to be driven into obscurity again? It might be noted that he went to Deheubarth from Ireland soon after his escape: if this was in 1088, there might be a connection with his old ally Rhys ap Tewdwr's Hiberno-Scandinavian supporters in that year.[280] There is no absolutely compelling reason to doubt Orderic's information that Gruffudd was free in 1088, and Gruffudd's failure to act after that time demonstrates the likelihood that he was an obscure figure,

---

275 Orderic Vitalis, *Historia Ecclesiastica* (ed. Chibnall, iv.140).
276 A possible candidate is the *Historia*'s '*Gothrei*' – probably either Godfrey Meranach, king of Dublin and the Isles in the early 1090s, or Godred Crovan of Man. *Historia*, ed. Evans, p. 17; *A Mediaeval Prince*, ed. & transl. Evans, p. 72; Maund, *Ireland, Wales and England*, p. 181; Orderic Vitalis, *Historia Ecclesiastica* (ed. Chibnall, iv.140).
277 *Historia*, ed. Evans, pp. 17, 18, 22; *A Mediaeval Prince*, ed. & transl. Evans, pp. 70–1, 72, 74–5; Orderic Vitalis, *Historia Ecclesiastica* (ed. Chibnall, v.224).
278 *Historia*, ed. Evans, pp. 18–21; *A Mediaeval Prince*, ed. & transl. Evans, pp. 70–5.
279 Orderic Vitalis, *Historia Ecclesiastica* (ed. Chibnall, iv.144).
280 *Historia*, ed. Evans, p. 18; *A Mediaeval Prince*, ed. & transl. Evans, p. 71; *ByT* (Pen.

and that the kingship now lay elsewhere, probably with Cadwgan ap Bleddyn. It may be that Cadwgan's rise was facilitated by a withdrawal of Norman recognition of Gruffudd after he killed Robert: is this why the *Historia* blames Hugh of Chester for the war of 1098?[281]

Speculation apart, it is clear that the *Domesday* agreement made very little practical difference once Gruffudd asserted himself. There was nothing to prevent him from killing the *Domesday* tenant and taking the kingdom himself. There is no evidence that Rhys ap Tewdwr ever paid his £40, and his tenure was not *de rege* or *ad firmam*, as Robert of Rhuddlan's was.[282] Indeed, since Welsh sources refer to the Conqueror's visit after their accounts of Mynydd Carn, it appears that the king was simply confirming Rhys in what he had won already.[283] It seems that the Welsh were not bound to the king as closely as the Normans, and Gruffudd ap Cynan was not unduly inconvenienced by the contract. If Owain ab Edwin was indeed under Norman influence in 1098, it was probably as no more than a client. The Normans had not undermined Venedotian *regalitas*, which was preserved intact after Gruffudd's return to the political spotlight. The *Historia* boasts that a campaign of William Rufus (perhaps that of 1097) was forced to retreat without taking even one cow,[284] and Henry I, whilst he compelled Gruffudd to make peace on his first campaign, had no choice but to make peace himself on his second expedition, despite his apparent intention of destroying Gruffudd's lands. Gruffudd's tactics of retreating to Snowdonia paid off this time, and Henry was afraid of Welsh ambushes in the mountains. The armies of the Norman king clearly held no fear for the king of Gwynedd. Moreover, the *Historia* implies that these campaigns were intended more as support for the earl of Chester than as an extension of royal power, in that the account of the war of 1121 is followed by a declaration that the earls of Chester and Shrewsbury, the men of Powys and Trahaearn ap Caradog's men had all failed to overcome Gruffudd.[285] This impression is supported by a study of Rufus's campaigns in 1095 and 1097: the *Historia* cites Hugh of Chester, rather than the king, as the cause of one of these ('*gureid er holl drwc*'), and Rufus may well also have been reacting to Welsh attacks on Chester and Montgomery in 1094 and 1095.[286] The king's

20) [1086=1088]; *ByT* (RB) [1088]; *ByS* [1088]. The *Historia* says that Gruffudd arrived by accident, whereas Rhys's men were brought deliberately.
[281] *Historia*, ed. Evans, p. 25; *A Mediaeval Prince*, ed. & transl. Evans, p. 75.
[282] *Domesday Book*, i. fos 179b, 269b.
[283] *ByT* (Pen. 20) [1079=1081]; *ByT* (RB) [1081]; *ByS* [1079=1081]; *AC* [1079=1081].
[284] *Historia*, ed. Evans, pp. 22–3; *A Mediaeval Prince*, ed. & transl. Evans, pp. 74–5.
[285] *Historia*, ed. Evans, pp. 29–30; *A Mediaeval Prince*, ed. & transl. Evans, pp. 80–1.
[286] *Historia*, ed. Evans, p. 23; *A Mediaeval Prince*, ed. & transl. Evans, p. 75; Henry of Huntingdon, *Historia, Anglorum* (ed. Arnold, p. 218); Symeon of Durham, *Opera omnia* (ed. Arnold, ii.226).

military aims in North Wales were essentially defensive, and Henry's first campaign was not even aimed primarily against Gwynedd.[287] Gruffudd's readiness to accept a bribe not to give refuge to Gruffudd ap Rhys, who fled from the king in 1115, and his threat to fight the men of Powys if they came anywhere near him when Maredudd ap Bleddyn appealed for his help against Henry in 1121, do not necessarily imply that he feared the king:[288] these were the actions of a pragmatist, concerned primarily with the problems of Gwynedd.

That the king was far from a dominant influence in Gwynedd is indicated by the limited practical results of his interference in *pura Wallia*. The 1114 campaign, for example, was seen as an attempt to drive the Welsh into the sea, but the only result was a payment of tribute – and that after Owain ap Cadwgan had twice rejected his terms – whilst the 1121 expedition was a military failure.[289] John of Worcester's judgement that the king subjected the Welsh to his will should therefore be examined more closely: the same phrase, '*sibi subjugavit*', is also used of William I's visit to St. Davids, so, although it clearly indicates an assertion of authority, it does not necessarily reflect any radical change.[290] Despite Henry's interference in Wales, it is significant that his gift of lands to Iorwerth ap Bleddyn in 1102 did not include payment, and Owain ap Cadwgan paid nothing after his defeat in 1114.[291] The king also played no part in the internal struggle which followed the exile of Cadwgan ap Bleddyn and his son, Owain, in 1109. Nor was Henry any more successful in his most important rôle, as a provider of patronage: none of his threats and promises is known to have been carried out.[292]

A useful measure of Henry's power is the revival of Powys after the mid-1130s. Whilst the king's death clearly removed a major annoyance, it also revealed that his influence had not been such that the fundamental strength of the kingdom had been sapped. His authority was no more than that of a troublesome neighbour: he did not represent the kind of constitutional menace to Welsh kingdoms that John, Henry III and Edward I were

287 The target was Owain ap Cadwgan in Powys. *ByT* (Pen. 20) [1111=1114]; *ByT* (RB) [1111=1114]; *ByS* [1111=1114].
288 *ByT* (Pen. 20) [1112=1115], [1118=1121]; *ByT* (RB) [1112=1115], [1118=1121]; *ByS* [1112=1115], [1118=1121]. See Maund, *Ireland, Wales and England*, p. 152.
289 *ByT* (RB) [1111=1115], [1118=1121].
290 John of Worcester, *Chronicon*, 1121; Roger of Howden, *Chronica* (ed. Stubbs, i.179); Robert of Torigny, *Chronica* (ed. Howlett, p. 43); Ralph of Diceto, *Opera historica* (ed. Stubbs, i.210).
291 *ByT* (Pen. 20) [1100=1102]; *ByT* (Pen. 20) [1111=1114].
292 *ByT* (Pen. 20) [1100=1102], [1106=1109], [1107=1110], [1111=1114]; *ByT* (RB) [1100=1102], [1105=1109], [1106=1110], [1111=1114]; *ByS* [1106=1109], [1107=1110], [1111=1114]. For an alternative view, see Davies, 'Henry I and Wales', p. 139; it was clearly believed that there was some substance behind the king's words.

to become. Although Henry I can be found exploiting political divisions, destabilising dynasties and 'hoodwinking client princelings to act on the king's behalf while at the same time persuading them that they were acting in their own interests',[293] there is no comparison between this and the way in which Henry III promoted dynastic conflict in the 1240s.[294] Henry I intervened directly to prise open a dynastic rift only once, when his sheriff of Shropshire bribed Llywarch ap Trahaearn, Uchdryd ab Edwin and the sons of Rhirid ap Bleddyn to drive out Cadwgan ap Bleddyn and Owain ap Cadwgan in 1109. The circumstances in this case were exceptional, following a personal insult (the abduction and violation of the king's former mistress, Nest). Moreover, unlike Henry III, he lacked sufficient military power to threaten to do the work himself, and was forced to rely upon the Arwystli and Meirionnydd dynasties and an unsuccessful segment of the Powys dynasty.[295] Consequently, it seems unlikely that any of the Norman kings was able to manipulate the Venedotian succession, or even that they attempted to.

The *Historia*'s claim that Gruffudd ap Cynan was on friendly, and by implication equal, terms with his royal neighbours therefore seems justified,[296] especially in view of the fact that Gwynedd was more separate from England than other Welsh kingdoms.[297] There was no significant reduction of his status. Whether or not he was part of the *Domesday* agreement, his position was no more subordinate than that of Cadwgan ap Bleddyn, who paid for his '*kyuoeth*' but not for his status.[298] There was no contractual relationship. Unlike other native rulers, Gruffudd paid no tribute and gave no hostages to Henry I, so it is hard to believe that he ever paid £40 for his kingdom.[299] There were few obligations to the king, and the terminology of

---

[293] *Ibid.*, p. 139; an example of the latter occurred in 1114, when he split the Welsh opposition by telling each of them that the others had made peace. *ByT* (Pen. 20) [1111=1114]; *ByT* (RB) [1111=1114]; *ByS* [1111=1114].

[294] See Smith, 'Dynastic succession', pp. 221–2 and throughout; Smith, 'The succession to Welsh princely inheritance', p. 73 and throughout; Smith, *Llywelyn ap Gruffudd*, chapter 2. In 1241, Henry III acquired the legal right to adjudicate the succession dispute between Gruffudd and Dafydd ap Llywelyn ab Iorwerth.

[295] *ByT* (Pen. 20) [1106=1109]; *ByT* (RB) [1105=1109]; *ByS* [1106=1109].

[296] *Historia*, ed. Evans, p. 30; *A Mediaeval Prince*, ed. & transl. Evans, p. 81. See also Lewis, below, pp. 73, 74.

[297] As an example of this, there was only one grant of lands within the diocese of Bangor to an ecclesiastical house in England or on the continent in the whole of the two centuries after 1066. Evans, in *Historia*, ed. Evans, p. xxvi; Davies, *Episcopal acts and cognate documents* i.35.

[298] *ByT* (Pen. 20) [1107=1110]; *ByT* (RB) [1106=1110]; *ByS* [1107=1110]. It is not clear whether this 'large tribute' was greater or smaller than £40.

[299] It can only be speculated whether Gruffudd was among those who gave hostages in 1114 and 1121. Roger of Howden, *Chronica* (ed. Stubbs, i.179); Symeon of Durham, *Opera omnia* (ed. Arnold, ii.264).

41

overlordship had hardly changed since Anglo-Saxon times.[300] It may be significant that Gruffudd's meeting with the Norman earls soon after his assumption of kingship in 1081 was on the border (he travelled '*hyd en lle y deillyadaeth*'): he may have expected these *ex officio* royal proxies to accept *hommage de paix*, a vague form of homage which usually had connotations of peace and concord between equals.[301]

Overlordship was indeed an 'elastic concept', which could mean 'as much or as little as the relative power of suzerain and dependant warranted'.[302] Although Gruffudd went to the king's court, there is no sign that pressure was brought upon him for any substantial length of time. Unlike the thirteenth century, the ruler of Gwynedd could still afford to keep his distance from the king – there was no real threat to Venedotian *iura*. Gwynedd was in effect beyond the reach of regularly enforceable royal authority, and native regality or sovereignty was therefore autogenous: this was the essential core of Llywelyn ab Iorwerth's '*principatus*'.[303] The situation under Gruffudd ap Cynan was primarily military and political, not constitutional, and the right to make war, and therefore independence from the king, naturally followed.[304] Simply by restoring Gwynedd as a military power, Gruffudd had laid the foundations of the later principality of Wales.

The principality was to be fuelled by a revitalised consciousness of Welsh nationality, and Gruffudd's rule saw important developments in the evolution of political and cultural unity. To a certain extent, this already existed, created by a common language and law.[305] There was no doubt that the Welsh were a separate *gens*,[306] and an awareness of Wales as a cultural and territorial whole is found in *Pedeir Keinc y Mabinogi* and the designation of Deheubarth as '*Dextralis Britanniae*' in the eleventh century.[307] The sense

---

300 The term '*regulus*', used to describe Hywel Dda in the tenth century, was also applied in the twelfth century to Rhys ap Gruffudd and Dafydd ab Owain. Loyn, 'Wales and England in the tenth century', p. 296; Roger of Howden, *Chronica* (ed. Stubbs, ii.134).

301 *Historia*, ed. Evans, p. 17; *A Mediaeval Prince*, ed. & transl. Evans, p. 69; Lemarignier, *Recherches sur l'hommage en marche et les frontières féodales*, pp. 1–8, 73–125; this was unlike *hommage vassalique*, in that there was no clear subordination or feudal obligations. Examples included the relations of the dukes of Normandy with France, Anjou, Maine and Brittany, and that between England and Scotland.

302 Davies, 'Henry I and Wales', p. 138.

303 See Smith, 'The Lordship of Glamorgan', p. 10; Rymer, *Foedera* I.i.84.

304 See Davies, 'Kings, Lords and Liberties', pp. 43–8, for a comparison with the thirteenth- and fourteenth-century marcher lords.

305 For Welsh nationality in this period, see Richter, 'The political and institutional background', pp. 37–55.

306 *Giraldi Cambrensis Opera* (edd. Brewer *et al.*, i.132).

307 *AC* (B) [1022], [1023], [1049]; *AC* (C) [1023]; [1049], [1073]; *ByT* (Pen. 20) [1037=1039], [1047=1049], [1050=1052]; *ByT* (RB) [1039], [1049], [1052]; *ByS* [1037=1039], [1047=1049], [1050=1052]; *Historia*, ed. Evans, p. 13 ('*Deheubarth Kemry*'); *A Mediaeval Prince*, ed. & transl. Evans, p. 66. The *Pedeir Keinc* seem to have

of a Welsh polity is also shown in the *Pedeir Keinc* when Gwydion promises to muster the forces of Gwynedd, Powys and Deheubarth.[308] Yet this nationality was both greater and smaller than Wales itself. Britain was seen as a single country with a single kingship (held by the Saxons),[309] but the unit of allegiance was local: Ieuan ap Sulien said that his *gens* was that of the Britons, but his *patria* was Ceredigion.[310] Political unity in Wales existed only in as far as that rulers such as Hywel Dda and Gruffudd ap Llywelyn were seen as pan-Welsh figures – there was no kingship of Wales. Yet there were signs of change. Whereas native rulers had hitherto confined themselves to the 'quarters of Wales', most of those in the period 1011–1063 ranged physically over the whole of Wales, and Bleddyn ap Cynfyn was said to have held the kingdom of all the Britons.[311]

The sense of nationality was helped by the presence of Irish, Norse and Normans in Wales in the eleventh century. These foreigners were often described as not being of the same language (*'anghyfiaith'*),[312] and Gerald said that the Welsh would fight for their *patria* against *'gentem inimicam'*, whilst there was concern that Henry I intended to destroy the Britons.[313] This appellation of 'Britons' was used almost without exception in the eleventh century,[314] but it does not appear in the Welsh chronicles after 1135.[315] The Welsh were now the *'kymry'*,[316] a name which first appears in *Brut y Tywysogion* in 1124.[317] This was an adoption from the tenth-century *Armes Prydein*, possibly inspired by a sense of defiance against the over-bearing Henry I, who was not unlike Æthelstan.[318] The idea of a *cenedl* grew

---

been brought together in the 1060s. *Pedeir Keinc y Mabinogi* ed. Williams, p. xli; for the possibility that this is a twelfth- or thirteenth-century source, see Charles-Edwards, 'The date of the Four Branches of the Mabinogi', pp. 263, 288.

[308] *Pedeir Keinc y Mabinogi* ed. Williams, p. 68.
[309] *ByT* (Pen. 20) [681=682]; *ByT* (RB) [680=682].
[310] Lapidge, 'The Welsh Latin Poetry', p. 83; for the small scale of awareness of group identity, see Charles-Edwards, 'Some Celtic kinship terms', p. 122.
[311] Davies, *Patterns of Power*, pp. 42–4, 83–4; *ByT* (Pen. 20) [1073=1075].
[312] *Historia*, ed. Evans, pp. 25, 30–1; *A Mediaeval Prince*, ed. & transl. Evans, pp. 77, 81–2; *Red Book of Hergest*, ed. Rhys, p. 181; *Llyfr Iorwerth* (ed. Wiliam, pp. 30–1).
[313] *Giraldi Cambrensis Opera* (edd. Brewer *et al.*, i.131); *ByT* (Pen. 20) [1111=1114]; *ByT* (RB) [1111=1114]; *ByS* [1111=1114].
[314] *ByT* (Pen. 20) [1073=1075], [1089=1091], [1091=1093], [1092=1094], [1093=1095], [1094=1096], [1095=1097], [1097=1099]; *ByT* (RB) [1075], [1091], [1090=1093], [1094], [1091=1095], [1092=1096], [1093=1097], [1095=1099]; *ByS* [1073=1075], [1089=1091], [1091=1093], [1092=1094], [1093=1095], [1094=1096], [1095=1097], [1097=1099].
[315] *AC* [1135] and following.
[316] *Historia*, ed. Evans, pp. 20, 22, 23, 25, 33 (*'kymry'* and *'kemry'*).
[317] *ByT* (Pen. 20) s.a. 1121.
[318] *Armes Prydein*, ed. Williams, pp. 2, 12.

from that of a kin group into a feeling of nationality,[319] and the military coalition at Corwen in 1165 was aware of its identity as a Welsh nation.[320] This was an unprecedented display of Welsh solidarity: these were not Britons any longer, but '*yr holl Gymry*' and '*omnes Wallenses*'.[321] The '*Nortwalensibus*' and the '*Dextralibus*' were brought together in concerted action for the first time,[322] and the term '*Kymry*' became common thereafter,[323] whilst Wales itself was now called '*Kymry*'.[324] If Owain Gwynedd harnessed Welsh nationality in 1164 and 1165, the roots of his success lay in the time of his father.

Gruffudd ap Cynan was one of the targets of the royal campaign in 1114, the intention of which, according to a native chronicler, was to exterminate even the name of the Britons.[325] Such ethnic definitions became common at the turn of the twelfth century, largely because of the cultural diversity of a Wales which was home to Welsh, Anglo-Saxons, Normans, Danes, Irish and Flemings, although the paranoid ferocity of *Brut y Tywysogion*'s 1114 entry was rarely matched. Gwynedd was ruled by '*estraun genedloed*' in Gruffudd ap Cynan's time, whilst Gruffudd freed Gwynedd from lords who came from 'other places', and the Normans are described as '*angkyfyeith*' in 1098. Gruffudd's appanages were intended for defence against '*estrawn genedloedd a rhei agkyfyeith*', and minor kings came to him for help against '*estrawn genetloedd*'. The Welsh also revolted against 'the tyranny and injustice of the French' in 1094.[326] Although Gruffudd still belonged to the old world of the Britons, as Meilyr's elegy makes clear,[327] he was also part of a world that was changing. It is interesting that the rebellion against the Normans in 1096 (which mainly affected the south and was dominated by the Powys dynasty) is said to have started in the north. Was this a

---

319 Pierce, *Medieval Welsh society*, pp. 22–3; in 1158, Rhys ap Gruffudd set out to '*dileu kethiwet y genedyl*'. *ByT* (Pen. 20) [1157=1158]; *ByT* (RB) [1156=1158]; *ByS* [1157=1158].

320 *AC* (B) [1165]: '*omnes Wallenses Norwalliae, Suthwalliae, Powysorum, jugum Francorum unanimiter respuerunt.*'

321 *ByT* (Pen. 20) [1163=1164]; *ByT* (RB) [1162=1164]; *ByS* [1163=1164]; *AC* (B) [1165].

322 *AC* (B) [1166].

323 *ByT* (Pen. 20) [1163=1164], [1164=1165], [1166=1167], [1193], [1196], [1198]; *ByT* (RB) [1162=1164], [1163=1165], [1165=1167], [1193], [1195=1196], [1197=1198]; *ByS* [1163=1164], [1164=1165], [1166=1167], [1193=1196], [1198]; *AC* (B) [1190], [1192], [1193], [1198] ('*Walenses*').

324 *Llawysgrif Hendregadredd*, ed. Morris-Jones and Parry, p. 174; *Historia*, ed. Evans, p. 14; *A Mediaeval Prince*, ed. & transl. Evans, p. 66; *ByT* (Pen. 20) [1169=1170], [1187], [1197]; *ByT* (RB) [1170], [1196=1197].

325 *ByT* (Pen. 20) [1111=1114]; *ByT* (RB) [1111=1114]; *ByS* [1111=1114].

326 *Historia*, ed. Evans, pp. 6, 9, 25, 30–1; *A Mediaeval Prince*, ed. & transl. Evans, pp. 58, 61–2, 77, 81–2; *ByT* (Pen. 20) [1092=1094]; *ByT* (RB) [1094]; *ByS* [1092=1094].

327 He was '*prydein briawd*', and was allegedly known beyond the '*Bannawc*' in Scotland. (French, 'Meilyr's Elegy', 264, Williams, 'Meilyr Brydydd', below p. 178 and n. 63).

co-ordinated Welsh effort, with Gwynedd at the forefront?[328] If so, this may be a precedent for the 1160s. Moreover, when he died, Gruffudd was seen by the *Brutiau* as the 'head and king and defender and pacifier of all Wales'.[329] Such a eulogy raises him to the level of the thirteenth-century princes, and invites further investigation.

There were very few precedents for overlordship, but several rulers had held the kingship of more than one kingdom since the tenth century. Hywel Dda was king of Seisyllwg, Dyfed, Gwynedd and probably Powys, Maredudd ab Owain ruled Gwynedd and Deheubarth, and Gruffudd ap Llywelyn was king of Gwynedd, Deheubarth, Powys, Morgannwg and probably Gwent.[330] These men were dominant figures in their time: almost all the major chronicle entries in Welsh in the mid-eleventh century (except obits and a number of entries about the Hiberno-Norse) concern Gruffudd ap Llywelyn.[331] Walter Map testifies to Gruffudd's revered status by the twelfth century,[332] as does the *Historia*'s association of Gruffudd ap Cynan with him.[333] Furthermore, that·there was a tendency towards the dominance of one kingdom is shown by the fact that kings of Gwynedd are said to have taken tribute repeatedly from the south-east in the eleventh century.[334] The existence of a pan-Welsh aristocratic polity in Gruffudd ap Cynan's time is attested by the fact that the future of Gwynedd was decided at Mynydd Carn in Deheubarth in 1081. Both Gruffudd and Trahaearn were leagued with southern rulers: Gruffudd with Rhys ap Tewdwr, and Trahaearn with Caradog ap Gruffudd and Meilyr ap Rhiwallon.[335] Moreover, Gruffudd is also later found in a dominant rôle, receiving and supporting Welsh kings who were attacked by foreigners.[336] This assumption of leadership of Welshmen against foreign enemies is reminiscent of Llywelyn ap Gruffudd in 1256,[337] and marks an important step in the forging of a nationality. The later principality was dependent on ethnic definition, and Gruffudd ap Cynan made a clear contribution to the process.

Gruffudd and his sons emerged as prominent figures in early twelfth-century Wales, as Gwynedd became the natural refuge of native rulers in

---

328 See Maund, *Ireland, Wales and England*, p. 151.
329 *ByT* (Pen. 20) [1136=1137]; *ByT* (RB) [1136=1137].
330 Lloyd, *A History*, i.333, 337, 345–6, ii.364.
331 Maund, *Ireland, Wales and England*, p. 66.
332 Walter Map, *De nugis curialum* (ed. James, pp. 188–94).
333 *Historia*, ed. Evans, p. 7; *A Mediaeval Prince*, ed. & transl. Evans, p. 60.
334 Davies, *Wales in the Early Middle Ages*, p. 129.
335 *Historia*, ed. Evans, p. 14; *A Mediaeval Prince*, ed. & transl. Evans, p. 66. For the reasons for Trahaearn's presence, and the possibility that Trahaearn and Caradog's understanding had lasted since *ca* 1078, see Maund, 'Trahaearn', pp. 473–4; and Maund, *Ireland, Wales and England*, pp. 79–80.
336 *Historia*, ed. Evans, p. 31; *A Mediaeval Prince*, ed. & transl. Evans, p. 82.
337 Smith, *Llywelyn ap Gruffudd*, pp. 77–8.

trouble. In 1114, Owain ap Cadwgan sheltered in Snowdonia during Henry I's campaign, and, with Goronwy ab Owain, joined Gruffudd in agreeing to stand together. Since they were in Gwynedd, and Gruffudd held the ultimate advantage of the mountains, the superiority of the Venedotian king is implied. Similarly, Gruffudd ap Rhys asked for help in 1115; his request was accepted at first, but he was then refused, hunted down and almost dragged out of Aberdaron church.

Maredudd ap Bleddyn also requested help in 1121, and other 'small kings' came to Gruffudd for protection, help and counsel.[338] There is no evidence of a formal contract, but it is clear that Gruffudd was in a position to dispense generosity to rulers from all over *pura Wallia*. His sons, Owain and Cadwaladr, are also said (in a a panegyric in the *Brutiau*) to have helped all those who fled to them; concrete evidence of this is provided in 1136, when Gruffudd ap Rhys again came to Gwynedd for assistance.[339] In the same year, the brothers are portrayed as the superior partners in alliances with Madog ab Idnerth, Hywel ap Maredudd and his sons, and Gruffudd ap Rhys, and are called 'the splendour of Britain and her defence and her freedom'.[340] During Gruffudd's lifetime, his son Owain was already becoming accustomed to the rôle he would play as leader of the Welsh alliance in 1165.[341]

The *Historia* makes great claims for Gruffudd himself as a leader of other kings: in 1081, he is given the credit for taking the initiative and winning the battle of Mynydd Carn, while Rhys ap Tewdwr followed gratefully behind. Moreover, Gruffudd is portrayed as an overlord. When he promises Rhys much-needed military aid, Rhys reciprocates by promising not only half his kingdom ('*kyuoeth*') but also his homage ('*guryogaeth*'), calling Gruffudd his lord ('*argluyd*'). Rhys goes onto his knees, addressing Gruffudd as 'king of the kings of Wales', and, with supreme confidence, Gruffudd replies loftily, 'Who are you?' After the victory, when Rhys, fearing treachery from Gruffudd, captures and hides one of Gruffudd's men, Gruffudd responds by ravaging Rhys's '*kyuoeth*'.[342] Clearly, the *Historia* is keen to stress Gruffudd's superiority over other native rulers. Whether this pretension was a reflection of the reality of the eleventh century, or merely a product of the 1160s, is another matter. Apart from the *Historia*, there is no evidence that Gruffudd was in a sufficiently strong

---

338 *ByT* (Pen. 20) [1111=1114], [1112=1115], [1118=1121]; *ByT* (RB) [1111=1114], [1112=1115], [1118=1121]; *ByS* [1111=1114], [1112=1115], [1118=1121]; *Historia*, ed. Evans, p. 31; *A Mediaeval Prince*, ed. & transl. Evans, p. 82.

339 *ByT* (Pen. 20) [1135=1136]; *ByT* (RB) [1135=1136]; *ByS* [1135=1136]; *Giraldi Cambrensis Opera* (edd. Brewer *et al.*, vi.79).

340 *ByT* (Pen. 20) [1135=1136]; *ByT* (RB) [1135=1136]; *ByS* [1135=1136].

341 *ByT* (Pen. 20) [1164=1165]; *ByT* (RB) [1163=1165]; *ByS* [1164=1165].

342 *Historia*, ed. Evans, pp. 13–16; *A Mediaeval Prince*, ed. & transl. Evans, pp. 66–8.

position to justify such a condescending attitude towards Rhys ap Tewdwr. His power base was minimal before Mynydd Carn, and that he was removed from power soon afterwards leaves very little room for the overlordship hinted at in the *Historia*. Moreover, there is nothing to suggest that Gruffudd ever received tribute or hostages from other Welsh rulers, and even the *Historia* admits that the 1081 alliance was made primarily on the basis of friendship, rather than domination: at St. Davids before the battle, Gruffudd and Rhys undertook to be '*gyueillyon fydlaun*'.[343] Mynydd Carn was essentially part of a southern conflict in any case, rather than a battle for Gwynedd.[344] Gruffudd's rôle in the *Historia* is probably greatly exaggerated.

Whilst the idea of overlordship in Deheubarth can be discarded, it remains that Gruffudd was a prominent figure in north Wales. What might his authority have been over those who performed '*guryogaeth*' to him, such as the men of Môn, Arfon and Llŷn?[345] There are instances of *gwrogaeth* in the *Pedeir Keinc*: Hafgan's men do *gwrogaeth* to Pwyll and become his men ('*gwyr*'), and Pryderi performs '*gwrogaeth*' to Caswallon ap Beli. These are more akin to traditional submissions or promises of allegiance than they are to later, more binding forms of homage,[346] and similarly, the '*kerenyd*' made between Pwyll and Arawn is no more than a legal relationship of peace between kings.[347] The concept of *gwrogaeth* is sometimes found in connection with the idea that land is held of a king, but this was merely a personal bond. Teirnon Twryf Uliant of Caerleon is described as having previously been the man of Pwyll of Dyfed, implying some kind of overlordship. However, it is said that he was no longer Pwyll's man; for an Anglo-Norman to break a bond of homage was seen as an act of hostility, yet Teirnon was on good terms with Pwyll – their bond could be broken.[348] Although the laws mention a payment of '*mechteyrn dyled*' to the king of Aberffraw in Gwynedd,[349] there is no sign in Gruffudd ap Cynan's reign of any contract involving homage and tenure of the kind which appears in the thirteenth-century principality, and which was essential for the transformation of a

---

[343] *Historia*, ed. Evans, p. 14; *A Mediaeval Prince*, ed. & transl. Evans, p. 67.
[344] Maund, *Ireland, Wales and England*, pp. 79–80; in the *Brutiau*, Gruffudd is merely said to have brought fleets to help Rhys. This may, however, be a mistranslation. (*ByT* (Pen. 20) [1079=1081]; *ByT* (RB) [1081]; *ByS* [1079=1081]; see Jones, transl., *ByT* (Pen. 20), p. 155.)
[345] *Historia*, ed. Evans, pp. 8, 13–14; *A Mediaeval Prince*, ed. & transl. Evans, pp. 61, 66–7.
[346] *Pedeir Keinc y Mabinogi*, ed. Williams, pp. 6, 50–1; Charles-Edwards, 'The date of the Four Branches of the Mabinogi', p. 276.
[347] *Pedeir Keinc y Mabinogi*, ed. Williams, p. 31; Charles-Edwards, 'The date of the Four Branches of the Mabinogi', p. 279.
[348] *Pedeir Keinc y Mabinogi*, ed. Williams, p. 24; Ellis, 'Legal References', pp. 23–4.
[349] *The Latin texts of the Welsh laws*, ed. Emanuel, pp. 207, 277, 437–8.

leader into a lord and a follower into a tenant.[350] This may be a somewhat unfair dismissal of Gruffudd's achievements, since demands for homage were rare in his time, even in England,[351] but it is important to note that Gruffudd never acted in a way which might suggest that he was at the head of a hegemonic power. There is no evidence that he manipulated the succession to rival kingdoms, as Llywelyn ab Iorwerth did in Deheubarth in 1216, or that he held councils of Welsh princes, as Llywelyn did in 1212, 1216, 1226 and 1238.[352]

If Gruffudd does not seem to have instituted any formal overlordship over neighbouring rulers, he also did not assert the military supremacy of Gwynedd in Wales. Whilst Gwynedd was a significant force, there was limited territorial expansion, and no attempt to emulate Gruffudd ap Llywelyn in acquiring other kingdoms. The sources are largely silent about Gruffudd's actions after his accession to the kingship, to the extent that it is not even certain that his 'furthest *cantrefi*' were outside Gwynedd Uwch Conwy.[353] Gruffudd's external relations were conducted primarily through his sons in this period, and, whilst he made good use of dynastic marriages, only one of his daughters, Susanna, married a man who represented no direct threat to Gruffudd's position as king of Gwynedd.[354] This was a period of consolidation rather than expansion, as his involvement in Ceredigion makes plain. Some interest in the region is suggested by the *Historia*'s account that Gruffudd secured a promise of half of Rhys ap Tewdwr's lands in 1081, and later ravaged Rhys's *cyfoeth*. He visited Deheubarth again, apparently accidentally, on a journey from Ireland to Gwynedd, when the wind carried him to Porth Hodni, and he won three battles there against '*kiudaut y wlat honno*', who remain unidentified. Neither the causes nor the consequences of these events are given.[355] A more active interest in the south was initiated by Owain and Cadwaladr in 1136, when they attacked Walter's castle, Aberystwyth, Dineirth, Caerwedros and Cardigan in two campaigns,[356] but Gruffudd himself can not be said to have been particularly concerned with Deheubarth; the events of 1136 may signify a change of policy as he handed over the reins of power to his sons.

Nor did Gruffudd establish a firm control of the Perfeddwlad, the strategic region between Gwynedd and Chester in which there was a

---

[350] Smith, *Llywelyn ap Gruffudd*, pp. 136–7, 204–5.
[351] The 1086 Salisbury oath was exceptional, and William I had no automatic right to it. (Charles-Edwards, 'The date of the Four Branches of the Mabinogi', p. 276.)
[352] See Davies, *Conquest, Co-existence and Change*, pp. 227, 245–6.
[353] *Historia*, ed. Evans, p. 30; *A Mediaeval Prince*, ed. & transl. Evans, p. 82.
[354] Lloyd, *A History*, ii.566; for the importance of marriage alliances, see Roderick, 'Marriage and Politics', pp. 3–20.
[355] *Historia*, ed. Evans, pp. 14, 16, 18–19; *A Mediaeval Prince*, ed. & transl. Evans, pp. 67, 68, 71.
[356] *ByT* (Pen. 20) [1135=1136]; *ByT* (RB) [1135=1136]; *ByS* [1135=1136].

traditional Venedotian interest. He is said to have expanded to the 'cantrefi bordering England' on his first expedition, and was possibly responsible for a Welsh attack on Chester in 1094,[357] but he is not known to have taken advantage of the flight of Hywel ab Ithel to Ireland in 1099. Hywel is not heard of again until 1118, when he was killed fighting the sons of Owain ab Edwin in Rhos and Rhufoniog, and the presence of Maredudd ap Bleddyn and the sons of Cadwgan ap Bleddyn on that occasion suggests that Hywel may have been a client of Powys, although it is also likely that the '*brenhinedd bychein*' to whom Gruffudd ap Cynan gave support were in this region.[358] Although the Powys dynasty disposed of Owain ab Edwin, they did not follow up their victory for fear of their erstwhile Norman allies.[359] Whether Gruffudd was able to do better is not known. His son, Cadwallon, was active on the Dee, and was killed in Nanheudwy in 1132,[360] and Gruffudd made gifts to churches outside Gwynedd uwch Conwy on his death in 1137, when 10s. was given to Meifod, Llanarmon (yn Iâl?) and *Dineirth* (Llandrillo yn Rhos).[361] Yet Venedotian control of the Perfeddwlad was not secure until Owain Gwynedd's campaigns there in 1146–1150.[362] There was no attempt at all to intervene in Powys, possibly because Powys was the stronger kingdom. Maredudd ap Bleddyn and the sons of Cadwgan seem to have rivalled Venedotian influence in the Perfeddwlad,[363] and that the mediator between the two kingdoms before 1127 was a man from Powys, Daniel ap Sulien, bishop of St. Davids and archdeacon of Powys, hints strongly that the balance of power lay with Powys.[364] It is significant that Powys emerged strongly in the 1130s;[365] indeed, had it not been afflicted with dynastic problems before 1132, Powys might have posed a much more serious threat to Gwynedd. A rare example of the possible extension of Venedotian power is Meirionnydd, which may have been brought under closer control when the Powys dynasty attempted to assert its authority there in 1124. Gruffudd's sons joined forces with Maredudd ap Cadwgan against Maredudd ap Bleddyn, and also made a pact with Llywarch ap Trahaearn.

---

[357] *Historia*, ed. Evans, p. 8; *A Mediaeval Prince*, ed. & transl. Evans, p. 61; William of Malmesbury, *De gestis regum Anglorum* (ed. Stubbs, ii.376).

[358] *ByT* (Pen 20) [1115=1118]; *ByT* (RB) [1115=1118]; *ByS* [1115=1118]; *Historia*, ed. Evans, p. 31; *A Mediaeval Prince*, ed. & transl. Evans, p. 82.

[359] *ByT* (Pen 20) [1115=1118]; *ByT* (RB) [1115=1118]; *ByS* [1115=1118].

[360] Lloyd, *A History*, ii.467; *AC* (B) [1132]; *Annales Cestriensis* 1132.

[361] *Historia*, ed. Evans, p. 31; *A Mediaeval Prince*, ed. & transl. Evans, pp. 82–3.

[362] *Annales Cestriensis* 1146; *ByT* (Pen. 20) [1148=1149], [1149=1150]; *ByT* (RB) [1148=1149], [1149=1150]; *ByS* [1148=1149], [1149=1150]; Lloyd, *A History*, ii.492.

[363] *ByT* (Pen. 20) [1115=1118]; *ByT* (RB) [1115=1118]; *ByS* [1115=1118].

[364] *ByT* (Pen. 20) [1124=1127]; *ByT* (RB) [1124=1127]; *ByS* [1124=1127]. Powysian concern about Venedotian power is shown by the anger exhibited against Llywarch ap Trahaearn in Meirionnydd when he aided Gruffudd's sons.

[365] Davies, *Conquest, Co-existence and Change*, pp. 45–6.

They allegedly tried to drive all of the dynasty of Powys into exile, and that Llywarch may have been on the point of becoming a Venedotian client is suggested by the harsh retribution exacted on him by Maredudd ap Bleddyn and the sons of Cadwgan.[366]

Many of the limitations of Gruffudd's power stemmed from the internal weaknesses of his kingdom. The only meaningful bond between a Welsh ruler and his authority was the concept that kingship was a possession.[367] The *Historia* condemns the men of Llŷn for turning against Gruffudd, their 'lord proprietor' ('*hargluyd priodaur*') in 1075,[368] and describes his enemies as '*ampriodorion argluydi*'.[369] Gwynedd was Gruffudd's inheritance ('*tref tat*') and propriety ('*priodolder*'); his kingship (*brenhiniaeth*) seems to have been separate from these, a remote abstraction of much less practical use.[370] There is no evidence in Gruffudd's time for the *regalia* possessed by the thirteenth-century princes; contemporary royal institutions appear rather to have looked backwards – the 1081 raid on Arwystli is strikingly similar to the ancient king's raid, of which a very late example can be found in Connacht in 1228.[371]

Moreover, mediaeval Welsh kingdoms were not pre-ordained entities. It was no easy task for a king to gain control of his dominions, given that consolidation of royal power, sophistication of administration, and urbanisation were all negligible before the eleventh century.[372] The concept of centralised authority is not found until the arrival of the Normans, who revived the ecclesiastical idea of the *caput* and brought the castle,[373] and the economy was very traditional, livestock being used to define currency.[374]

366 *ByT* (Pen. 20) [1121=1124]; *ByT* (RB) [1121=1124]; *ByS* [1121=1124].
367 A king was said to own ('*byey*') his country ('*gwlad*'), and Rhys ap Gruffudd was called '*proprietarius princeps*' of Deheubarth in the twelfth century. *Llyfr Iorwerth* (ed. Wiliam, p. 10); *The Myvyrian archaiology of Wales* (edd. Jones, Williams and Owen, v.632).
368 *Historia*, ed. Evans, p. 10; *A Mediaeval Prince*, ed. & transl. Evans, p. 62. Gruffudd was the '*hargluyd dyledauc*' of the men of Llŷn, Eifionydd, Ardudwy, Arfon, Rhos and Dyffryn Clwyd, and supposedly told the men of Môn and Arfon that he ruled them as their '*hargluyd priodaur*' against usurpers from elsewhere. *Historia*, ed. Evans, pp. 7, 10, 20; *A Mediaeval Prince*, ed. & transl. Evans, pp. 59, 62, 73.
369 *Historia*, ed. Evans, p. 7; *A Mediaeval Prince*, ed. & transl. Evans, p. 59.
370 *Historia*, ed. Evans, pp. 6, 7, 8, 16; *A Mediaeval Prince*, ed. & transl. Evans, pp. 58–9, 61, 669; that Gruffudd is said to have been told 'what *tref tat* was his and what *brenhiniaeth*' suggests that these were two separate things.
371 *Historia*, ed. Evans, p. 16; *A Mediaeval Prince*, ed. & transl. Evans, p. 69; Lydon, 'Lordship and Crown', p. 49.
372 Davies, *Wales in the Early Middle Ages*, pp. 84, 195.
373 Davies, *Conquest, Co-existence and Change*, p. 89.
374 A campaign of William Rufus is said to have failed because he did not take cattle, *Historia*, ed. Evans, p. 22; *A Mediaeval Prince*, ed. & transl. Evans, p. 75; Williams, 'Meilyr Brydydd', below, pp. 178, 184; and Maredudd ap Bleddyn paid ten thousand

The greatest problem in Wales was one of insufficient exploitable economic surpluses and a lack of movable wealth, but there were many other weaknesses.[375] One of these was a lack of modern military technology,[376] but more fundamental was a lack of social adherence to native kings.[377] Gruffudd's war-band in 1081 was no more than a '*gedymdeithas*',[378] implying an absence of strong bonds of leadership, and the fact that Welsh society was less hierarchically defined than that of the Anglo-Normans meant that Welsh kings had less freedom of action.[379] Aristocratic defiance was therefore not unusual: the *uchelwyr* of Gwent trapped the household of Gruffudd ap Llywelyn in 1047, and those of Ystrad Tywi killed Bleddyn ap Cynfyn in 1075.[380] The military nature of the ruler-client relationship seems to have been weakened further by the use of external military aid, and clients grew more powerful as a result.[381] The development of these *uchelwyr* groups, outside the traditional social structure of the kin group and the *teulu*, naturally clashed with the interests of kings.[382]

A result of these problems was that those kingdoms which could not live with the strength of powerful neighbours, especially the king of England, saw a significant diminution of the titles of their rulers in the twelfth century. In early mediaeval terminology, there was an idea that a king (*rex*) could be pre-eminent over *reges*, *reguli* and lesser kings,[383] and in all the sources, Gruffudd ap Cynan and his contemporaries are referred to by the traditional Welsh equivalent of *rex*, *brenin*.[384] In the twelfth century, however, there was only one king in southern Britain. Titles now reflected power rather than royalty.[385] The status of the *rex* declined dramatically,[386] and *Brut y Tywysogion*'s obit for Gruffudd, which calls him prince (*tywysog*) of

---

cattle as tribute to Henry I in 1121. *ByT* (Pen 20) [1118=1121]; *ByT* (RB) [1118=1121]; *ByS* [1118=1121].

[375] Wormald, 'Celtic and Anglo-Saxon Kingship', p. 171; for the development of the Welsh economy, see Davies, 'Land and power', pp. 3–23.

[376] The first Welshman known to have thought of building a castle is Cadwgan ap Bleddyn in 1111. *ByT* (Pen. 20) [1108=1111]; *ByS* [1108=1111].

[377] For the relationships between kings and their followers, see Davies, 'Land and power', pp. 3–23.

[378] *Historia*, ed. Evans, p. 16; *A Mediaeval Prince*, ed. & transl. Evans, p. 68.

[379] Davies, *Conquest, Co-existence and Change*, pp. 69–70.

[380] *AC* (B) [1047]; *AC* (C) [1047]; *ByT* (Pen. 20) [1073=1075].

[381] Davies, *Patterns of Power*, pp. 77–8.

[382] Davies, *Wales in the Early Middle Ages*, p. 84.

[383] Davies, *Patterns of Power*, pp. 10–15.

[384] See, for example, *Historia*, ed. Evans, throughout.

[385] Richter, 'The political and institutional background', p. 46.

[386] See Jenkins, 'Kings, lords and princes', pp. 451–62; since the *Historia* was probably written in the 1160s, or possibly later, the adherence to the old nomenclature is interesting.

Gwynedd, reflects this trend.[387] *Tywysog* was a new title in the twelfth century. Its Latin equivalent, *princeps*, simply denoted a ruler, and, since it is very rarely found in the singular, indicated a much less exalted status than that of a *rex*. The Welsh *tywysog* had the connotation of leader – usually, like the Latin *dux*, a military one – but it seems that this style was adopted deliberately because of its novelty and ambiguity, and its consequent quality of disguising a diminution of status.[388] Yet this same ambiguity could also allow the use of 'prince' as an assertion of power: in 1165, at the height of Owain Gwynedd's power, Henry II complained to Pope Alexander III that the Venedotian ruler '*se principem nominat*', and William of Newburgh says that the Welsh were '*tanto principi per insolentiam*' in 1157.[389] This was the elevated status to which the thirteenth-century princes of Gwynedd aspired. That Gruffudd is styled a prince by the *Brutiau* may well reflect the broad extent of his influence, rather than its limitations, but it remains that he lived most of his life in a world where every ruler was a king. His was no principality, even in name.

Yet the seeds of the later principality were undoubtedly present in Gruffudd's time. The idea of overlordship – as applicable to Wales as it was to Britain – was probably derived from centuries of contact with the king of England,[390] and the laws mention a tribute called '*mechteyrn dyled*' which was payable to Gwynedd.[391] Nevertheless, the political apparatus necessary to go beyond mere overlordship and create a kingship of Wales simply did not exist in the tenth and eleventh centuries. Hywel Dda, for example, appeared to unite Gwynedd and Dyfed, but the kingdoms retained their separate identities. Wales was not developing into a kingdom: the careers of Rhodri Mawr, Hywel Dda and Gruffudd ap Llywelyn were not milestones in a progress towards unity; rather the pattern of Welsh politics was 'increasing chaos'.[392] A ruler might take more than one kingship, but there is very little evidence of overlordship. Destruction of kingships by a new

---

387 *ByT* (Pen. 20) [1136=1137]; *ByS* [1136=1137]; *ByT* (Pen. 20) [1085] and *ByT* (RB) [1087] also call William the Conqueror a prince.

388 Smith, *Llywelyn ap Gruffudd*, pp. 199–203; the *Historia* uses the term '*dywyssogyon*' of the men who guided the armies of Gruffudd's enemies before Bron yr Erw – '*a chanorthuyau eu gelynyon a bot en dywyssogyon udunt y'r kuyoeth*'. It also declares that 'the people without a "*tywyssawg*" shall perish'. *Historia*, ed. Evans, pp. 10, 24; *A Mediaeval Prince*, ed. & transl. Evans, pp. 63, 77.

389 Haddan and Stubbs, *Councils and ecclesiastical documents* i.367; William of Newburgh, *Historia rerum Anglicarum* (ed. Howlett, ii.106); Owain styled himself '*princeps Walliae*' in 1166; Robertson, ed. *Materials for the history of Thomas Becket*, v.239.

390 Davies, *Patterns of Power*, pp. 79, 88; Meilyr called God '*rex regum*'. *The Myvyrian archaiology of Wales* edd. Jones, Williams and Owen, ii.142.

391 *The Latin texts of the Welsh laws*, ed. Emanuel, pp. 207, 277, 437–8; it can not be certain, however, that legal texts do not include material from the thirteenth century. (Pryce, 'The prologues', pp. 151–87.)

392 Davies, *Patterns of Power*, pp. 35–6, 81.

pan-Welsh kingdom was unheard of, and was not tried even in the thirteenth century. Yet, whatever the reality, Gruffudd ap Llywelyn is still portrayed in *Liber Landavensis* as '*monarchia Britonum*', '*regis Britannie*' and '*regis totius Gualie*'.[393] Did Gruffudd attempt to establish a kingship of Wales? Owain Gwynedd, the next Venedotian ruler to command national support, revived the theme, calling himself '*rex Gualliae*' and '*princeps Walliae*' in the 1160s.[394] It is not unreasonable to suspect that Gruffudd ap Cynan was aware of the same ambition, although he could not realise it: the *Historia* was ahead of the reality even of its own time in calling him 'king of the kings of Wales',[395] but it may well reflect an aspiration which was present in Gwynedd from the time of Gruffudd ap Llywelyn. That neither Gruffudd ap Cynan, Bleddyn ap Cynfyn nor Madog ap Maredudd attempted to emulate Gruffudd's domination of Wales does not necessarily mean that it was not a recognised objective: the destruction of Gruffudd ap Llywelyn had not only thrown Wales into confusion; it had shown that the king of England would not countenance a king of Wales, and that he had the power to have his way. The Welsh leaders of the late eleventh and early twelfth centuries knew that they did not have the military and political strength to take such a defiant step, and that only an unprecedentedly powerful hegemony could dare attempt such a radical alteration of the *status quo*. Such caution was later shown to be justified by the career of Llywelyn ap Gruffudd.

By the late twelfth century, other factors were at work to encourage Welsh unity. The political idea of Wales was aided by a growing sense of ethnicity, as well as a feeling that Welsh solidarity was necessary, if only for a short time, in order to repel the Anglo-Normans, and especially the king.[396] It was these sentiments which prompted Gerald to say that the Welsh should submit to one good prince, for their own defence.[397] Yet an aspiring prince of Wales was still hampered by considerable practical problems. Since the administration of Gwynedd itself lacked centralisation, how could a unitary government be imposed on the rest of Wales? There was also a difficulty with traditional notions of the legitimacy of conquest. In calling Gruffudd ap Cynan '*ysgororyt*' ('one who makes free with the border'), Meilyr was not alone in urging his patron to take lands by force[398] – Prydydd y Moch, for instance, told Llywelyn ab Iorwerth '*ac ar bob terfyn torri*'[399] – but

---

[393] *The Text of the Book of Llan Dâv*, edd. Rhys and Evans, pp. 266, 269, 275.
[394] Robertson, ed. *Materials for the history of Thomas Becket*, v.229, 239.
[395] *Historia*, ed. Evans, p. 13; *A Mediaeval Prince*, ed. & transl. Evans, p. 66.
[396] Davies, *Conquest, Co-existence and Change*, p. 75.
[397] *Giraldi Cambrensis Opera* (edd. Brewer *et al.*, vi.204); Gerald was also inspired by the notion of an archbishopric of Wales.
[398] Williams, 'Meilyr Brydydd', below, pp. 179–80, 185.
[399] *The Myvyrian archaiology of Wales*, edd. Jones, Williams and Owen, ii.307.

tradition was against mere conquest. *'Nid meddwl meddu hefyd namyn Dduw ddim o'r byd'* was Cynddelw's judgement, and Elidir Sais warned Llywelyn ab Iorwerth, *'ystyrwch pan dreisych dros ffin'*,[400] whilst possession or conquest (*goresgyn*) was not sufficient grounds for ownership or right in the laws.[401] The odds against a principality of Wales were enormous.

There is, however, evidence that Gruffudd's rule saw the development of a territorialisation of power, as well as a nascent feudalism, which would underpin the later principality. Between the ninth and eleventh centuries, territorial definition of kingship was limited, although it was increasing. By the 1020s, a Welsh *rex* was clearly associated with a territorial region.[402] His growing identification of rule with territory,[403] when coupled with the growth in national aspirations, probably encouraged an awareness of Wales as a geopolitical entity. It seems to have been made particularly explicit in the styles used of Gruffudd ap Cynan: whilst Madog ap Maredudd of Powys was given styles relating to his subjects – *'Powysorum princeps'* and *'rex Powissensium'* – Gruffudd's appellations were more territorial: *'regis Guenedotie'* and *'Gruffut Gwyned'*.[404] That Gruffudd is said by the *Historia* to have freed Gwynedd from lords who came from 'other places' also suggests a territorialisation of dynasties.[405]

This process was carried further in the twelfth century, to the extent that Henry II seems to have recognised Dafydd ab Owain Gwynedd and Rhys ap Gruffudd as rulers of North and South Wales respectively in 1177.[406] Gwynedd and Deheubarth (possibly with some encouragement from the king) were carving Wales up between them, as two separate spheres of influence. It is possible that a precedent for this can be found in 1081, when Gruffudd ap Cynan and Rhys ap Tewdwr made an agreement before Mynydd Carn: that Rhys was apparently a royal tenant in 1086, and that Gwynedd is said to have been in the king's gift, implies English recognition of their status; and that this arrangement was recorded in *Domesday Book*, whilst William I was in West Wales in 1081, encourages speculation that some new three-way agreement was reached under the *aegis* of royal authority.[407] Was this a new reaction to the legacy of Gruffudd ap Llywelyn:

[400] *Red Book of Hergest*, ed. Rhys, p. 226; *The Myvyrian archaiology of Wales*, edd. Jones, Williams and Owen, ii.240.
[401] Pierce, *Medieval Welsh society*, p. 372.
[402] Davies, *Wales in the Early Middle Ages*, p. 102; Davies, *Patterns of Power*, p. 41.
[403] *Ibid.*, pp. 81–2.
[404] *AC* (B) [1161]; *AC* (C) [1161]; Rees, ed. *Cartulary of Haughmond abbey*, p. 222; *The Text of the Book of Llan Dâv*, edd. Rhys and Evans, p. 5; Williams, 'Meilyr Brydydd', below, p. 00.
[405] *Historia*, ed. Evans, p. 9; *A Mediaeval Prince*, ed. & transl. Evans, p. 61.
[406] Roger of Howden, *Chronica* (ed. Stubbs, ii.134); Richter, 'The political and institutional background', pp. 44, 49.
[407] *Historia*, ed. Evans, pp. 13–14; *A Mediaeval Prince*, ed. & transl. Evans, pp. 34–6;

a realisation of the failure to achieve centralisation in Wales, and a resolve to compromise rather than seek a single kingdom? This hypothesis is somewhat weakened by the failure of either Gwynedd or Deheubarth to squeeze Powys into a submissive position in this period, unless it is accepted that neither was sufficiently strong to do so. Yet a north-south polarisation is certainly found after Gruffudd's death, possibly as early as the 1140s, when the sons of Owain Gwynedd intervened in Ceredigion. That most of their activities there were to the benefit of the sons of Gruffudd ap Rhys suggests that the two dynasties worked in conjunction. Hywel and Cynan ab Owain operated without local support only before the emergence of Cadell ap Gruffudd in 1146, and Hywel's only hostile act against Gruffudd's sons was defensive.[408] Hywel's rôle is particularly intriguing. He helped the native dynasty in 1146 and 1147,[409] but he lost Ceredigion Is Aeron to them in 1150, as well as Ceredigion Uwch Aeron in 1151 and Penweddig in 1153.[410] That he was rapidly dispossessed by the very men whom he had helped, and that his father did nothing about it, is suspicious: did Owain consciously seek the recovery of the native dynasty of Deheubarth against the Normans, and consequently a north-south polarisation of power in Welsh hands? He seems to have been in a position to do this, since he is said to have been supreme in the south,[411] and it is perhaps significant that all his battles there were against Normans.[412] What is certain is that Gruffudd ap Rhys relied on Gruffudd ap Cynan's support more than once. In supporting him in 1136, Gruffudd clearly took an interest in the re-establishment of the dynasty of Deheubarth, and with it the possibility of a *pura Wallia* dominated by Gwynedd in the north and Deheubarth in the south.[413]

The existence of a form of feudalism in Wales in this period, however negligible, was both to aid Gruffudd's successors in binding their followers to military service and also to facilitate a re-structuring of the relationship between Gwynedd and the king. Although the '*guryogaeth*' taken by Gruffudd from the men of Môn, Arfon and Llŷn was personal, rather than

---

Domesday Book i fos 179b, 269b; *ByT* (Pen. 20) [1079=1081]; *ByT* (RB) [1081]; *ByS* [1079=1081].

[408] *ByT* (Pen. 20) [1144=1145], [1145=1146], [1150=1151], [1152=1153]; *ByT* (RB) [1143=1145], [1144=1146], [1150=1151], [1152=1153]; *ByS* [1144=1145], [1145=1146], [1150=1151], [1152=1153].

[409] *ByT* (Pen. 20) [1145=1146], [1146=1147]; *ByT* (RB) [1144=1146], [1145=1147]; *ByS* [1145=1146], [1146=1147].

[410] *ByT* (Pen. 20) [1149=1150], [1150=1151], [1152=1153]; *ByT* (RB) [1148=1150], [1150=1151], [1152=1153]; *ByS* [1149=1150], [1150=1151], [1152=1153].

[411] *Red Book of Hergest*, ed. Rhys, p. 331 (Llywelyn Fardd).

[412] *Red Book of Hergest*, ed. Rhys, pp. 330, 331 (Llywelyn Fardd), 204, 206, 207, 213 (Cynddelw), 190, 194 (Gwalchmai).

[413] *ByT* (Pen. 20) [1112=1115]; *ByT* (RB) [1112=1115]; *ByS* [1112=1115]; *Giraldi Cambrensis Opera* (edd. Brewer *et al.*, vi.79).

feudal,[414] the Welsh laws said that there could be no land without a king, that every man was the man (*'gwr'*) of a king, and that the bond between a king and his man transcended that between a man and his kindred bond. *Gwrogaeth* was therefore bound up with the *priodolder* of land,[415] and this might be interpreted as a form of feudal tenure. Welsh investiture practice resembled feudal enfeoffment, and a lord's rights (including his authority to deprive a man of land for failure to pay tribute, death without an heir within four degrees of consanguinity, felony or treason) were very similar to feudal incidents.[416] In South Wales, there are also indications of military obligations which bear similarity to feudal practices. In a document perhaps as early as 1045, Caradog ap Rhiwallon is described as one of the *'comitibus'* of Meurig of Morgannwg, and *Braint Teilo* has an early twelfth-century charter referring to a late tenth-century exemption of the church and bishops of Llandaff from military service to the king of Morgannwg. A charter of *ca* 950x1090 also mentions military service, and the late eleventh-century *Vita Cadoci* says that Gwynllŵg sent men for three days and three nights to serve the same king. A comparable example from Powys in the early twelfth century is found when Cadwgan ap Bleddyn gave Meirionnydd to Uchdryd ab Edwin in 1116 on condition that Uchdryd helped him and his sons against their opponents.[417] Similarly, according to the *Historia*, Gruffudd ap Cynan gave the three sons of Merwydd in Llŷn, and also Tewdwr and Collwyn in Môn, a gift called *'kyuarwys'* after they joined him and Gwrgeneu ap Seisyll in a military alliance. *'Kyuarwys'* probably represents some sort of tribal rights, which were usually given to a innate Welshman (*'bonhedyc kanhuy-naul'*), a category which encompassed clergy, *priodorion* and the king's court (*'llys'*).[418] Yet the five recipients of Gruffudd's gift do not seem to fit any of these descriptions: was he rewarding them for military service?

The *Historia* also employs the terminology of feudalism. Gruffudd is said to have had *'varchogyon'*, or knights, in 1075, and Trahaearn ap Caradog had at least twenty five *'marchauc'*, who were killed in 1081.[419] Gruffudd is also said to have had barons – *'Guyncu'* was a *'barwn'* from Môn, and

414 *Historia*, ed. Evans, p. 8; *A Mediaeval Prince*, ed. & transl. Evans, p. 61; *Pedeir Keinc y Mabinogi*, ed. Williams, p. 24; Ellis, 'Legal References', pp. 123–4.
415 Pierce, *Medieval Welsh society*, p. 205.
416 *Ibid.*, pp. 25–6.
417 *The Text of the Book of Llan Dâv*, edd. Rhys and Evans, p. 261; Davies, 'Braint Teilo', pp. 134, 135; *Vitae sanctorum Britanniae*, ed. Wade-Evans, pp. 24–140; *ByT* (Pen. 20) [1113=1116]; *ByT* (RB) [1113=1116]; *ByS* [1113=1116].
418 Seebohm, *The tribal system in Wales*, p. 66; *Llyfr Blegywryd* (edd. Williams and Powell, p. 58).
419 *Historia*, ed. Evans, pp. 10, 15; *A Mediaeval Prince*, ed. & transl. Evans, pp. 62, 68. The translation of *marchog* as knight, rather than simply a horseman, is taken from the *Brutiau*, which record that Owain ap Cadwgan was made a *'marchog'* by Henry I in 1114. *ByT* (Pen. 20) [1111=1114]; *ByT* (RB) [1111=1114]; *ByS* [1111=1114].

Meirion Goch, who betrayed Gruffudd, was his *'varwn'*[420] – although the veracity of this information is undermined by the fact that the *Historia* mentions not only Robert of Rhuddlan (accurately) as a *'barwn enwauc'*, but also the *'varwneit'* of the king of Ireland at the time of Gwaed Erw.[421] These traces of feudalism are slight, but they were the roots of what feudalism existed in the time of Owain Gwynedd.[422] It may be that there was little potential for the feudalisation of relations with other princes while these processes were so feeble in the native polity, but they were to grow in strength, until a clear tendency towards classical continental feudalism is discernable in the thirteenth-century principality.[423]

When moves were made to feudalise *pura Wallia* into a Venedotian *principatus Walliae*, a dichotomy was reached. The assertion of princely *libertas* and *regalitas* under the king demanded change, whereas the maintenance of territory and authority against the king could only be achieved by retention of the *status quo*.[424] Llywelyn ap Gruffudd's great victory, the treaty of Montgomery in 1267, in fact marked a demotion in Venedotian relations with the king:[425] the power of the king was such that, by the 1280s, he assumed supreme power over his subjects, urged on by a sense of *imperium* over Britain.[426] The only course for a Welsh ruler who wanted to create a native principality was to accept greater royal domination. Furthermore, feudalisation created tensions within Wales. In extending Venedotian power, it was impossible to avoid conflict with tenants and neighbours, who found themselves placed under unacceptable restraints and suffered intrusions upon their own liberties.[427] The intensification of an overlordship such as that of Gruffudd ap Llywelyn was unfeasible. Moreover, because of the degradation of Welsh kingship, Venedotian *regalitas* was undermined jurisdictionally by John, Henry III and Edward I.[428] This merely worsened existing difficulties: even the thirteenth-century princes had no precedent of national unity, jurisdiction, homage or kingship, and it was still necessary

---

420 *Historia*, ed. Evans, pp. 11, 16; *A Mediaeval Prince*, ed. & transl. Evans, pp. 63, 69.
421 *Historia*, ed. Evans, pp. 7, 10; *A Mediaeval Prince*, ed. & transl. Evans, pp. 59, 62.
422 For feudalism in Owain's time, see Pierce, *Medieval Welsh society*, p. 30.
423 Smith, *Llywelyn ap Gruffudd*, pp. 136–7.
424 Richter, 'The political and institutional background', p. 52.
425 Smith, *Llywelyn ap Gruffudd*, pp. 232–3.
426 Davies, ed. *Welsh Assize Roll*, pp. 59–60, 266.
427 Smith, *Llywelyn ap Gruffudd*, p. 232.
428 There were interminable arguments about what Welsh law was and who should administer it. See Rymer, *Foedera*, I.i.84; Smith, *Llywelyn ap Gruffudd*, pp. 334–42. The legal issues which touched the nature of Welsh kingship concerned rights to meet the king on the border, to harbour the king's fugitives, to punish royal subjects for infringements of the princely *dignitas*, to build castles and establish markets, to retain spoils of war, and to take possession of wrecks. Hardy, ed. *Rotuli Chartarum*, p. 103; Edwards, *Calendar of Ancient Correspondence*, pp. 24–5, 60, 67, 86; *ByT* (Pen. 20) [1230]; *ByT* (RB) [1230]; *ByS* [1230].

to fight for recognition as the sole ruler of Gwynedd – there was no link between the kingdom and the dynasty.[429] The *regalitas* of the principality was therefore based merely on conquest and popular consent, rather than the status of a *rex*, founded on sacerdotal authority conferred by divine ordination.[430] Although there were *regalia*, there was no coronation:[431] *regalia* were not the same as *regalitas*.[432]

Gruffudd ap Cynan's Gwynedd was internally weak, had no major external conquests, and probably received little or no tribute. There was little precedent for overlordship, none at all for a kingship or principality of Wales, and a fierce debate about the legality of conquest. The main reason why Gruffudd did not seek a treaty with the king was that he did not have a Greater Venedotian *principatus* to be recognised: that his marriage alliances were confined to Gwynedd and Powys, rather than an Anglo-Norman and European stage, also highlights the fact that Gruffudd's horizons, in practice at least, were restricted to North Wales. Yet his rule laid the foundations for future expansion. Although Gwynedd was racked with problems before 1100, and also probably after that date, there was nothing unique about Gruffudd's troubles. Similar difficulties confronted Llywelyn ab Iorwerth in his early years, and the line of Bleddyn ap Cynfyn in Powys enjoyed unbroken succession for two hundred years, achieving a period of supremacy and surviving the Edwardian conquest despite partitions, opposition from neighbouring powers, conquest, changes of allegiance, rebellion, forfeiture and a dynastic bloodbath. Gruffudd made his successors' hegemony possible simply by his survival, and for this he depended upon the inherent stability of the native Welsh polity. Moreover, Venedotian *regalitas* was preserved intact, esconced within a carefully nurtured and slowly expanding power-base. The re-establishment of Gwynedd as a major source of patronage, the growing sense of nationality, the inchoate territorial polarisation and the presence of a form of feudalism were key ingredients in the later principality. When other kingdoms faltered and the opportunity arose for Gwynedd to assume national leadership after Gruffudd's death, his son, Owain, was ready. Gruffudd deserves credit for consolidating his kingdom and thereby preserving and enhancing the potential for the assertion of what Llywelyn ab Iorwerth was to term '*status Wallie*'.[433] At the same time, it was arguably his lack of a wider hegemony which allowed Gruffudd to remain aloof from the king and avoid many of the legal troubles

---

[429] This is in stark contrast to the kingdom of Scotland. (Smith, *Llywelyn ap Gruffudd*, pp. 192–5.)

[430] Nelson, 'Inauguration rituals', pp. 54–61.

[431] The *Pedeir Keinc* distinguish between a *brenhin* and a *brenhin corunawc*. Ellis, 'Legal References', p. 89.

[432] Jolliffe, *Angevin kingship*, p. 19.

[433] Edwards, *Calendar of Ancient Correspondence*, p. 9; Lewis, below, pp. 73–7.

which befell his successors. The experience of Gruffudd ap Llywelyn had shown that any attempt to upset the Anglo-Welsh *status quo* against the royal interest was fraught with hazards, and in the thirteenth century such an ambition was to lead to the destruction of Venedotian autonomy. It was no accident that, unlike Llywelyn ap Gruffudd, Gruffudd ap Cynan died in his bed and passed his kingdom safely to his successor.

II

GRUFFUDD AP CYNAN AND THE NORMANS

C. P. Lewis

The long years of Gruffudd ap Cynan's career were a critical time for the Welsh.[1] By 1075, when he first appeared in Wales, the Normans had an unshakeable grip on England and were already swinging the balance within southern Britain decisively against Welsh regal independence. On a long perspective it was the fulcrum of nine centuries between the emergence of the larger Anglo-Saxon kingdoms and Henry VIII's Acts of Union: never again after the middle eleventh century were the Welsh united as tributaries of a native king as powerful as Gruffudd ap Llywelyn or Bleddyn ap Cynfyn had been between 1055 and 1075. The arrival of the Normans began the slow strangulation of independent Wales, finally completing what had been begun in the sixth and seventh centuries. Not every Welsh kingdom disappeared at once. The most durable of those which survived into the twelfth century was Gruffudd's land, Gwynedd, which was ruled by his direct descendants until it, too, succumbed to the English in the late thirteenth century. Such dynastic continuity was itself remarkable, since it followed the chronic instability that had characterised the entire eleventh century in North Wales, when usurper had usurped usurper with bewildering regularity.[2]

Gwynedd's survival under the house of Gruffudd ap Cynan demands an explanation. Although the full story goes far beyond the scope of this chapter, the roots of Gwynedd's slow evolution into a state capable – for a time at least – of resisting English expansion are to be found in the years of Gruffudd's extraordinary life. There was a twist right at the beginning: the kingdom which for so long defied the kings of England was in a sense the creation of an English king. Gruffudd's relations with the Normans are thus arguably the most significant dimension of his career: not only the reason for his personal success as king of Gwynedd but beyond that the key to Gwynedd's survival long after he was dead.

[1] Earlier accounts of the subject are Lloyd, 'Wales and the Coming of the Normans'; Lloyd, *A History*, II.378–469.

[2] Maund, *Ireland, Wales, and England*, pp. 54–101, and see also Moore, above, pp. 1–59.

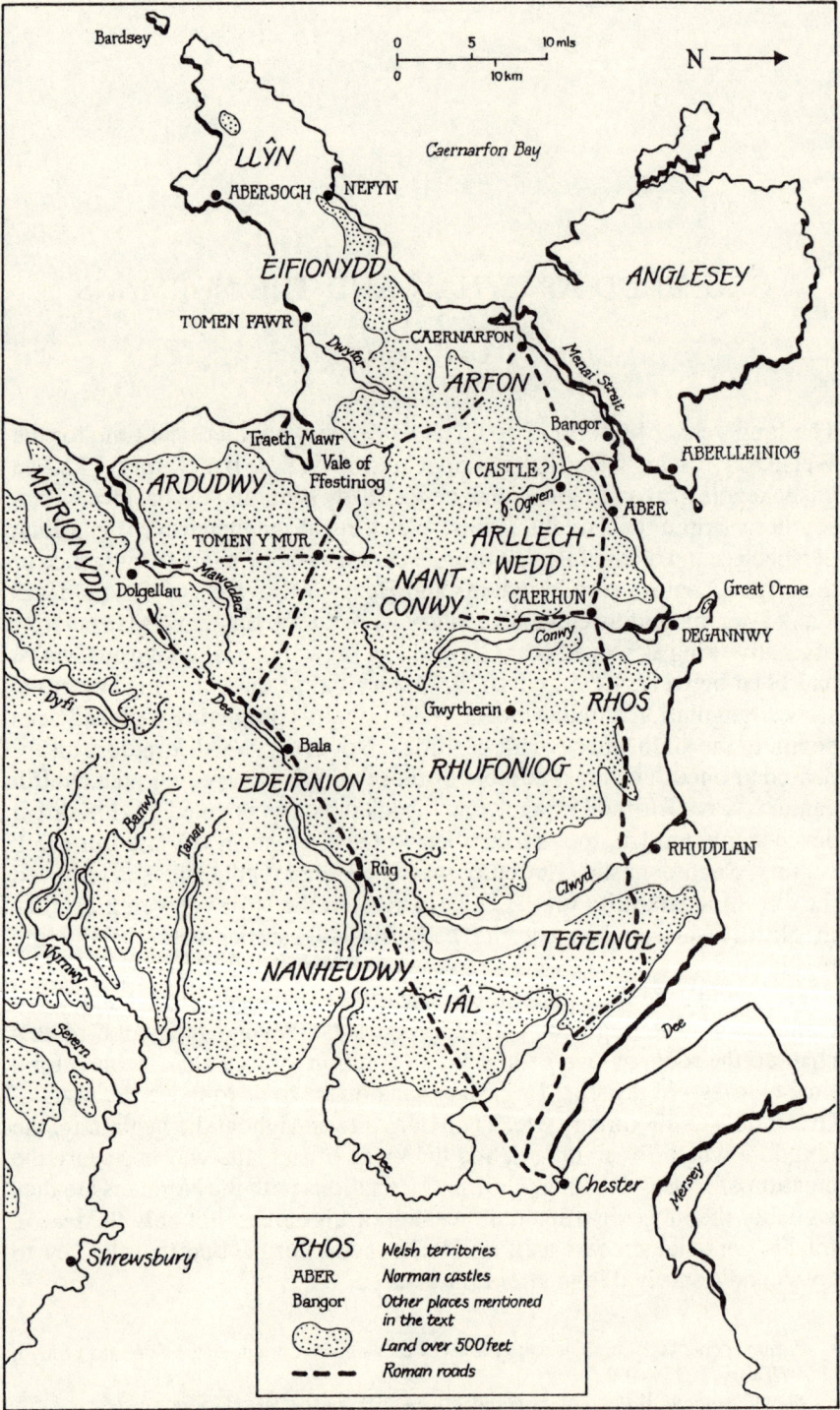

Bardsey

LLŶN

ABERSOCH   NEFYN

Caernarfon Bay

0   5   10 mls

0   10 km

N

ANGLESEY

EIFIONYDD

TOMEN FAWR

Dwyfor

CAERNARFON

ARFON

Bangor

Menai Strait

ABERLLEINIOG

MEIRIONYDD

ARDUDWY

Traeth Mawr

Vale of
Ffestiniog

(CASTLE ?)

Ogwen

ABER

TOMEN Y MUR

ARLLECH-
WEDD

Dolgellau

Mawddach

NANT
CONWY

CAERHUN

Great Orme

Dyfi

Dee

Conwy

DEGANNWY

Gwytherin

RHOS

Bala

RHUFONIOG

EDEIRNION

Banwy

Tanat

Rûg

Clwyd

RHUDDLAN

Wnion

TEGEINGL

Severn

NANHEUDWY

IÁL

Dee

Dee

Chester

Mersey

Shrewsbury

RHOS   Welsh territories
ABER   Norman castles
Bangor   Other places mentioned
            in the text
            Land over 500 feet
– – –   Roman roads

Gruffudd ap Cynan and the Normans in North Wales

Gruffudd interacted with the Normans at every stage of his life, as adventurer, prisoner, prince, king, and in retirement; at times an enemy, at times an ally or client; in the main matched against the earls of Chester and Kings William II and Henry I, but also dealing with the earls of Shrewsbury and Anglo-Norman churchmen. Exploring and explaining Gruffudd's relations with them raises the difficulty which faces all who venture into Gwynedd's history in this period: how to marry the rather full account in the problematical biographical *Historia Gruffud vab Kenan* with the scraps that can be gleaned from other more obviously reliable sources. The case cannot be argued here but there are grounds for thinking that the *Historia* embodied tales about Gruffudd's adventures that were told during his lifetime.[3] The author of the *Historia* was partial to Gruffudd but never a mere flatterer or eulogist. He had been close to the king and knew that his reign had ended gloriously for Gwynedd. Because of that knowledge he magnified Gruffudd's importance throughout his life, insisting that he was a major figure in the politics of North Wales from the very beginning. That hindsight is corrected by the other sources. Some of them were contemporary with the earlier part of Gruffudd's long life, as the *Historia* was not, and they were written far enough from North Wales to provide a more balanced perspective.

The Welsh annalists whose compilation lies behind *Brut y Tywysogion* knew little about Gruffudd until his last two decades. That was natural enough, since they were writing at St David's in the far south-west until about 1100, then at Llanbadarn on the coast of Ceredigion. The Llanbadarn author was mainly interested in Powys, and especially the kin of Bleddyn ap Cynfyn. Until 1114 Gruffudd had little to do with Powys and so figures hardly at all in the annals except as lord of Anglesey and an associate of Bleddyn's son Cadwgan, playing a minor role in the rather confusing events in the north. After 1114 the annals are still laconic about events within Gwynedd, but from a Powysian perspective Gruffudd was now looming offstage as an important client of Henry I, independent of Powys and potentially hostile to its rulers. The annalist was increasingly aware of Gruffudd's growing importance in Welsh affairs, especially when he sent his armies crashing into Meirionydd and Ceredigion in the 1120s and 1130s. In the annal for 1137, the year of Gruffudd's death, the Llanbadarn author lavished praise on the dead king and his sons, by then masters of Ceredigion and Llanbadarn.[4]

Anglo-Norman chroniclers and historians were for the most part unaware of Gruffudd's existence. For the Shropshire-born monk Orderic Vitalis, writing an ecclesiastical history of the Anglo-Norman realm in distant

---

3 Lewis, 'Status'.
4 *ByT* (RB) [1075]–1136 (*recte* 1137); *ByT* (Pen. 20) 1073–1136 (*recte* 1075–1137).

Saint-Evroul in the 1120s and 1130s, Wales was peripheral and usually irrelevant. He had no interest in its recent history, failed to mention the major Anglo-Norman royal expeditions of 1114 and 1121, and confined his attention in North Wales to the career of Robert of Rhuddlan in the late eleventh century. That was because Robert's brother, Orderic's fellow monk, had retrieved Robert's bones from England for reburial at Saint-Evroul and asked Orderic to write an epitaph. Orderic repeated what he was told by Robert's brother: from the family's point of view Gruffudd ap Cynan was just one of several Welsh kings against whom Robert fought, notable mainly because he was Robert's captive and in the end (or so Orderic believed) his killer.[5] Other Anglo-Norman writers were still less concerned with Welsh history: the Anglo-Saxon Chronicle, John of Worcester, and William of Malmesbury were aware of the main events and did not refer once to Gruffudd.[6] The lack of interest in him elsewhere in Wales and in England and Normandy is itself telling: he made little impact beyond the restricted circles accessible to his biographer until almost the end of his life. Nevertheless there remains a central problem: how did one among many Welsh kings become so spectacularly successful as to create a lasting dynasty amid the chaos of a Wales overrun by the Normans?

Gwynedd in the late eleventh and early twelfth century was a territory in transition. It possessed an ancient unity as one of the greater kingdoms of the Welsh; it was bound together by history and hagiography, by geography and a sense of difference from other parts of Wales; but as a political entity it was highly unstable. On the evidence of the *Historia* Gruffudd regarded himself as its rightful king even when beset or confined by his enemies, but what he actually ruled varied greatly over the years. At his zenith he commanded the rich corn-growing arable lands and lowland pastures of Anglesey and Llŷn, and the mountain strongholds of Arfon, Arllechwedd, Nant Conwy, Ardudwy, and Meirionydd. Success in fighting the Normans and the Welsh carried his authority eastwards into the Perfeddwlad (the middle country between the Conwy and the English border) and south into Powys. In 1132 one son was busy in Nanheudwy on the Shropshire border; 1136 and 1137, the last years of his life, saw his other sons raiding deep into Ceredigion.[7] In the 1130s Gwynedd was wherever Gruffudd's sons' mighty armies could reach. Earlier, however, his rule was limited to the far north-west of the country between the Conwy and Bardsey, or to Anglesey alone, or even to the solitary ship in which he made hair's-breadth escapes to Ireland. Without permanent structures of government Gwynedd was based

---

5 Orderic Vitalis, *Historia Ecclesiastica* (ed. & transl. Chibnall, IV.136–47).
6 ASC 1094–1098, 1114; John of Worcester, *Chronicon* (ed. Thorpe); William of Malmesbury, *Gesta Regum* (ed. Stubbs).
7 *ByT* (RB) 1129 (*recte* 1132), 1135 (*recte* 1136), 1136 (*recte* 1137); *ByT* (Pen. 20) 1129 (*recte* 1132), 1135 (*recte* 1136), 1136 (*recte* 1137).

on a king's strong personal rule; without strong personal rule it fragmented into rival and squabbling lordships.

The Normans who conquered England in 1066 were hardened frontiers-men, accustomed to campaigning beyond their own lands in Brittany and Maine, well aware of the possibilities in booty and land when their neigh-bours were fractious and divided. Probably William I believed that he had inherited from the West Saxon kings a claim to overlordship over the whole island of Britain which, properly pursued, could be made real in ways that had not been attempted since the tenth century. There were several means of exploiting the western frontier of England: raids to collect booty and captives; political interference to secure allies and cause mischief to en-emies; conquest to take tribute or even facilitate settlement. William, and the sons who succeeded him on the English throne, had a shrewd under-standing that Welsh dynastic politics were so unstable, so likely to cast up a dangerous neighbour in place of a compliant ally, that options had to be weighed carefully within each region and over time. One was to leave the Welsh to his marcher earls and barons; another was to intervene in person; a third was to seek Welsh allies and clients. In the north the first William gave Hugh d'Avranches as earl of Chester and Roger de Montgomery as earl of Shrewsbury unfettered access to conquer what they could, insisting only that they keep to separate zones so that rivalries over Welsh conquests would not spill into English politics. Gwynedd was assigned to Hugh, Powys to Roger, a division made clear by the fate of the commote of Iâl, Powysian but on the frontier of Cheshire, Earl Roger's as tenant-in-chief but Earl Hugh's as undertenant.[8]

Some general remarks are needed about military affairs. From the Norman point of view, the main strategic problem was to get behind the mountains of Snowdonia (where a Welsh army could disappear alarmingly yet remain ready to pounce) to the richer lands of Anglesey and Llŷn. There were ways by land and sea. Gruffudd ap Cynan was as much at home in a boat as he was on land; the Normans transported and supplied troops by sea, and put all their major castles in North Wales on the coast. Sea power has been underestimated, perhaps because it was evenly matched. All the peoples of the Irish Sea – Welsh, English, Normans, Irish, and Norse – built and used warships of the type perfected by the vikings. Oceanographic conditions did not give a decisive advantage to any one party but instead created hazards and uncertainty for everyone.[9] The strong tidal current that pushes into the Irish Sea from the south-west, often driven by the prevailing winds, could speed sailors trying to navigate round Anglesey and from

---

[8] *Domesday Book*, ed. Farley, I.254r.
[9] U.S. Naval Oceanographic Office, *Oceanographic Atlas*, pp. 3, 15, 17, 20, 54–64; Caton, *Map of Wind Speed*; Mason, *Bartholomew Gazetteer*, p. 120.

Anglesey to the Isle of Man, or hinder them on the return journey; it did not make much difference to ships making their way up and down the North Welsh coast. Passages between Wales and Ireland, across the current, were easy only in slack water when the tide was turning. There were large tidal ranges along the coast. The Menai strait was treacherous. Surprises could and did happen in the waters around North Wales, especially in severe weather. Ships were blown off course; passages might be delayed or unexpectedly rapid; whole fleets could arrive unheralded and to devastating effect.

On land, the most important route into North Wales was from Chester along the inland Roman road between the Dee estuary and the Menai strait. The advantages of keeping to fairly high ground with excellent visibility were unmistakeable to the Normans, whose military planners sited earthwork castles next to the road at Caerhun on the River Conwy and Aber on the Menai, at either end of a mountainous stretch where the road crosses the northern rim of Snowdonia. The routes taken by Norman armies originating further south are apparent in Henry I's expeditions of 1114 and 1121. In one direction or the other (it is not clear which) the 1114 army went by Tamworth, Cannock, Shrewsbury, and the valleys of the Severn, Vyrnwy, and Banwy to (or from) Dolgellau on the Mawddach, or possibly by the Severn, Vyrnwy, and Tanat to (or from) Bala on the Dee. On the other leg of the journey the army passed through Castle Holgate in Shropshire, following a southerly line to (or from) the Severn at Welshpool. The 1121 army was at Bridgnorth, Shrewsbury, and Condover on the Severn valley route.[10] In both years the army apparently moved forward from the Mawddach or the Dee (over a low pass in either case) to a base camp at the old Roman fort called Tomen y Mur. William II was certainly there in the 1090s, and an earlier expedition to Llŷn in the 1070s very likely marched the same way.[11] Probably the first Norman army to camp at Tomen y Mur raised the large motte which still occupies the centre of the Roman earthwork, with huge views over the Vale of Ffestiniog and the Traeth Mawr. From there, an army could strike west into Llŷn; or north-west to cross the Snowdon range to Caernarfon, Bangor, Menai, and Anglesey; or north into the Conwy valley.

As a young man and well into his middle years Gruffudd was simply one among several North Welsh leaders who fought against the Normans. His nearest and earliest antagonists were the men of Chester. As territories Gwynedd and Chester made a stark contrast. Where Gwynedd was unstable and impermanent, the earldom and honor of Chester, though a Norman

[10] Farrer, *Outline Itinerary*, pp. 69–71, 95–8; *Regesta*, II, ed. Johnson and Cronne, nos 1048–54, 1294–9.
[11] *The History*, ed. & transl. Jones, pp. 123–5, 141; *Historia*, ed. Evans, pp. 12–13, 22; *A Mediaeval Prince*, ed. & transl. Evans, pp. 65, 74–5.

invention, was a solid political fact from the moment of its creation by William I in 1070 or 1071 to the end of Gruffudd's life and beyond. All Cheshire, apart from a handful of episcopal manors, was under the earl's lordship. Although the county was poor agriculturally it included the wealthy regional capital of Chester, a town which the earls increasingly dominated. In any case Cheshire as a whole accounted for no more than a quarter of the earl's landed estate in England. The honor thus provided splendid resources in revenues and knights for an earl intent on conquering North Wales.[12]

The first Norman earl of Chester (setting aside the Fleming Gerbod who may have been earl around 1070) was Hugh, son of the viscount of Avranches, still a young man in the early 1070s, and throughout his life a capable and tireless warrior. Orderic Vitalis, who was acquainted with men who had been his knights, described how the earl's progresses even through his own provinces, hunting and feasting, laid the land waste.[13] His effect on enemy territory must have been dreadful: the *Historia* claimed that the Llŷn lay waste for eight years after Hugh and others raided it for the first time.[14] An even more ferocious enemy was Hugh's older cousin and general Robert of Rhuddlan, surnamed from the castle and town that he and the earl together built as their first forward base in Wales. From the mid 1070s for almost twenty years Hugh's and Robert's successes against the Welsh went on without check. From Rhuddlan they pressed forward to Degannwy, an ancient seat of the kings of Gwynedd on the Conwy. Already by 1086 they had penetrated the heart of Snowdonia, ringing it with castles, and Robert was holding Gwynedd from the king on the same terms as the native Rhys ap Tewdwr held the southern kingdom of Deheubarth.[15] In the early 1090s the Norman grip was beginning to tighten with the appointment of a Breton bishop at Bangor and Hugh's gift of lands and rights in North Wales to the new Benedictine abbey which he was founding at Chester.[16] A Norman principality of Gwynedd was in the making.

Gruffudd's relations with the Normans during that first dramatic phase when Hugh and Robert battled their way west to Anglesey were clearly drawn by the *Historia*. Their first contact was co-operative. Having established himself as ruler over Anglesey, Arfon, and Llŷn in or soon after 1075, and intent on furthering his claim to the wider kingship of Gwynedd against Trahaearn ap Caradog, Gruffudd went to Rhuddlan to seek Robert's help

12 Lewis, 'Formation of Honor of Chester'.
13 Orderic Vitalis, *Historia Ecclesiastica* (ed. & transl. Chibnall, II.260–3; III.216–17, 226–7).
14 *The History*, ed. & transl. Jones, pp. 123–5; *Historia*, ed. Evans, pp. 12–13; *A Medieval Prince*, ed. & transl. Evans, p. 65.
15 *Domesday Book*, ed. Farley, I.269r.; compare I.179r.
16 *Charters of Anglo-Norman Earls of Chester*, ed. Barraclough, no. 3; below for the bishop.

and won a promise of support and a contingent of sixty men from the province of Tegeingl.[17] Whether they were Normans or Welshmen is not stated. An alliance between Robert and Gruffudd is in line with the better documented history of South Wales in the 1070s, when Norman-Welsh alliances against other Welsh rulers were commonplace.[18] It gave Gruffudd additional armed strength to pursue his ambitions, and offered the Normans, still newcomers on the Welsh scene, a lever to use against their more powerful enemy Trahaearn.

It was not long before Gruffudd and the Normans fell out. The circumstances are unclear because so little is known about the course of Gruffudd's struggle with Trahaearn.[19] The *Historia* simply recounts an attack by Gruffudd on Rhuddlan in which the bailey was burnt, great plunder was taken, and many knights were killed, others escaping to the tower on the motte.[20] That episode was followed by others in which the Normans were the aggressors. At an unknown date a large army led by Earl Hugh and Robert of Rhuddlan, together with Warin, sheriff of Shrewsbury, and Walter de Lacy from Herefordshire, crossed the mountains and plundered Llŷn for a fortnight.[21] The *Historia* presents the raid as if it were an exceptional measure targeting an exceptional enemy, though more likely it was not the only raid into Western Wales. The third episode from those years told in the *Historia* was the capture of Gruffudd soon after he had – almost by chance – found himself on the winning side at the decisive battle of Mynydd Carn in South Wales in 1081. Suddenly victorious over Trahaearn (who was killed), Gruffudd went to central Wales to ravage Trahaearn's home cantref of Arwystli. From there he was persuaded to travel further north to meet the earls of Chester and Shrewsbury in conference at Rûg on the Dee in Edeirnion. It was a trap. He was captured and taken to Chester, where he languished for years in gaol.[22] The author of the *Historia* intended to show that Gruffudd had become the greatest danger to the Normans in North Wales. His capture was thus followed by their great surge forward: Earl Hugh invaded Gwynedd, built castles, filled them with horsemen and archers, and lorded it over the land.[23] In reality the precondition for the

---

17 *The History*, ed. & transl. Jones, pp. 113–15; *Historia*, ed. Evans, pp. 7–8; *A Mediaeval Prince*, ed. & transl. Evans, pp. 59–60.
18 Crouch, 'Slow Death'.
19 Maund, 'Trahaearn'.
20 *The History*, ed. & transl. Jones, p. 117; *Historia*, ed. Evans, pp. 9–10; *A Mediaeval Prince*, ed. & transl. Evans, p. 62.
21 *The History*, ed. & transl. Jones, pp. 123–5; *Historia*, ed. Evans, pp. 12–13; *A Mediaeval Prince*, ed. & transl. Evans, p. 65.
22 *The History*, ed. & transl. Jones, pp. 125–33; *Historia*, ed. Evans, pp. 13–17; *A Mediaeval Prince*, ed. & transl. Evans, pp. 66–70.
23 *The History*, ed. & transl. Jones, p. 133; *Historia*, ed. Evans, p. 18; *A Mediaeval Prince*, ed. & transl. Evans, p. 70.

Norman invasion of Gwynedd was not the capture of Gruffudd alone but rather the vacuum left by Trahaearn's death. Gruffudd was probably one of several Welsh princes reasonably well placed to take advantage, and he may have gone to Rûg hoping for Norman recognition and support.

From 1081 until 1093 Gruffudd was a prisoner of the Normans of Chester. The only direct statement of that fact is in the *Historia*, though Orderic wrote rather airily of (unnamed) Welshmen whom Robert of Rhuddlan 'kept for years in fetters' and knew that Gruffudd had been among them.[24] The fact of his imprisonment is plausible enough, though its duration is bound to remain controversial, since within the space of a few lines the *Historia* gives it as twelve and as sixteen years without apparently noticing the discrepancy.[25] The difference might have come about through a careless scribe (at some stage in what was clearly a complex evolution of the text as it now stands) confusing the Roman numerals 'xii' and 'xvi'. Although the *Historia* is wholly innocent of real dates, a twelve-year imprisonment does in fact fit neatly between Mynydd Carn in 1081 and the Welsh rebellion of 1093.[26]

Mynydd Carn left the kingship of Gwynedd vacant. The Normans moved decisively to fill it by disposing of Gruffudd and other potentially trouble-some leaders, then by invasion. What they achieved in the 1080s and early 1090s was an overlordship backed by military force, not intensive occupa-tion or settlement. Robert of Rhuddlan led the assault west of the Conwy and by 1086 held Gwynedd from King William in addition to the fief that he had earlier been granted in the cantrefs of Rhos and Rhufoniog east of the Conwy. He may also have had the lands of the bishopric of Bangor,[27] pending an appointment to the see.

Robert's control of Gwynedd in the late 1080s and early 1090s is still visible on the ground in a string of powerful earthwork castles. They have not been adequately surveyed and it would be unwise to be dogmatic about their dating, though in number, character, and disposition they seem to belong to Robert's and Earl Hugh's time.[28] In any case we know from the *Historia* that some castles were built by the Normans in Gwynedd after 1081: 'a castle in Anglesey, and another in Arfon in the old fort of the emperor Constantine . . . [and] another in Bangor and another in Meirionydd'.[29] Even adding those that were undocumented, their small

---

[24] Orderic Vitalis, *Historia Ecclesiastica* (ed. & transl. Chibnall, IV.138–9, 144–5).
[25] *The History*, ed. & transl. Jones, p. 133; *Historia*, ed. Evans, pp. 17–18; *A Mediaeval Prince*, ed. & transl. Evans, pp. 69–70.
[26] For an alternate view, see also Moore, above, pp. 36–9.
[27] *Domesday Book*, ed. Farley, I.269r.
[28] There is a helpful discussion of early castles in general in Pounds, *The Medieval Castle*, pp. 3–71.
[29] *The History*, ed. & transl. Jones, p. 133; *Historia*, ed. Evans, p. 18; *A Mediaeval Prince*, ed. & transl. Evans, p. 70.

numbers contrast with districts where military contact between Normans and Welsh was prolonged (as all along the Anglo-Welsh border)[30] or where conquest was followed by settlement and thus castles for strictly military purposes were succeeded by the castles of Anglo-Norman lordships (as in Glamorgan).[31] The Gwynedd castles are mostly substantial mottes without baileys and in positions of great strategic importance, commanding significant points around the coasts and in inland valleys.[32] The nearest to Robert's forward base at Degannwy were Aber on the Menai strait and Caerhun in the Conwy valley, at either end of the road over Snowdonia. Directly across Menai from Aber and in easy signalling contact was Aberlleiniog; they provided vantage points for observing ships entering the strait. Further west there may have been castles at Bangor (though the *Historia*'s reference was arguably to Aber), and a few miles up the Ogwen valley astride another route through Snowdonia (though there is only place-name evidence for it). There was certainly a sizeable motte at Caernarfon, watching over the south-eastern mouth of Menai, and three more castles circling the Llŷn peninsula: Nefyn on the north coast, a motte built to have superb views alike over Caernarfon Bay and the countryside; and on the south coast a motte (now destroyed) at Abersoch and a ringwork, Tomen Fawr, overlooking the mouth of the Dwyfor. Both had commanding outlooks to sea.

One further point needs to be made about the castles. There is much in their siting that foreshadows the permanent conquest of Gwynedd by Edward I two hundred years later, partly because of the logistical necessity for supply by sea: Edward's Conwy was planted immediately across the river mouth from Robert of Rhuddlan's Degannwy; Beaumaris a couple of miles down the coast from Aberlleiniog; Cricieth (a Welsh castle rebuilt by Edward) no further from Tomen Fawr; Caernarfon actually around Robert's motte, which survived in the upper ward until the late nineteenth century. In both periods a strategist of genius had understood how Gwynedd could be dominated from a few vital points on the coast. There was one major difference: the late eleventh-century castellation of Gwynedd did not lead to permanent conquest.

The promise of a Norman principality of Gwynedd was broken when Welsh resistance became more successful in the early 1090s. The key moment was the killing of Robert of Rhuddlan at Degannwy in 1093, an incident memorably described by Orderic Vitalis: 'Gruffudd, king of the Welsh', landed with three ships below the Great Orme and plundered the countryside, loading his ships with men and animals as they lay beached

30 Hogg and King, 'Early Castles'; Hogg and King, 'Castles'.
31 Royal Commission, *Glamorgan*, III (1A), esp. pp. 8–24.
32 The following account is based on personal visits and on King, *Castellarium*, I.1–3, 31–7; Royal Commission, *Anglesey*, pp. 123–4; Royal Commission, *Caernarvonshire*, I.10, 27, 134; II.125, 237–8; III.63, 85.

waiting for the tide; Robert, with only a few armed men on the spot at Degannwy, impetuously rushed to the shore accompanied by a single knight; he was fatally wounded, the Welsh cut off his head, fixed it to one of their masts, and made off.[33] Orderic attributed the feat to Gruffudd ap Cynan perhaps on his (or his informant's) assumption that the only Welsh leader capable of such audacity was the great king still ruling Gwynedd when Orderic was working on his History. While it is possible that Gruffudd, newly escaped from Chester gaol, was already marauding along the coast by July 1093, it is extremely odd that the *Historia*, normally so anxious to accredit its hero with anything and more that could be claimed for him, did not refer at all to Robert's death. On balance the *Historia*'s silence is to be preferred to Orderic.[34]

For the moment, Hugh of Chester fought on in North Wales with the support of William II and the earls of Shrewsbury. The earldom and honor of Shrewsbury had a less important role than Chester in the affairs of North Wales. Like Chester, the earls controlled valuable lands away from the Welsh marches, and organised them so as to give themselves and their barons the resources to campaign unceasingly and successfully in Wales.[35] Earl Roger (1068–1094) directed his energies towards Ceredigion and Dyfed in West Wales.[36] In the middle 1090s Roger's son Earl Hugh (1094–1098) co-operated more closely with the earl of Chester in the north.

The period from 1093 to 1102 was one of great confusion in North Wales, in which the Normans of Cheshire and Shropshire under their earls, and William II at the head of royal armies, battled in Snowdonia and Anglesey, but without decisively regaining the initiative lost with the death of Robert of Rhuddlan. Gruffudd ap Cynan was free and, according to the *Historia*, active and successful in harrying the Normans. The *Historia* tells a consistent story but rather less than the whole truth. If Gruffudd had learnt lessons about the value of working with the Normans during those long years of captivity in Chester he did not apply them straight away. First it depicts Gruffudd as a guerrilla, moving from place to place within Gwynedd, inflicting damage on the Normans wherever he could and in turn pursued by them from the safety of their castles. Then, with help from the Norse king of Man he undertook a more sustained campaign, beginning with an attack on Aberlleiniog in Anglesey which burnt it to the ground, and moving on to destroy the other castles in Gwynedd and chase the Normans east into the Perfeddwlad. That success provoked William II into leading a great army to Tomen y Mur, intent on retaliation, but Gruffudd prepared

---

[33] Orderic Vitalis, *Historia Ecclesiastica* (ed. & transl. Chibnall, IV.140–3).
[34] For the contrary view see Orderic Vitalis, *Historia Ecclesiastica* (ed. & transl. Chibnall, IV, pp. xxxvii–xxxviii). But see also Moore, above, pp. 134–9.
[35] Lewis, *Welsh Borders*.
[36] Lloyd, *A History*, II.388–90, 400–1.

ambushes against him and William led his army back into England without engaging the Welsh or securing plunder. After that (in 1098) Earls Hugh of Chester and Hugh of Shrewsbury mounted an expedition by land and sea to Anglesey. Although Gruffudd and his ally Cadwgan ap Bleddyn fled to Ireland, the Norman assault was disrupted by the unexpected arrival of King Magnus of Norway. Hugh of Shrewsbury was killed by the Norwegians; Hugh of Chester withdrew with booty and captives; and soon afterwards Gruffudd returned from Ireland and made peace with him.[37]

The *Historia* tries to show that between his escape from Chester in 1093 and 1099 Gruffudd was the chief – and often successful – resistance leader in North Wales. Even according to the *Historia* that picture can be called into question. The continuing depth and scale of Norman involvement in Gwynedd, the desperate adventures which befell Gruffudd after he got away from Chester, even his subordinate position in 1098 and 1099 are all too apparent. Other Welsh sources and English evidence further downplay his role. Notably, the Welsh annalist assigned him only a minor part in the conflict: when rebellion broke out in 1094 the leader was not Gruffudd but Cadwgan ap Bleddyn; indeed Gruffudd was not even mentioned. William II led two expeditions, in 1095 and 1097, not just the one recounted in the *Historia*, and on neither occasion was Gruffudd mentioned. In 1098 the annals made him a second leader of the Welsh after Cadwgan, but since the two took flight to Ireland neither played a part in the main events. When they returned in 1099 Gruffudd received only Anglesey, and by gift of the French not by force of arms.[38] Nevertheless the years 1093–1099 were not wasted. The Normans were being worn down – admittedly not by Gruffudd's efforts alone – marking the way for a change of policy by Henry I; and it may have been that Gruffudd struck up an acquaintance with the Normans' bishop of Bangor, Hervé, which in time made him the principal beneficiary of that new policy.[39]

Gruffudd's insignificance in 1099, precariously established as lord of Anglesey, makes it all the more pressing to explain what had happened by 1114, when he was secure as ruler of the whole of Gwynedd and had become the key figure in North Wales, a force to be reckoned with by the Normans on his eastern frontier and the ruler of Powys to his south.[40] The *Historia*, ambiguous as ever, makes it clear that Gruffudd came to prominence as a client of Henry I, but also suggests that afterwards he was able to defy him. Specifically it claims that after some years ruling Anglesey Gruffudd sought

[37] *The History*, ed. & transl. Jones, pp. 133–49; *Historia*, ed. Evans, pp. 18–27; *A Mediaeval Prince*, ed. & transl. Evans, pp. 70–9.
[38] *ByT* (RB) 1090–1095 (*recte* 1093–1099); *ByT* (Pen. 20) 1091–1097 (*recte* 1093–1099).
[39] Below, p. 74.
[40] *ByT* (RB) 1111 (*recte* 1114); *ByT* (Pen. 20) 1111 (*recte* 1114).

out Henry I and that Bishop Hervé of Bangor interceded on his behalf; the king granted him lands in North Wales; Gruffudd returned there and took possession, growing in strength as Welshmen from the Perfeddwlad slipped away from the territory of the earl of Chester to join him, enabling him eventually to take control of the whole of Gwynedd. The biographer then recounts two expeditions by Henry I to impress upon Gruffudd his continuing state of subjection. Peace was made between the two kings on each occasion and they reigned for many years in friendship.[41]

The explanation of Gruffudd's greatly enhanced position in the first two decades of the twelfth century thus lies, even on the evidence of the *Historia*, in England rather than Wales. Events on the English side of the border explain why: within the space of eighteen months in 1101–1102 first Cheshire then Shropshire fell under the direct control of Henry I. Earl Hugh of Chester, not an old man when he died in July 1101, was succeeded by his seven-year-old son Richard. Henry I took the honor of Chester into wardship and directed its affairs personally until Earl Richard came of age in 1115. Even after Chester returned to the rule of the earls (Richard until he died when the White Ship went down in 1120, his cousin Ranulph I 1120–1129, and Ranulph's son Ranulph II from 1129),[42] Henry I continued to play a large part in the affairs of North Wales. In Shropshire Earl Hugh de Montgomery's successor in 1098 was his elder brother Robert, who had little time for close involvement with the Welsh before rebellion against Henry I in 1101–1102 brought him dispossession and banishment.[43] The king appointed as governor of Shropshire Richard de Belmeis, who had already served both the king and the Montgomery earls and who in 1108 was further rewarded with the bishopric of London. Richard's sphere of activity in Wales was confined to Ceredigion and Dyfed, as Earl Roger's had been, and as his successor Payn fitz John's was from the middle 1120s.[44] With both earldoms in his hand Henry I was freer than William II had been to formulate a new policy for North Wales.[45] Direct intervention had failed because the king had not been able to give continuous attention to the region; Henry I instead turned to clientage and assisted Gruffudd ap Cynan to the kingship of Gwynedd. Gruffudd built on that start, but the turning point in his career, even as presented in the *Historia*, was Henry I's patronage. On his return from exile in 1099 he had received Anglesey from the French. Henry awarded him Llŷn, Eifionydd, Ardudwy, and Arllechwedd, and Gruffudd later added Arfon and Nant Conwy.

---

[41] *The History*, ed. & transl. Jones, pp. 151–5; *Historia*, ed. Evans, pp. 28–30; *A Mediaeval Prince*, ed. & transl. Evans, pp. 79–81.
[42] *Complete Peerage*, ed. C[okayne], III.165–7.
[43] *Complete Peerage*, ed. C[okayne], XI.687–93.
[44] Cox, 'County Government', pp. 10–11.
[45] In general see Davies, 'Henry I'.

The role of Bishop Hervé in Gruffudd's promotion deserves closer inspection. According to orthodoxy the bishop was imposed upon the Welsh during the Norman ascendancy in Gwynedd in 1092 and fled during the revolt of 1093–1094. Since Gruffudd was at large only from 1093 the conventional chronology hardly gives time for the two men to have crossed paths. But the usual date for Hervé's expulsion is mere supposition: he may in fact have remained in post through the middle 1090s as Gruffudd began to secure a toe-hold in Gwynedd. The story of Bishop Hervé's expulsion was preserved by several twelfth-century authors writing in his lifetime or shortly afterwards. In William of Malmesbury's version, Hervé left Bangor in hope of a richer see and because he and the Welsh could not live together.[46] A fuller account, written down at Ely after Hervé's death (presumably from what he had told people while he was bishop there after 1109), mentions friction between Hervé and his flock over their intolerably perverse customs, his attempt to coerce them by anathema, Welsh rebellion and threats against his person, the murder and wounding of many of his men, and finally his flight to the protection of the English king.[47] When did that happen? The fact is that we do not know anything of what Hervé was doing until the end of the 1090s, except that about 1097 William II confirmed Hascoit Musard's gift to him of the manor of Aston Somerville in Gloucestershire.[48] The manor was a delectable piece of the Vale of Evesham just below the dramatic scarp of the Cotswolds at Broadway and only a day's ride from the royal palace at Gloucester. It had a well-stocked home farm, plenty of slaves, and a comfortable rental:[49] highly suitable as a income-generating residence for a bishop in exile from his see, when he was not at court. It may well have been only then, towards the end of the 1090s, that Hervé no longer visited his Welsh diocese. That would have given him ample time to become acquainted with Gruffudd ap Cynan.

In the ensuing period of Gruffudd's greatest prominence between about 1110 and the middle 1120s, he was busy consolidating and extending his dominant position in North Wales. The annals mark him as an important ruler by 1114, when Henry I needed to buy him off separately from the Powysians, and when he in turn treated independently with Henry's generals, Earl Richard of Chester and the Scottish prince Alexander. The annals for 1115–1121 further underline his position: exiles sought his protection and he attended Henry I at court. But he was not independent: in 1121, for example, he stood fast by Henry when Powysians beleaguered by the Norman king sought his help.[50]

46 William of Malmesbury, *Gesta Pontificum* (ed. Hamilton, p. 326).
47 *Liber Eliensis*, ed. Blake, p. 245.
48 *Liber Eliensis*, ed. Blake, pp. 207–8.
49 *Domesday Book*, ed. Farley, I.169v.
50 *ByT* (RB) 1111–1118 (*recte* 1114–1121); *ByT* (Pen. 20) 1111–1118 (*recte* 1114–1121).

Further evidence of the co-operation between Gruffudd and Henry I comes from the arrangements made to fill the long-vacant see of Bangor in 1120. The native church in Wales before the Norman invasion stood apart from the western European mainstream, its bishops not diocesans of the English type, its dioceses not fully territorial.[51] Three Welsh bishops of Bangor in succession were later said to have been consecrated by the bishops of St David's, the last in the 1070s or early 1080s.[52] The Normans intruded an alien model of diocesan organisation when the archbishop of York consecrated Hervé in 1092, but it presumably lapsed when he fled.

Elsewhere in Wales, at St David's and Llandaff, Welsh or Anglo-Welsh bishops were busy modernising in the early twelfth century, but both those sees were in areas where there was substantial Norman settlement.[53] Hence the decision by Gruffudd in 1120 to appoint a proper diocesan and have him approved by Henry I and consecrated at Canterbury is highly significant. It was a deliberate political act to bring the church of Gwynedd into line with the other Welsh churches and thus with England. Bishop David was an interesting choice. He has been regarded as a Welshman, but only on the strength of an unprovenanced entry in the Annals of Worcester priory, compiled as late as the fourteenth century: the statement that David was 'Welsh by birth' (*Walensem natione*) does not appear in any of the annalist's known sources and was probably his own assumption from the Welsh forename, compounded by misreading or confusing the corresponding entry in the continuation of the Chronicle of John of Worcester.[54]

David's name was certainly Welsh in origin, but his cognomen *Irensis* or *Scottus* (as used by Orderic Vitalis and William of Malmesbury, who knew his written works) points unambiguously to Ireland. Perhaps David, like King Gruffudd himself, was of mixed Welsh-Irish parentage or upbringing. David's career before Bangor is even more interesting: a student at Würzburg in Bavaria; a clerk of Henry I in England; the ambassador who accompanied the king's daughter Maud to Germany when she was sent to marry Henry V; Henry V's literary apologist in 1111 when he went to Rome to browbeat Pope Paschal II and be crowned emperor.[55] David's connexion with Henry I shows that it was important for Gruffudd to appoint a bishop acceptable to the Normans, but David, cosmopolitan in background, widely travelled and widely connected, was more than the minimum necessary for

---

51 Davies, *Wales in Early Middle Ages*, pp. 157–64.
52 Davies, ed. *Episcopal Acts*, I.92–3, 99.
53 Crouch, 'Urban'.
54 *Annales Monastici*, ed. Luard, IV.377; compare John of Worcester, *Chronicon* (ed. Thorpe, II.74).
55 Orderic Vitalis, *Historia Ecclesiastica* (ed. & transl. Chibnall, V.198–9); William of Malmesbury, *Gesta Regum* (ed. Stubbs, II.498–502); Leyser, 'England and the Empire', pp. 77–8.

acceptability in England. His appointment was a statement that Gruffudd aspired to make Gwynedd a European principality.

Others besides Gruffudd and Henry might have had a hand in David's elevation. The month after he was consecrated at Canterbury, Bishop Urban of Llandaff (who had assisted at the ceremony) had relics of St Dyfrig translated from Bardsey Island off the Gwynedd coast to his own cathedral, with the assent of Bishop David and in the presence of King Gruffudd.[56] Dyfrig was an important symbol for Urban, one of the saints around whom he was building traditions for his own newly created territorial diocese. The timing of consecration and translation seems more than a coincidence. David and Urban must have known each other at Henry I's court before 1120, and Urban's Llandaff might well have been the model for David's Bangor. As bishop, David is known to have spent some time on the affairs of the English church but must also have been active in his diocese. All we know for certain is that he appointed an archdeacon, but the sources are pitifully thin and it would be a mistake to read too little into them.[57]

In the final period of Gruffudd's life, from the early 1120s until his death in 1137, he remained king in name but had handed effective authority to his sons. The moment of his retirement can probably be dated. By 1124 he had given up leading his warbands in person, and in the next year there was one of those family massacres which punctuate the history of Wales so frequently in the twelfth century (Gruffudd's eldest son killed his three maternal uncles),[58] a slaughter best read as the first blow in a struggle for power within the ruling kin after the retirement of its head. The *Historia* presents the last period of Gruffudd's life as one of peace and harmony (not altogether convincingly in view of the bloodletting which heralded it). It also adds evidence for a growing web of relations between Gruffudd and the Normans, since he made death-bed gifts not only to Welsh churches but also to the Benedictine monasteries of Chester and Shrewsbury.[59] The negotiations which led to the translation of the bones of St Winifred from Gwytherin in Gwynedd to Shrewsbury abbey also took place in the very year of Gruffudd's death.[60] Since the monks of Chester were closely involved with their Shrewsbury brethren in the translation, it may be that Gruffudd's bequests to the two houses were connected with St Winifred.

Gruffudd's survival and at the end his prosperity no doubt owed a great deal to luck, not just the sort of luck that a resourceful and intelligent

---

56 *The Text of the Book of Llan Dâv*, edd. Evans and Rhys, pp. 84–5.
57 Davies, ed. *Episcopal Acts*, I.99–101.
58 *ByT* (RB) 1121–1122 (*recte* 1124–1125); *ByT* (Pen. 20) 1121–1122 (*recte* 1124–1125).
59 *The History*, ed. & transl. Jones, p. 155; *Historia*, ed. Evans, p. 31; *A Mediaeval Prince*, ed. & transl. Evans, p. 82.
60 Owen and Blakeway, *History of Shrewsbury*, II.33–42, summarising the Lives of St Winifred printed in *Acta Sanctorum: Novembris*, I (Paris 1887).

adventurer could make for himself, but the luck to have two chances. Twice he found himself well placed to bid for the kingship of Gwynedd. On both occasions he sought Norman help. The first time, after Mynydd Carn in 1081, he walked into the earls' trap; the second, during the years after Anglesey in 1098, he fell into Henry I's greedy embrace just at the moment when royal policy was switching from direct intervention to arm's-length clientage and Henry was looking for a prince to sponsor. But as well as luck Gruffudd had the cunning to adapt the age-old skills of statecraft among the Welsh princes – mayhem and murder – to the new era of Norman dominance in Britain. The principality of Gwynedd thus took its first shape under Anglo-Norman protection.

III

THE GENEALOGY OF GRUFFUDD AP CYNAN

David E. Thornton

The genealogy of Gruffudd ap Cynan is preserved in the *Historia Gruffud vab Kenan*, which it introduces, and also in Welsh genealogical manuscripts of the fifteenth and later centuries.[1] While the latter material is demonstrably derived from a version of that in the *Historia*, it contains some additional information lacking in the main text. The following discussion will concentrate on the genealogy as it is given in the *Historia* but will also refer to the later copies where it is useful to do so. The genealogy of Gruffudd in the *Historia* can be described as 'ego-focal' in that its various elements all converge upon Gruffudd and it is divided into two, very unequal halves: one describing his paternal and Welsh ancestry and the other his maternal and Hiberno-Scandinavian heritage. These two parts of the genealogy differ from one another both in their respective genealogical structures (the total number of generations covered, the degree of segmentation involved, and so forth) and in the amount of strictly non-genealogical information or narrative material associated with them. These differences depended, in part perhaps, on the functions which the two halves were intended to perform, and also on the foreknowledge of the Welsh author of the original *Historia*.

The Welsh side of the genealogy comprises the Venedotian pedigree to Rhodri Mawr, the ninth-century founder of the Second Dynasty of Gwynedd. Here the pedigree diverges into two lines (tracing Rhodri's paternal and maternal ancestries respectively) which eventually converge again at the grandson of Beli Mawr. Beli's descent, through various legendary, Galfridian, classical and biblical names, is then given down to Adam ('mab Duw'), thus concluding this side of Gruffudd's genealogy. As is

---

[1] The texts are available in *Historia*, ed. Evans, pp. 1–3; *A Mediaeval Prince*, ed. & transl. Evans, pp. 23–7, 53–7; Bartrum, ed., *Tracts*, pp. 35–7; *The History*, ed. & transl. Jones, pp. 102–11. For some longer discussions of the material see Bartrum, ed., *Tracts*, pp. 35, 134–6, 152 (see Bartrum, 'Achau Brenhinoedd a Thywysogion Cymru', pp. 219–20); Charles, *Old Norse Relations with Wales*, pp. 56–8; Charles-Edwards, *Early Irish and Welsh Kinship*, pp. 220–4; *Historia*, ed. Evans, pp. cci–ccxix; *A Mediaeval Prince*, ed. & transl. Evans, pp. 85–98; *The History*, ed. & transl. Jones, pp. 33–47, 159–63; Maund, *Ireland, Wales, and England*, pp. 85–90, 178–9.

apparent, with the exception of the divergence between Rhodri Mawr and Beli Mawr, this material is otherwise linear (that is, one name given per generation). Seven generations separate Gruffudd from Rhodri Mawr, who is in turn separated from Beli by either thirty-two or twenty-seven names; and the final stage, above Beli, contains forty-eight generations. This would give totals of eighty-seven or eighty-two generations for the whole paternal genealogical scheme, depending which line is followed above Rhodri Mawr. Furthermore, if various 'corrections' are made to this scheme in accordance with other genealogical collections,[2] then these totals would increase to ninety-one or eighty-six. We thus have a genealogy of covering between eighty and ninety generations in total with minimal segmentation of two names per generation for less than half of the scheme.

This stands in marked contrast to the Hiberno-Scandinavian ancestry of Gruffudd ap Cynan through his mother *Ragnell*. The backbone of this side of the genealogy is Ragnell's ancestry through the Ostmen rulers of Dublin traced to *Harfagyr Vrenhin mab Brenhin Denmarc*. Into this line are married the female representatives of various Irish dynasties, providing links thereby to the ruling lines of Munster, Leinster, Ulster and Meath. The total number of generations separating Gruffudd from the ultimate generation (an anonymous 'king of Denmark') is a mere eight. Determination of the degree of segmentation is hindered by a series of errors in the text, which are apparent when it is compared with extant Irish sources (below), but the maximum possible is up to to seven names in a single generation.[3]

These structural differences between the two sides of Gruffudd's ancestry are compounded by the amount of non-genealogical and narrative material which is associated with them. The Welsh side takes the form of linear sequences of names (some combined with cognomena, such as Rhodri *Mawr*), but even the entries *Kenan o Gastell Dindaethue* ('Cynan from Castell Dindaethwy') and *Brut Tywyssauc o Ruvain* ('Brutus Prince from Rome') hardly constitute major asides! The Hiberno-Scandinavian material, however, contains a large amount of non-genealogical and often sequential narrative information, in particular a lengthy account of the deeds of Harald Fairhair (*Harald Harfagyr*) and his alleged brothers. It is of course likely that the Welsh audience of the original *Historia* would not have needed to be informed who, for instance, Rhodri Mawr was and where he ruled, whereas it would have been less knowledgeable about the likes of the Dubliner Olaf Cuarán. Even if this likelihood is taken into account, the differences between the two sides of the genealogy of Gruffudd still stand. As the Welsh part of the genealogy is essentially a long pedigree, tracing its subject's ancestry back to the Creation, only about a fifth of the names

---

2   For instance, on the alterations to the Welsh genealogy of Gruffudd made by John Jones of Gelli Lyfdy in his copy of the *Historia*, see below, pp. 81–82.
3   See Figure 2 below.

mentioned can be identified in other, non-genealogical sources as being in some way 'historical' (and perhaps a fifth errs a little on the generous). The far shorter and more segmented Hiberno-Scandinavian material, on the other hand, cannot be pushed back beyond the late ninth century at the most (in the person of Harald Fairhair) and only a handful of the names cannot be identified in extant Irish and Scandinavian sources (mostly women married into the Dublin line) or are of doubtful historicity. But while most of the Hiberno-Scandinavians and Irish can be identified with historical figures with some degree of certainty, the relationships in which they are put in the *Historia* do not all agree with the Irish sources (see below); and in some cases names are repeated for different figures when clearly a single personage is intended. These errors may have arisen in the course of translation from the Latin and in subsequent copying or they may have been part of the original text.

One of the problems faced when discussing the genealogy of Gruffudd ap Cynan in the *Historia* is that we no longer possess this original Latin version of the text, but only later copies based on a translation into Middle Welsh of the original. The extent to which the surviving versions accurately represent the Latin text is by no means clear. Indeed comparison of the genealogy in the *Historia* with other sources (other Welsh genealogical sources for the paternal side and various Irish genealogies and chronicles for the maternal) demonstrates that a number of apparent 'irregularities' exist in our extant text. Thus, John Jones of Gelli Lyfdy, who copied the *Historia* in 1641 into Aberystwyth, National Library of Wales, MS. Peniarth 267, drew attention to the errors (as he perceived them) in the account of Gruffudd's Welsh ancestry in his source when compared with what he termed his *llyfyr acheu* (probably Cardiff, Public Library, MS. 3.77, copied 1640). Furthermore, Jones 'corrected' his version of the paternal side of the genealogy in agreement with the other Welsh genealogical manuscripts.[4] Most of these corrections involve the insertion of names seemingly 'omitted' in Peniarth 17;[5] and in one case Jones omitted a name which occurs in Peniarth 17 but not in the other genealogical manuscripts.[6] Jones also gave the Welsh form of the cognomen of Geoffrey of Monmouth's *Brutus Uiride*

---

[4] Jones made no similar correction to the Hiberno-Scandinavian side of the genealogy, with which he would have been less familiar. Indeed it would appear (from Bartrum's critical apparatus) that Jones did not copy the relevant Hiberno-Norse material of the tract *Achau Brenhinoedd a Thywysogion Cymru* (= ABT §§ 6[a]–[h]) in his *llyfr achau*: Bartrum, ed., *Tracts*, pp. 78–9, 100. Anyway, this section of ABT is evidently based ultimately on the *Historia* and (with a few exceptions) agrees with it, including the errors.

[5] These include Idwal Foel (as son of Anarawd ap Rhodri Mawr), Enid (as son of Eudos ab Euddolen), Cunedda (as son of Rhegau ferch Llŷr), Efrawg (as son of Membyr ap Madog), and Cetun (as son of Javan ab Japheth).

[6] Namely, Elise as son of Meurig ab [Idwal Foel].

Scutum which was usually to be found in the manuscripts (*Darianlas*) as opposed to the translated-form *Ysgwyt Ir* given in Peniarth 17 and the other copies of the *Historia*.[7] Jones' corrections may bring the genealogy of the *Historia* into line with other genealogical sources, but it is by no means certain that he was thereby producing a text more faithful to the Latin original: at least some of these so-called anomalies may well have been part of the archetype. And, of course, it is possible that similar revisions have been made to the genealogy by earlier scribes which we now lack the means of detecting.

The Hiberno-Scandinavian material could conceivably be closer to the original text since the Welsh scribes (including, it would seem, John Jones) would have been less familiar with it and thereby less likely to 'correct' it in their redactions. As we shall see in greater detail below however, this section contains a series of errors when set alongside surviving Irish 'books of pedigrees' and chronicles (such as identifiable figures being in the wrong relationship to one another, or the repetition of names) which have led modern scholars to emend this side of the text in accordance with these sources, as Jones did with the Welsh side. Again, the possibility that the extant material does not accurately represent its Latin source must be considered (either through mistakes in translating or subsequent scribal errors) but we must not necessarily assume that the original Welsh author possessed our (admittedly much later) knowledge of affairs Irish or that his Latin text must have agreed perfectly with what can be reconstructed from the genealogies and chronicles.

THE WELSH ELEMENT

As we have seen, the Welsh ancestry of Gruffudd ap Cynan as described in the extant versions of the *Historia* constitutes a coherent genealogical scheme comprising eighty-two or eighty-seven generations back to Adam son of God which (for a time) branches into two collateral lines. The greater part of the genealogy is wholly unhistorical, incorporating names taken from Geoffrey of Monmouth's *Historia Regum Brittanie*, classical tradition, and the Old Testament. An outline of the scheme is given in Figure 1, containing only the main, apical names.

Other versions of the genealogy occur in Welsh genealogical manuscripts, both dating before and after the material in the *Historia*, though that before is only useful up to Beli Mawr. The earliest extant version of the genealogy of the rulers of Gwynedd forms part of the patriline of Owain ap Hywel Dda of Dyfed (*ob.* 988) which begins the collection in London,

---

[7]   On this see Thornton, 'A neglected genealogy of Llywelyn ap Gruffudd', p. 21.

British Library, MS. Harley 3859 (= HG; *ca* 1100).[8] The pedigree of Llywelyn ap Gruffudd (*ob.* 1282), preserved in Exeter, Cathedral Library, MS. 3514 (1280s; in Latin) and Aberystwyth, National Library of Wales, MS. Mostyn 117 (1300 × 1350; in Welsh), contains some 'unorthodox' features which must be taken into account.[9] The collection in Oxford, Jesus College, MS. 20 (1350 × 1400) contains some relevant material.[10] A different version of the pedigree of Llywelyn ap Gruffudd occurs in London, British Library, MS. Harley 673, probably fifteenth-century in date.[11] Also Bartrum has edited the genealogical material known as Hanesyn Hen, including the tract called *Achau Brenhinoedd a Thywysogion Cymru* (ABT), from late mediaeval and early modern manuscripts, suggesting that it is derived from two codices of *ca* 1400 and *ca* 1450.[12] Finally it is worth noting that Gerald of Wales recorded a handful of pedigrees of contemporary Welsh rulers in his *Descriptio Cambrensis* (written 1193-4) including that of Gruffudd's grandson Dafydd ab Owain Gwynedd (*ob.* 1203).[13]

In general the Venedotian matter of the genealogy in the *Historia* compares favourably with these other versions, but there are a number of differences, not all of which can necessaily be attributed to scribal error. I offer below a discussion of this part of Gruffudd's genealogy by drawing attention to its important members and to particular textual readings characteristic of the *Historia*, without giving a lengthy and tedious commentary on each of the over a hundred different names contained therein.

The genealogy begins by describing Gruffudd's descent through Rhodri Mawr to Beli Mawr. The first part, to Rhodri, reads thus:

Canys mab oed Gruffud y Gynan Vrenhin m. Yago m. Idwal m. Elissed m. Meuryc m. Anaraut m. Rodri [. . .]

The description of Cynan ab Iago as *brenhin* seems to be erroneous as he does not appear in the chronicles in this capacity. His father, Iago ab Idwal, however, was king of Gwynedd and was killed in 1039. This non-kingly status of Cynan may explain why Gruffudd was called *wyr Iago* in some instances.[14] The line demonstrates Gruffudd's Venedotian heritage as a descendant of Rhodri Mawr: according to a (demonstrably false) tradition,

---

8   *Tracts*, p. 9; Phillimore, 'The *Annales Cambriæ* and Old-Welsh genealogies from *Harleian MS.* 3859'.
9   Thornton, 'A neglected genealogy'; *Tracts*, pp. 38–9.
10 *Ibid.*, pp. 42–50; Phillimore, 'Pedigrees from Jesus College MS. 20'.
11 Thornton, 'A neglected genealogy', pp. 21–2.
12 *Tracts*, pp. 75–120; Bartrum, 'Achau', pp. 205–18.
13 *Giraldi Cambrensis Opera*, edd. Brewer *et al.*, VI.167; *Gerald of Wales. The Journey through Wales/The Description of Wales*, transl. Thorpe, p. 222.
14 On the function of the royal element in the genealogy see below, pp. 104–5; and Charles-Edwards, *Early Irish and Welsh Kinship*, pp. 220–4.

for which Gerald of Wales is our earliest extant witness, Rhodri ruled the whole of Wales and on his death (878) the kingdom was divided between his three sons. His consequent role as dynastic founder and ancestor is well-documented in the sources.[15] The Venedotian portion is said to have passed to his son Anarawd (*ob.* 916), Gruffudd's ancestor.[16] This line of descent can be compared with the other pedigrees of the kings of Gwynedd as well as the chronicles.[17] Such comparison reveals a number of discrepancies, which John Jones duly 'corrected' (above). For example, *Elissed* (Elise) appears to have been inserted here between Idwal (*ob.* 996) and Meurig. His 'father' Meurig, furthermore, can be shown to be son of Idwal Foel ab Anarawd (*ob.* 942/3), that is, the grandson, not son, of Anarawd ap Rhodri. *Elissed* may have been derived from Elise ab Anarawd (*ob.* 942/3) who is represented variously in the sources also as son of Rhodri Mawr and of Idwal Foel.[18]

The pedigree continues by connecting Rhodri Mawr to the so-called First Dynasty of Gwynedd through his mother Esyllt and thence to Beli Mawr:

[. . .] Rodri m. Etill (Esyllt) verch Kenan o Gastell Dindaethue, m. Idwaldere m. Catwalader Vendigeit m. Catwallaun m. Catvan m. Yago m. Beli m. Run m. Maelgun m. Catwallavn Llauhir m. Einnyavn Yrth m. Cuneda Vrenhin m. Edern m. Padern Peisrud m. Tagit m. Yago m. Guidauc m. Kein m. Gorgein m. Doli m. Gurdoli m. Dwuyn m. Gorduvyn m. Anwerit m. Onnet m. Diuwng (Diawng) m. Brychwein m. Ewein m. Auallach m. Aflech m. Beli Maur.

This part of the genealogy can be compared with the pedigree of the First Dynasty as preserved in both earlier and later Welsh genealogical sources.[19] The *Historia* agrees with MG and ABT, against HG and JC, in rendering Rhodri Mawr (and not his father Merfyn Frych) as the son of Esyllt ferch Cynan Dindaethwy. The connection between the First and Second Dynasties was therefore not agnatic, and is among a series of unions with ruling Welsh dynasties which the line of Merfyn and Rhodri is said (according to the genealogical tracts) to have entered. Scholars have regarded this as one of the means by which the Second Dynasty was able to establish its rule over most of Wales, but a closer analysis of the texts suggests that things are not quite so simple.[20] Thus, the link with the First Dynasty (above) is the only such union to be witnessed (or implied) in the Harleian genealogical

---

15 For Rhodri's obit see: *AC* (A) 877 [= 878]; *ByT* (RB) [878]; *ByT* (Pen. 20) [877=878]; *ByS* [877=878].

16 *AC* (A) [915=916]; *ByT* (RB) [916]; *ByT* (Pen. 20) [916]; *ByS* [913=916].

17 JC § 26; MG § 1; Exeter 3415; ABT § 1(a); Harley 673; *Giraldus*.

18 *AC* (A) [942= 943]; *ByT* (RB) [943]; *ByT* (Pen. 20) [943]; *ByS* [941=942]; JC § 20; ABT § 1(b, f); see Lloyd, *A History*, I.337, n. 64. We may, of course, have more than one Elise here.

19 HG § 1; JC § 22; MG § 1; Exeter 3514; ABT § 1(a); Harley 673.

20 I hope to return to this material in a further discussion.

collection. Textual features of this part of the genealogy include the omission of Rhodri Molwynog (*ob.* 754) as father of Cynan Dindaethwy, and the name-form *Idwaldere* for Idwal Iwrch (*dere* 'deer' tanslating Welsh *iwrch* 'roe-buck'). According to the ninth-century *Historia Brittonum* and the tenth-century and later genealogies, the First Dynasty was founded by Cunedda Wledig (called here *Cuneda Vrenhin*), who migrated from Manaw of Gododdin (in Northern Britain) with his numerous sons to rid Wales of Irish settlers and in so doing established a series on dynasties in North and West Wales.[21] The historical accuracy of this dynastic origin-legend is debatable, but its significance is probably best understood in terms of ninth-and tenth-century politics, rather than those of the twelfth. The names above Cunedda are wholly unhistorical, probably serving primarily to link this founder to Beli Mawr (below). Points of interest include the Latin origin of the names of Cunedda's immediate forebears – Aeternus (*Edern*), Paternus (*Padern*), and Tacitus (*Tagit*) – and the paired sequence *Kein-Gorgein*, *Doli-Gurdoli*, and *Dwuyn-Gorduvyn*.

At this point the genealogy returns to Rhodri Mawr, tracing the ancestry of his father Merfyn Frych to Beli and beyond. The first part, to Beli, reads thus:

Rodri Maur m. Mervyn Vrych m. Guryat m. Elidir m. Sandef m. Alcwn m. Tagit m. Gveir m. Dwc m. Llewarch Hen m. Elidir Lledanwyn m. Meirchyaun Gul m. Gorwst Ledlumm m. Keneu m. Coel Godebauc m. Tecvan Gloff m. Deheweint (Deueweint) m. Vrban m. Grad m. Riuedel m. Rideyrn m. Euteyrn m. Eudygant m. Eudos m. Eudolen m. Avallach m. Aflech m. Beli Mavr [. . .]

The role of the line of Merfyn Frych ap Gwriad is clearly to provide Rhodri Mawr with some suitably 'royal' paternal ancestry to match that of his Venedotian mother.[22] Politically the line was intrusive, but from where is not at all certain: the Isle of Man is a common suggestion (based, in part, on mediaeval sources) though others have suggested Scotland or Ireland.[23] Above Gwriad (who *may* be attested on a Manx inscription)[24] the line does not contain any historically-known figures. Llywarch Hen is renowned as an early but legendary poet associated with both Northern Britain and Powys.[25] His ancestor Coel Godebog (or *Hen*) – and otherwise known as 'Old King Cole'! – is an important figure in northern British genealogy, but his original historical significance (if any) is now obscured.

---

21 See Thornton, 'Power, Politics, and Status', pp. 57–66; Miller, 'The foundation-legend of Gwynedd', pp. 515–32.
22 Compare the above version with JC § 17; ABT § 1(c, e); the names above Coel can also be found in HG § 10.
23 I hope to return to this material in a further discussion.
24 See *ibid.*
25 For Llywarch in the genealogies see Ford, 'Llywarch, ancestor of Welsh princes', pp. 442–50.

This Welsh section of the genealogy of Gruffudd ap Cynan concludes by tracing the descent of Beli Mawr to Addaf ap Duw, 'Adam son of God', thus:

[. . .] Beli Mavr m. Manogan m. Eneit m. Kerwyt m. Krydon m. Dyvynarth m. Prydein m. Aet Maur m. Antonius m. Seiryoel m. Gurust m. Riwallaun m. Regat uerch Lyr m. Rud m. Bleidud m. Lliwelyt m. Brutus Ysgwyt Ir (Ysgwyd Wyn/Darian Las) m. Membyr m. Madauc m. Llocrinus m. Brut (Brutus) Tywyssauc o Ruvein, m. Siluius m. Ascanius m. Eneas Ysgwyt Wyn m. Anchises m. Capis m. Assaracus m. Trois m. Herictonius m. Dardanus m. Iupiter m. Sedurn m. Celius m. Cretus m. Ciprius m. Iauan m. Iaphet m. Noe Hen m. Lamech m. Mathussalem m. Enoc m. Iaret m. Malaleel m. Cainan m. Enos m. Seth m. Adaf m. Duw.

The figure Beli Mawr (*Beli Magnus*) of the genealogies has been derived variously from the Briton *Bellinus filius Minocanni* who opposed Caesar according to the ninth-century *Historia Brittonum*; or from some vaguely-recalled Celtic deity.[26] However, the problem of his original significance in the genealogies is more relevent to the tenth-century Harleian collection than for the pedigree of Gruffudd ap Cynan and other later mediaeval genealogies. Beli's ancestry falls into a number of distinct parts depending on the apparent source of the names involved.[27] Overall the effect is of an ancestry created from various sources in order to trace the line of descent ultimately up to God by providing a connection to the Old-Testament 'Table of Nations' of Genesis 10. As such, it is not without precedent in mediaeval Europe: indeed, the mediaeval Christian need to demonstrate one's genealogical link with a religious text thought to account for the origins of all peoples but which in fact reflects the limited geographical knowledge of the Old-Testament writers could produce some ingenious instances of genealogical acrobatics![28] In the genealogy of Gruffudd, the names from Seiryoel up to Sadwrn ap Celius and from Iauan ab Iaphet to Addaf ap Duw represent Galfridian (and Trojan) and biblical borrowings respectively. However, the source(s) for the remaining two groups of names cannot be so readily identified. Some scholars have argued that the names above Mynogan to Aedd Mawr ab Antonius were drawn from genuine 'Welsh tradition' but there is little evidence to support this view either way.[29] The next sequence of names, up to Sadwrn ap Celius, is derived from Geoffrey of Monmouth's *Historia Regum Britannie*, and follows the genealogy of his Kings of Britain

---

26 On Beli Mawr see Thornton, 'Power, Politics, and Status', pp. 109–16.
27 Various version of Beli's ancestry have been preserved: see, for example, ABT § 1(a) and Harley 673 against MG § 1 and Exeter 3514: Thornton, 'A neglected genealogy', pp. 18–20.
28 For a discussion of this phenomenon with some non-Celtic christian and islamic examples, see Thornton, 'Power, Politics, and Status', pp. 30–49.
29 Bromwich, ed., *Trioedd*, pp. cxxvii, 198, 228, 495–6; Bartrum, 'Was there a British "Book of Conquests"?', pp. 4–5.

to the Brutus 'Prince from Rome' and the eponym of Britain, and continues with his Trojan ancestry and thence to classical antecedents. It is worth noting that Geoffrey did not invent the Trojan origins of his Kings through Brutus, but took the idea from the aforementioned *Historia Brittonum*. The use of these patently Galfridian names is not without importance for the *Historia* since some scholars have argued that the time-span between the publication of Geoffrey's *Historia* (*ca* 1135×1138) and the incorporation of these names (perhaps through a vernacular translation) into the royal Venedotian genealogy no more than four decades later is 'possible but improbable'.[30] The next few names above Saturn son of Caelius (*Cretus, Ciprius*) provide the link with the biblical Javan son of Japheth son of Noah, and appear to be eponyms of the islands Crete and Cyprus. This element seems to be based on early christian exegesis (derived from Josephus) which associated Kittim son of Javan with these islands.[31] Comparison of the genealogy of Gruffudd with other Welsh sources (genealogical and non-genealogical) would suggest that the name equivalent to this Kittim has been omitted, and naturally John Jones obligingly corrected his version (above).

THE SCANDINAVIAN ELEMENT

According to the *Historia*, Gruffudd ap Cynan's mother was called *Ragnell* (also written Raonell, Racvell, Ranillt, etc.) the daughter of *Avloed*, king of Dublin and a Fifth part of Ireland.[32] Her name is normally regarded as the Old Norse *Ragnhildr* and that of her father *Óláfr* (=Olaf; Irish *Amlaíb*). Her ancestors included (in the patriline) Scandinavian rulers of Dublin and (through intermarriage into the line of Dublin) 'native' rulers of various parts of Ireland. The pedigree of the Dublin kings thus forms the backbone of the Hiberno-Scandinavian section of Gruffudd's genealogy into which the Irish element is plugged. We shall begin therefore by considering the Hiberno-Scandinavian pedigree and the associated Scandinavian material and then proceed to the more strictly Irish names.

The Dubliners

This maternal pedigree of Gruffudd ap Cynan follows the direct line of Scandinavian kings of Dublin back to the Norwegian king Harald Fairhair. As we have seen, Gruffudd's maternal grandfather was Olaf who is described as '*[b]renhin Dinas Dulyn a phymhet ran Ywerdon ac Enys Vanaw*'; his dominions are said to have encompassed 'other islands' as well as

---

30 Bartrum, ed., *Tracts*, p. 35; Maund, *Ireland, Wales and England*, p. 178.
31 For a fuller discussion see Thornton, 'Power, Politics, and Status', pp. 41–3.
32 *Historia*, ed. Evans, p. 1; *A Mediaeval Prince*, ed. & transl. Evans, pp. 23–4, 53–4.

Denmark, Galloway, the Rhinns, Anglesey, and Gwynedd.[33] Ragnhildr (Olaf's daughter according to our text) may be identified with the *Radnailt ingen Amlaíb Arnaid* mentioned in the Irish tract *Banshenchas*,[34] but her son is said to have been Muirchertach ua Congalaig Cnogba, who died in 994, which is chronologically too early for a half-brother of Gruffudd (*ob.* 1137). *Radnailt* may rather have been the daughter of an earlier Olaf of Dublin (nicknamed Cuarán) whom we shall consider below. Gruffudd's mother is not otherwise mentioned in any extant source and the coincidence of the female name and her patronymic is perhaps significant. Olaf's own descent is given in the *Historia* thus:

Avloed . . . vab y Sutric Vrenhin mab Avloed Vrenhin Cuaran mab Sutric mab Avloed Vrenhin mab [Harald] Harfagyr Vrenhin mab Brenhin Denmarc.

The tract ABT (§ 6[a]) gives the same pedigree with some variant readings which will be noted below. As others have demonstrated, the first four names of this pedigree can be identified with figures named in the Irish annals in association with Dublin and, as such, they support the line of descent described in the Welsh text. Above this level however, there is no independent witness for the relationships which seem to be inaccurate.

Gruffudd's maternal grandfather Olaf, king of Dublin, may be identified with the Amlaíb who was killed by the English in 1034.[35] Alternatively, some have identified him with the *Amlaíb mac Sitriucca* who was slain in 1013 and is described as *mac ríg Gall* in the Annals of Ulster and the Annals of the Four Masters.[36] In either case, Olaf's death would have preceded that of his father Sihtric Silkenbeard (below) and, despite the grand claims made by the author of the *Historia* for the extent of his dominions, it is usually thought that he did not rule as king of Dublin.[37] These claims were made either through ignorance or through a desire to bolster the reputation of

---

33 *Historia*, ed. Evans, p. 2; *A Mediaeval Prince*, ed. & transl. Evans, pp. 24, 54–5.
34 Dobbs, 'The Ban-Shenchus' (1930) 337; (1931) 188, 227.
35 AU *s.a.* 1034; *CS* [1032=1034]; ALC *s.a.* 1034; AFM *s.a.* 1034. For this identification see, for example, Byrne *et al.*, *A New History of Ireland*, IX.139; Duffy, 'Irish and Islemen', p. 99.
36 AU [1012=1013]; *CS* [1011=1013]; AI *s.a.* 1013; AFM [1012=1013] (= *mac tigherna Gall*). For this identification see, for example, *A History*, ed. & transl. Jones, p. 39; Charles, *Old Norse Relations*, p. 57; Bartrum, ed., *Tracts*, p. 136; *A Mediaeval Prince*, ed. & transl. Evans, pp. 86–7; Maund, *Ireland, Wales and England*, p. 178.
37 This statement may only be partially true. In 1029 an *Amlaíb mac Sitruicca rí Gall* was taken hostage by Mathgamain Ua Riacáin ('king of Brega') and ransomed at high cost: AU *s.a.* 1029; AT [1029]; ALC [1029]; AFM *s.a.* 1029; also *CS* [1027=1029] which does not call this Olaf *rí*. This is likely to be the Olaf son of *Sitriucc* who died in 1034 (above). Sihtric Silkenbeard had gone on a pilgrimage to Rome in the previous year (AU *sa* 1028; AT [1028]; CS [1026=1028]; AI *sa* 1028; ALC [1028]; AFM *s.a.* 1028) and it is possible that (assuming that he was Sihtric's son) Olaf had ruled in his father's stead: thus, for example, Ryan, 'Pre-Norman Dublin', pp. 119–20.

Olaf's alleged grandson Gruffudd. This evidence may in fact suggest that at least part of the Welsh king's Hiberno-Scandinavian ancestry was not wholly fictitious: why state that Gruffudd was descended from such a 'weak link' as the non-ruling Olaf, thereby necessitating such elevated but demonstrably false territorial claims, when there would have been numerous other eligible Hiberno-Scandinavians to fulfil the role?

Olaf's father Sihtric Silkenbeard (ON *Sigtryggr Silkiskeggi Óláfsson*) was king of Dublin from 989 until he was deposed in 1036.[38] He died in 1042, which, as we have noted, was well after his son Olaf.[39] In fact, Sihtric's immediate successor in the Dublin kingship was a representative of the rival rulers of Waterford (called Echmarcach mac Ragnaill) who vied for the position with Ímar mac Arailt, probably Sihtric's nephew (below). According to the Welsh genealogy Sihtric was the son of *Avloed Vrenhin Cuaran*, that is the famous Olaf Cuarán ('the Crooked'; ON *Óláfr Kváran*). This relationship is supported by the Irish chronicles, though in one instance Sihtric is called *mac meic Amlaím rí Gall*, that is the grandson of Olaf.[40] Olaf Cuarán ruled as *ardrí* of the Gaill of Dublin from 945 to 980 when he abdicated and embarked on a pilgrimage to Iona, dying in the following year.[41] According to the version of the maternal pedigree of Gruffudd in ABT, this Olaf's position is occupied by a figure called *Glinaru* (Glinvarn, Gwriarn): this may be a (very) corrupt form of Olaf's cognomen Cuarán, but seems more likely to be a corruption of the Irish personal-name *Glún Iairnn* (Glún Iarainn: lit. 'Iron Knee'; ON *Járnkné*). Indeed, Olaf Cuarán had a son by this name who ruled Dublin between his reign and that of Sihtric Silkenbeard.[42] Whether this figure was intended at this point in ABT or whether the name-form given represents an attempt to make sense of a very corrupt original is unclear.

Olaf Cuarán was the son of yet another Sihtric, nicknamed in Irish *Caech* ('the Blind') or *Gale*, thus agreeing again with the Welsh text. This Sihtric ruled Dublin from 917 to 921 and subsequently ruled York, dying in 927 as *rí Dub Gall ocus Finn Gall*.[43] At this point, however, the genealogy of Gruffudd ap Cynan ceases to be supported by the Irish annalistic sources and seems to become historically unreliable. According to the pedigree Sihtric Caech was son of *Avloed Vrenhin mab Harfagyr* (=Olaf son of [Harald] Fairhair). However, in the Irish chronicles Sihtric is invariably

---

38 AT [1036].
39 AI *s.a.* 1042; AT [1042]; AFM *s.a.* 1042.
40 AU *s.a.* 1028; see Broderick, 'Irish and Welsh strands', p. 35.
41 AT [980]; *CS* [978=980], [980=981]; AFM [978=980], [979=981]; AClon. [974=980].
42 AU [988=989]; AT [988]; *CS* [987=989]; AI *s.a.* 989; AFM [988=989]; AClon [982=989]; also *ByT* (Pen. 20) [988=989]; *ByT* (RB) [989]; *ByS* [988=989]. Also Sihtric Silkenbeard seems to have had a son (and not a father, as ABT would suggest) called Glún Iairn who died in 1031: AT [1031]; AFM *s.a.* 1031.
43 AU [926=927]; *CS* [926]; AFM [925=927]; AClon. [922=927].

called *Ua Ímair* ('grandson of Ímar').[44] This Ímar has been taken to be *Ívarr inn Beinlausi* ('the Boneless') son of the legendary Viking leader Ragnarr Loðbrók. While some scholars have made Sihtric 'Caech' the son of Ímar's own son called *Sitriuc* (*ob.* 986),[45] the extant sources do not state the exact relationship so that it is unclear whether this elder Sihtric or his brother Sigfrith was the relevant genealogical intermediary. Alternatively, it has been suggested that Olaf, father of Sihtric according to the pedigree of Gruffudd, represents a third son of Ímar who is not otherwise witnessed.[46] As this hypothesis cannot be verified independently it cannot be employed to prove the reliability of the genealogy without resorting to a circular argument. Indeed, this elder Olaf may be a misnomer because the version of this pedigree in ABT omits Olaf and has *Swtrig* (that is, Sihtric Caech) as son (not grandson) of Harald Fairhair: perhaps the Olaf son of Harald in the extant copies of the *Historia* represents a scribal error arising from the repeated alternation of the names *Avloed* and *Sutric* in the genealogy.

Harald Fairhair

The point is to some extent moot since the next name in the pedigree, *[Haralld] Harfagyr*, is wholly unconnected. This is Harald Fairhair (ON *Haraldr [inn] Hárfagri*) who according to mediaeval Scandinavian pseudo-history was the first ruler of all Norway and probably flourished in the late ninth and early tenth centuries. He has gained additional notoriety as the ruler whose centralizing policies compelled many Norwegian nobles to seek fortune abroad, particularly in Iceland, according to later Icelandic accounts. Of course, it is likely that much of the material which is associated with Harald Fairhair represents subsequent legend or propaganda, and so, in keeping with his role as dynastic founder, it is not surprising to find that he is credited with a large progeny in the thirteenth-century Scandinavian sources.[47] One of his sons is in fact called *Óláfr Digrbeinn*, which, given the popularity of this name, is not to be unexpected, but who may theoretically be identical with the *Avloed mab [Harald] Harfagyr Vrenhin* of the Welsh genealogy.[48] Furthermore, he was the grandfather of Olaf

---

44 Note, for example, AU [916=917], [926=927]; AI *s.a.* 919; *Fragmentary Annals*, ed. & transl. Radner, p. 181; *CS* [926=927].
45 For instance Smyth, *Scandinavian York and Dublin*, II.316.
46 Broderick, 'The Irish and Welsh strands', p. 35.
47 *Monumenta*, ed. Storm, pp. 104–5; Snorri Sturluson, *Heimskringla* (ed. Aðalbjarnarson, Íslenzk Fornrít XXVI–XXVIII, I.119); *Ágrip. Fagrskinna*, ed. Einarsson, Íslenzk Fornrít XXIX, pp. 5, 71.
48 Harald Fairhair is also said to have had a son called *Sigtryggr* who could have been identified with Sihtric Caech in the version of the genealogy in ABT. For this son and *Óláfr Digrbeinn* see *Ágrip. Fagrskinna*, ed. Einarsson, pp. 5, 19, 71, 141; *Íslendingabók. Landnámabók*, ed. Benediktsson, I.14; also *Monumenta*, ed. Storm, pp. 11, 104–5; and Snorri Sturluson, *Heimskringla* (ed. Aðalbjarnarson, I.119.

Tryggvason. If this was the case (and there is no way of being certain) then this Olaf may have been selected because he was suitably anonymous (at least when compared with the likes of his brother Eric Bloodaxe) when grafting the line of Dublin onto Harald. Whether the *Avloed* of the Welsh genealogy represents a forgotten son of Ívarr inn Beinlausi, or an insignificant son of Haraldr Hárfagri, or merely the invention of the author of the *Historia*, the direct connection between the line of Dublin and this king of Norway described in the pedigree is totally unhistorical.

This connection may have been made to provide Gruffudd with a suitably famous royal ancestry, or may in fact reflect the garbled accounts of Scandinavian history current amount the Dubliners in the twelfth century. The latter is supported by the fact that additional material relating to Harald Fairhair is given in the *Historia* immediately after Gruffudd's maternal pedigree which appears equally confused and inaccurate.[49] Harald is described as son of the King of Denmark and later of the King of *Llychlyn*. The latter is evidently *Lochlann* in Irish, which is usually taken to be Norway, not Denmark, but may have included western parts of Scotland.[50] The Danish link, as we have seen, is incorrect. Furthermore, Harald is accorded two brothers called *Alyn* and *Rodulf*. It is stated in the *Historia* that Harald and his 'three' brothers sailed to Ireland but that previously Harald had subdued Ireland, had built Dublin and other *dinasoed a chestyll a leoed cadarn*. Furthermore, he is said to have established as ruler in Waterford (*Porthlarg*) one of his brothers whose descendants continued to rule there. Harald's own rule is said to have encompassed Ireland and the 'Islands of Denmark'. No reflex of these events can be found in any other Insular sources, suggesting that they have little basis in fact. Indeed the Icelandic accounts of two expeditions by Harald Fairhair to the British Isles are concerned primarily with the Northern and Western Isles and have been shown equally to have little basis in fact.[51] The main purpose of this material about Harald seems to have been to reinforce his reputation as a powerful king, not only in Norway, but in the very areas where Gruffudd ap Cynan's alleged Hiberno-Scandinavian ancestors were active.

Of Harald Fairhair's brothers Alyn and Rodulf, the former personal-name has no immediately apparent Old Norse source, but the latter is probably derived from the name *Hróðúlfr* or the hypocoristic *Hrólfr*.[52] Neither can

[49] On this material see Van Hamel, 'Norse history', pp. 336–44; and Jesch, below, pp. 117–47.
[50] Marstrander, 'Lochlann', p. 250, argued that the Irish *Lochlann* originally designated 'a particular Norse tribal-territory, which can only be *Rogaland* . . . the district around the Stravanger Fjord', that is a Norwegian region with which the Irish may have mostly familiar, and that it only subsequently came to refer to the whole of Norway. This latter meaning is no doubt intended in the Welsh text.
[51] See Sawyer, 'Harald Fairhair's expeditions to the British Isles', pp. 105–9.
[52] Van Hamel argued that it is unclear whether Alyn was the brother of Harald or of his father: 'Norse history', p. 337; see also Jesch, below, pp. 117–47.

be identified directly as brothers of Harald Fairhair in the Scandinavian sources. Alyn is described in the Welsh text as *brenhin kyssygredicaf ac enwocaf ymphith holl Denmarc*, that is 'most holy and renowned king of all Denmark'.[53] He is said to have been slain by a *tywyssauc* called *Thur* (ON *Þórr*), who was subsequently known as *Thur Kiaul* ('Thor the Doglike'?) on account of having killed such a guiltless king.[54] It has been suggested that this figure Alyn represents a corrupt form of *Óláfr inn Helgi Haraldsson* ('St Olaf'), great-great-grandson of Harald Fairhair according to the Scandinavian sources and king of Norway: he was killed by one *Þórir Hundr* ('Thori the Dog') according to Icelandic texts.[55] St Olaf did have a brother (or, more accurately, a half-brother) called Harald, namely that Harald Hardrada (*Haraldr Harðráði*), king of Norway, who fell at Stamford Bridge in 1066. It is possible that St Olaf, as Alyn, has been incorporated into Gruffudd's genealogy as brother of Harald Fairhair because of a confusion of the two namesakes' cognomena, *Hárfagri* and *Harðráði* (lit. 'Hard-Counsel').[56] This would not be the first time these two men were confused with one another because of the similarity of their nicknames and not the only time the confusion was made in a Welsh genealogical source (see below).[57] The other brother, Rodulf, is more easily identifiable, though again not as an immediate relation of Harald Fairhair. He is said to have subdued a large part of France, now called *Nordmandi* (Normandy), and to have been ancestor of *Guilim Vrenhin* and subsequent English kings. This shows that he is to be regarded as the legendary viking founder of the Duchy of Normandy, remembered in Norman tradition as *Rollo* and in Icelandic as *Göngu-Hrólfr*.[58] Hrólfr's father was *Rǫgnvaldr*, Earl of Møre, who is shown in the sagas to have been a contemporary (but not a direct kinsman) of Harald Fairhair and to have given the latter his cognomen *hárfagri*.[59] If Alyn and Rodulf are correctly identified, these confused versions of Scandinavian pseudo-history may reflect the legends current among Gruffudd ap Cynan's relatives in Dublin, or may be fictions, concocted by the author of the

---

53 *Historia*, ed. Evans, p. 3; *A Mediaeval Prince*, ed. & transl. Evans, pp. 25, 55.
54 Thur is not specified to have been a further brother of Harald, as Jones suggested: *The History*, ed. & transl. Jones, p. 42.
55 Van Hamel, 'Norse history', pp. 342–4; *Historia*, ed. Evans, p. cxci.
56 *Historia*, ed. Evans, p. cxciii, n. 504; but see Jesch's discussion below, pp. 117–47.
57 For the Welsh instance see below p. 94. The D-text of the Anglo-Saxon Chronicle (1066) calls Harald Hardrada *Harold Harfager*; for an Icelandic instance of the confusion see Power, 'Magnus Barelegs' expeditions to the west', p. 111, n. 4.
58 *Historia*, ed. Evans, p. cxcii. For the Icelandic accounts see *Ágrip. Fagrskinna*, ed. Einarsson, p. 291; *Íslendingabók. Landnámabók*, ed. Benediktsson, II.314–16; *Heimskringla*, ed. Aðalbjarnarson, I.123–4; *Orkneyinga Saga*, ed. Guðmundsson, p. 7. For the Norman account see Douglas, 'Rollo'.
59 Norman tradition (at least as preserved by Dudo of St-Quentin) claimed that Rollo was of Danish, not Norwegian, origin: see Douglas, 'Rollo'. It seems likely that most of the Scandinavian settlers in Normandy were of Danish extraction.

Historia from such material, in order to link his subject with suitably royal ancestors.

As we have seen, the *Historia* states that Harald Fairhair's father was the anonymous king of Denmark or of Lochlann. The related material in ABT, however, gives Harald's patriline for five additional generations thus:[60]

Harallt Harfag ap Haldan Ddu ap Gwythrig (Gwythrid) Vrenin Helgwr ap Haldan Milde ap Eisten ap Haldan Chinbein y brenin kyntaf a ddoeth y Lychlyn o Suesia.

This can be paralleled exactly in Icelandic accounts of the paternal ancestry of *Haraldr Hárfagri*:[61]

Haraldr Hárfagri son of Hálfdan(r) inn Svarti son of Guðrøðr Veiðikonungr son of Hálfdan(r) inn Mildi ok Mátarilli son of Eysteinn son of Hálfdan(r) Hvítbeinn.

In two cases the Welsh pedigree translates the Old Norse cognomen (Welsh *ddu* for *svartr*, 'black'; *brenhin helgwr* for *veiðikonungr*, 'hunting king') while in others a form based on the Norse original is retained.[62] The claim that *Haldan Chinbein* was 'the first king who came to Llychlyn [*recte* Norway] from Sweden' is a reflection of the apical importance which *Hálfdan(r) Hvítbeinn* assumed in the pseudo-history of the Norwegian dynasty as worked out by Icelanders.[63] This particular pedigree could not have been derived from the *Historia*, and must reflect another (probably later) input of Norse material into the Welsh corpus. There are other such Scandinavian genealogies in the later Welsh collections which are omitted in the *Historia*. It is worth noting that this traffic of genealogical matter was not all one way, but that it has been shown that the higher levels of the long pedigrees of mediaeval Scandinavian dynasties contain names similar to those characteristic of the post-Galfridian Welsh genealogies (such as ABT) and which may be derived from an ultimately Welsh source.[64]

[60] ABT § 6(c). As extant, ABT § 6(a) continues the maternal pedigree of Gruffudd above Harald Fairhair for four generations which are lacking in the *Historia*. These additional names can be shown (below) to have been grafted onto the line at this point as they differ from the pedigree quoted here from ABT § 6(c) and because they culminate in Harald Fairhair, who cannot occur in the same patriline twice!

[61] *Íslendingabók. Landnámabók*, ed. Benediktsson, I.3; *Monumenta*, ed. Storm, pp. 102–3.

[62] Thus, for example, *milde* for the weak declension of *mildr*, 'generous'. Presumably the translated nicknames are based on a Latin intermediary.

[63] On this see Turville-Petre, 'The genealogist'.

[64] Faulkes, 'Descent'.

More Scandinavians

As we have seen above, a part of the tract *Achau Brenhinoedd a Thywysogion Cymru*, corresponding to the genealogical introduction of the *Historia*, contains additional Scandinavian material (such as Harald Fairhair's patriline) which is lacking in this earlier text. This material comprises pedigrees of rulers of Scandinavian ancestry who were active in the British Isles in some capacity in the eleventh to the thirteenth centuries and whose pedigrees (at least in the forms given here) share common names with that of Gruffudd discussed above. They will be briefly considered here.

A line descending from Harald Fairhair is given in ABT § 6(a), where it occurs somewhat erroneously as an extension of the maternal pedigree of Gruffudd through this same Harald. As the latter can hardly occur in the same patriline twice and as his ancestry is given (in agreement with Icelandic accounts) at ABT § 6(c) (above), Bartrum correctly regarded this material as a separate pedigree.[65] This collateral line occurs thus:

[. . . m.] Siwyrder Sur m. Beor m. Siwyrder Ris m. Harallt Harfagyr.

As Bartrum has pointed out, this pedigree is evidently a version of the ruling line of the sub-kingdom of Ringerike in Norway which can be reconstructed from Icelandic and Norwegian sources thus:[66]

Sigurðr Sýr son of Hálfdan(r) Heikilnef/Hvítbeinn son of Sigurðr Hrísi son of Haraldr Hárfagri.

Sigurðr Sýr ('Sow') was the father of Harald Hardrada, who ruled Norway from 1045 until 1066. It seems likely that the Welsh text is probably based on a pedigree of this younger Harald and that it was grafted onto Gruffudd's genealogy at Harald Fairhair because of the similarity of the namesakes' cognomena. (We have already had recourse to mention the possible confusion of these men as a cause of the incorporation into the *Historia* of St Olaf [*Alyn*] as Harald Fairhair's brother.) This view is supported by Hardrada's Insular importance for the events of 1066 which might explain why his pedigree was included at all in the collection. Comparison of the Welsh version of the line with that based on Scandinavian sources shows that Hálfdan Heikilnef occurs as *Beor* (=ON *Bjǫrn*?).

The pedigree edited by Bartrum as ABT § 6(c) reads as follows:

Rhanallt m. Gwythryg ap Afloyd m. Gwrthryt Mearch m. Harallt Ddu m. Ifor Gamle m. Afloyd m. Swtrig.

65 *Tracts*, p. 152.
66 *Ágrip. Fagrskinna*, ed. Einarsson, pp. 36–7, 226; *Heimskringla*, ed. Aðalbjarnarson, I.310; *Morkinskinna*, ed. Jónsson, I.56; *Monumenta*, ed. Storm, pp. 109–10.

This is the pedigree of Ragnall (*Rhanallt*), king of Man from 1187/8 to 1229 through the dynastic founder Godred Crovan (or Godred Méránach) who ruled Man from 1079 to 1095.[67] The first half of the pedigree can be verified by reference to the Irish and Manx chronicles; the second half (above Godred Crovan), however, cannot and presents a number of problems. Ragnall succeeded his father Godred (*Gwythryg*; ON *Guðrøðr*; Ir. *Gofraid*) who ruled Man from 1154 to 1187/8 and who in turn had succeeded his father Olaf Bitling (*Afloyd*) (*ca* 1112/3–53). Olaf was the son of Godred Crovan who conquered Man *ca* 1079 and eventually asserted some influence in Dublin. He died of the plague in 1095.[68]

All this agrees with the Welsh pedigree, but the ancestry of the earlier Godred is a matter of uncertainty. According to the Manx chronicle (fo 32) Godred Crovan was *filius Haraldi Nigri*, adding that the latter was *de Ysland* (Iceland?).[69] This would support the genealogy which has Harallt Ddu (*du*, 'the Black', for *niger*). The Irish chronicles, however, call him *Gofraid mac meic Arailt*, that is 'grandson of Harald'.[70] It seems likely that the same Harald is intended in both cases. Munch rendered Godred as son of the Harald son of the *Gofraid mac Arailt rí Innsi Gall* who died in 989.[71] This would make Godred Crovan into a descendant of the rulers of Limerick. Bartrum followed this interpretation and was thereby compelled to emend the Welsh pedigree above Godred by starting a fresh pedigree with *Ifor Gamle*.[72] An alternative approach has been to associate the line of Godred Crovan with the Ostmen of Dublin descended from Olaf Cuaran through the Harald (*Aralt*) who died in 999 (above).[73] The disagreement in the sources mentioned above as to Godred's precise relationship to his forebear Harald (son or grandson?) means that the genealogy remains unclear. *Ifor Gamle* (probably ON *Ívarr Gamli*) of the Welsh line could be identical with *Ímar mac Arailt* (*ob.* 1054), though according to the pedigree Ifor was son of *Afloyd mab Swtrig* (possibly Olaf Cuaran son of Sihtric Caech).[74] Ifor's son *Harallt Ddu* may therefore be the *Aralt*, father of *Ímar*. We would thereby need to amend the pedigree in order to make it agree witht the annalistic sources: either by reversing the order of the names *Ifor Gamle*

---

[67] On this material see Broderick, 'The Irish and Welsh strands'; Duffy, 'Irishmen and Islemen', pp. 106–8. For Ragnall see Ó Cuív, 'A poem in praise of Raghnall'; and on Godred's cognomen see *ibid.*, pp. 283[–4], n. 6.

[68] AI *s.a.* 1095; AFM *s.a.* 1095; AClon. [1094=1095].

[69] *Cronica Regum Mannie & Insularum*, ed. & transl. Broderick, fo 32.

[70] AT [1091].

[71] Munch, *The Chronicle of Man and the Sudreys*, p. 144; AT [989]; *CS* [987=989]; AClon. [982=989].

[72] Bartrum, ed., *Tracts*, p. 152.

[73] Thus see Broderick, 'The Irish and Welsh strands', p. 33; Duffy, 'Irishmen and Islesmen', p. 106.

[74] The cognomen *Gamle* is evidently ON *gamli*, weak declension of *gamall*, 'old'.

and *Harallt Ddu*, making Godred son of Ivar the Old son of Harald the Black
(= *Gofraid mac meic Arailt*); or (as Broderick suggests) inserting an
additional Harald as son of Ímar mac Arailt, making Godred son of Harald
the Black son of *Ímar mac Arailt*.[75]

We shall conclude this aside by mentioning the genealogy of Eidio Wyllt
which, though not given in ABT, does comprise an ultimately Scandinavian
ancestry connected with that of Gruffudd ap Cynan. This pedigree is
preserved in some late sources, London, British Library MS. Harley 5835
(*ca* 1610) and Lewis Dwnn's *Heraldic Vistitations* (1686 × 1613) and has
been edited by Bartrum in diagramatic form.[76] Eidio Wyllt is said to have
been the product of a union between Llin (or Nest) daughter of Tewdwr ap
Cadell and *Sutrick* (=ON *Sigtryggr*) the son of *Allrid* (*Anloed* = Avloed)
grandfather of Gruffudd ap Cynan, that is Olaf Sihtricsson (above).[77] It is
said that Rhys ap Tewdwr gave the district of Llywel in Brycheiniog to his
nephew Eidio. Bartrum thought that this scheme 'seems quite reasonable',[78]
but it is not clear whether much reliance can be placed on such a late
document. I know of no explicit reference to a son Sihtric of Olaf and the
Sutrick mentioned here may have arisen from the alternation of the name
Olaf and Sihtric in the pedigree. However, the Irish chronicles do contain
an enigmatic notice of a *Sitruic mac Amlaíb* dying in the Isle of Man in
1073:[79] chronologically, this could be the father of Eidio but there is no
means of being certain.

THE IRISH ELEMENT

While the Hiberno-Scandinavian line represents the patriline of Gruffudd's
mother, the strictly Irish element in the genealogy is introduced by means
of a series of unions by the Dubliners into various Irish dynasties: in each
case therefore the Irish line is represented by a female whose parentage and
pre-marital political associations are stated. Gruffudd's maternal grand-
mother is said to have been Mael Corcraig (daughter of Dúnlaing of
Leinster) and her husband Olaf was in turn the product of a union between

---

[75] Broderick, 'The Irish and Welsh strands', pp. 34–5.
[76] Bartrum, 'Pedigrees of the Welsh Tribal Patriarchs', pp. 123, 142–3. Bartrum states here
that Harley 5835 dates from the late sixteenth century, but he later dated it to the early
part of the following century: Bartrum, 'Further notes on Welsh genealogical manuscripts', p. 117. The Eidio Wyllt genealogy is also discussed in Jones, 'The Scandinavian
settlement in Ystrad Tywi', pp. 153–6.
[77] Elsewhere, however, Eidio is said to have been the son of Gerald of Windsor: *Llyfr
Baglan*, ed. Bradney, p. 89.
[78] Bartrum, 'Welsh Tribal Patriarchs', p. 142.
[79] AU *s.a.* 1073; ALC *s.a.* 1073. Note Duffy, 'Irishmen and Islemen', p. 102.

Sihtric Silkenbeard and Sláine (daughter of Brian Bóruma of Munster). Sihtric was himself the son of Gormfhlaith (daughter of Murchad of Leinster). Of these women only the much-married Gormfhlaith ingen Murchada can be identified with certainty in independent, Irish sources. The scheme as extant is given below as Figure 2, and an emended version as Figure 3. The reasons for the amendations will be discussed below with reference to the successive parts of the scheme. We will begin with Gormfhlaith.

Gormfhlaith

One of the more renowned women in Gruffudd's genealogy is represented by *Gurmlach verch Mwrchath vrenhin Laine* or Gormfhlaith daughter of Murchad, king of the Laigin (Leinster). She can be identified with the much-married Gormfhlaith ingen Murchada meic Fhinn who died in 1030.[80] According to the usual interpretation of this part of Gruffudd's genealogy Gormfhlaith had four sons, by two (or more) men. There are, however, a number of errors (both textual and historical) which must be taken into account when intrepreting this material. The relevant part of the text reads:[81]

Ac odena Gurmlach oed vam Sutric vrenhin; merch oed honno y Vwrchath vrenhin Laine. Ac y *hvnnw* y bu tri meib clotvaur, nyt amgen Dunchath vrenhin Muen, a Sutric vrenhin Dinas Dulyn, a Moelchelen vrenhin Midif. Maelmorda eissyoes oed vab y'r vrenhines honno o Vwrchath brenhin Laine.

Modern scholars invariably emend *y hunnw* ('to him') italicized in the quotation above to *y honno* ('to her') in order to achieve a more satisfactory reading.[82] The original reading would seem to render Murchad, father of Gormfhlaith, as the father of the three famous sons. The emendation is supported by the fact that Gormfhlaith has already been called the mother of a Sihtric, the name of one of the three; and the Irish sources show her to have been mother of Sihtric Silkenbeard and of Donnchad mac Briain Bóruma *rí Muman*, as well as *wife* of Mael Sechlainn mac Domnaill.[83] It is interesting to speculate to what extent we are justified in emending a corrupt text on the basis of our subsequent, superior knowledge. As Bartrum has noted, neither version is absolutely correct.[84] The mediaeval genealogists were evidently faced with a text not dissimilar to the extant copies of the

---

80 *CS* [1028=1030]; AFM *s.a.* 1030. She is not to be identified with her namesake who died in '840': Bromwich, ed. & transl., *Trioedd*, p. 467. On her see Stacpoole, 'Gormflaith'.
81 *Historia*, ed. Evans, p. 4; *A Mediaeval Prince*, ed. & transl. Evans, p. 26; Bartrum, ed., *Tracts*, p. 37.
82 See *Historia*, ed. Evans, p. clxxvi.
83 *CGH*, ed. O'Brien, I.13 (note on LL); Dobbs, 'The Ban-Shenchus' (1930) 314, 338; (1931) 189, 227; AT [1030]; AFM *s.a.* 1030.
84 Bartrum, ed., *Tracts*, p. 135, n. 1.

David E. Thornton

Historia in that they claimed that *tri meib a vu y Wrthach*.[85] This use of the personal-name (as opposed to the demonstrative pronoun of the *Historia*) removes any uncertainty although it does not necessarily imply that it represents a lost Latin original. Further complications arise from the fact that we are presented with two Murchads (*Mwrchath*) both kings of Leinster: one her father (Murchad mac Finn as is witnessed in the Irish sources)[86] and the other her husband by whom she had a son Mael Mórda (*Maelmorda*) (who is not thus witnessed). The latter is evidently the same Murchad as Gormfhlaith's father since he had a son Mael Mórda (slain at Clontarf in 1014) who was therefore Gormfhlaith's brother, not her son.[87] It is not immediately apparent how one might emend this part of the genealogy in order to correct it: the word *vab* in the passage quoted above might be changed to *vraut*, for example, perhaps deriving from an earlier confusion of the abbreviations of *filius* and *frater*.

Maylcorcre

According to the *Historia* the wife of *Avloed vrenhin Dinas Dulyn*, that is Olaf Sihtricsson, was *Maylcorcre*, the daughter of *Dunlug (Dwling) mab Tethel (Dwthil)*, king of Leinster. Her father can be identified with Dúnlaing mac Tuathail meic Augaire of Uí Muiredaig of Uí Dúnlainge who died in 1014.[88] This Dúnlaing is not credited with a daughter *Maylcorcre* in any known Irish source, but, it is worth noting, he is said to have had a daughter called Cacht in the *Banshenchas*.[89] The name Maylcorcre is certainly not common in the extant sources and scholars have been in disagreement as to the underlying Irish form of the second element *-corcre*. M. A. O'Brien listed the name *Máel-corcrae*, presumably suggesting *corcra* (*corcair*) 'purple' as the second element.[90] On the other hand, the forms *Mael-Curcaigh* and *Máelcorcaig* have been given, thus omitting the second *-r-* of the Welsh version.[91] This latter form may have been influenced by the name of *Melkorka* who, according to various mediaeval Icelandic sources was the daughter of an Irish king *Mýrkjartan* and who was captured and eventually brought as a slave to Iceland during the mid-tenth century.[92] Whitley Stokes

85 ABT § 6(g); also the so-called 'North Welsh Genealogical Tract': Bromwich, ed. & transl., *Trioedd*, pp. 256–8.
86 AU [971=972]; *CS* [970=972]; AI *s.a.* 972; AFM [970=972].
87 *CGH*, ed. O'Brien, I.13, 423; AU *s.a.* 1014; *CS* [1012=1014]]; AI *s.a.* 1014; AB § 281; AFM [1013=1014]; also *ByT* (Pen. 20) [1014]; *ByT* (RB) [1014]; *ByS* [1013].
88 AU *s.a.* 1014; ALC [1014]; AFM [1013=1014]; *Corpus*, ed. O'Brien, I.12. Tuathal died in 958: AU [957=958]; *CS* [957=958]; AI *s.a.* 958.
89 Dobbs, 'The Ban-Shenchus', pp. 193, 231.
90 O'Brien, 'Old Irish personal-names', p. 229: the element *mael* ('servant') can be combined with adjectives.
91 *Historia*, ed. Evans, p. clxxiii; Charles-Edwards, *Early Irish and Welsh Kinship*, p. 223.
92 *Historia*, ed. Evans, p. clxxiii, and n. 375. For the Icelandic accounts see *Íslendingabók*,

98

etymologized *Melkorka* as being in Irish *Mael Curcaig*, from the personal-name Curcach borne by several female saints.[93] Stokes also suggested that her father would have been called Muirchertach in Irish, though the two forms are not entirely compatible.[94] There are no grounds for identifying our *Maylcorcre* with *Melkorka* directly, but the possibility that the name of the latter princess (united with a Scandinavian) influenced the choice of name for the former (also engaged in such a union) cannot be discounted outright.

Kings of Ulaid

According to his genealogy, Gruffudd ap Cyan had two Irish half-brothers called *Ranalld m. Mathgavyn* and *Ethumachgavyn* who were kings of the Ulaid (*Wltw* = OI dat. *Ultu*). The patronymic *mab Mathgavyn* suggests a father called Mathgamain in Irish; this personal-name would appear also to underlie the second element -*machgavyn* of the other half-brother. The identification of these three names in Irish sources (two of whom are said in the *Historia* to have been kings of the Ulaid) has presented some difficulties for historians, a fact which is as much caused by the problematic nature of the Irish sources as by the Welsh ones.

The name *Mathgavyn*, which we have identified with the Irish personal-name Mathgamain, occurs in the Welsh genealogical sources also as Amachaden, Machawn, Mathawn, and Wrchadd. No Mathgamain occurs in the Ulaid genealogies at a chronologically convenient level, but one must be inferred from the fact that a series of kings of that Irish kingdom in the eleventh and twelfth centuries bore the surname Ua Mathgamna.[95] Margaret Dobbs suggested that these Uí Mathgamna rulers of the Ulaid were of the

Landnámabók, ed. Benediktsson, I.143; *Egils Saga*, ed. Nordal, p. 242; *Laxdœla Saga*, ed. Sveinsson, Íslenzk Fornrít V, pp. 27–8. For translations see *The Book of Settlements*, transl. Pálsson & Edwards, p. 54; *Egil's Saga*, transl. Pálsson & Edwards, p. 201; *Laxdœla Saga*, transl. Magnusson & Pálsson, p. 68. For a brief discussion see Smyth, *Scandinavian Kings*, pp. 164–5.

93 Stokes, 'On the Gaelic names', p. 189; also Craigie, 'Gaelic words and names', p. 449; *Corpus*, ed. Ó Riain, pp. 11, 18, 21, 114 (nos 61, 110, 125, 670.36).
94 Scholars have identified this Muirchertach with Muirchertach *na Cochall Craicinn* ('of the Leather Cloaks') mac Néill Glúnduib of Cenél nEogain who was killed by the Danes in 943: see for example, *Cogadh*, ed. & transl. Todd, p. 265. The name Muirchertach is represented as *Mýrjartak* elsewhere in Icelandic sources: for example, see Snorri Sturluson, *Heimskringla* (ed. Aðalbjarnarson, III.224, 233–4). However, reservations have been made regarding the historical accuracy of the Melkorka episode, suggesting it may depend more on the royal aspirations of medieval Icelanders of Celtic or slave ancestry: Karras, *Slavery*, pp. 57–8. According to the *Banshenchas*, Muirchertach had a daughter called Dúnlaith who was the mother of Glún Iairn mac Amlaíb Cuaráin (*ob.* 989; see above): Dobbs, 'The Ban-Shenchus', pp. 314, 337; 188, 227.
95 Byrne, 'Clann Ollaman', pp. 72, 79; Dobbs, 'The History of the Descendants of Ir', pp. 86–7.

neighbouring Airgialla, presumably linking them with Mathgamain mac Laidgnein of Fir Fernmaige (*ob.* 1022).[96] According to some Airgialla genealogies this Mathgamain was eponymous ancestor of the Mac Math-gamna (MacMahons) of Fernmag,[97] but the eponym of the latter has been identified alternatively as Mathgamain mac Néill (*ob.* 1273) who could not have been the father of Gruffudd's half-brothers.[98] Byrne, however, argued against this association with the Airgialla, but added that '[u]nfortunately it is by no means so clear who they [Uí Mathgamna] actually were'.[99] In order to explain the Ulaid material, he suggested that 'by some quirk of fancy' the surname Ua Mathgamna was here derived from the personal-name Matudán.[100] In such a case there would be more than one candidate for identification in the Ulaid genealogies: for example, Matudán mac Aeda (*ob.* 950) or Matudán mac Domnaill (*ob.* 1007).[101] It is worth stressing that the Irish genealogies and their modern commentators are as confused and uncertain about Ua Mathgamna and the precise affiliations of the half-brothers of Gruffudd ap Cynan as is the *Historia,* so it is perhaps not too surprising that the author of the latter had some apparent difficulty in interpreting and representing this material. An alternative identification for Mathgamain has been proposed by some scholars as the Mathgamain son of Dubgall (or Dubgilla) mac Amlaíb who died in 1013.[102] Dubgall died a year later at Clontarf.[103] Some scholars have regarded Dubgall as the son of Olaf Cuarán and thereby father of Sihtric the grandfather of Rhanillt; others have seen him as the son of Olaf, Rhanillt's father. The former seems to be the chronologically more suitable identification.[104] What basis for identifying this Mathgamain with our man? Our Mathgamain is given no patronymic or association, but his sons are specified as *brenhinedd Wltw.* The link to the Ulaid would support the association with the surname Ua Mathgamna, even if the precise genealogical ramifications are no longer available.

Turning to the half-brothers of Gruffudd, and kings of the Ulaid. *Ranalld*

---

96 *Ibid.,* p. 87, n. 11.
97 *Corpus,* ed. O'Brien, I.422, 435.
98 Ó Maolagáin, 'Uí Chremthainn', p. 162.
99 Byrne, 'Clann Ollaman', pp. 89–90.
100 *Ibid.,* p. 90.
101 AU [949=950], [1006=1007].
102 AU 1013.8 (has *Dubgilla* as the name of Mathgamain's father); *CS* [1011=1013]; AI *s.a.* 1013; Brian Ó Cuív has argued that Dubgall is the superior reading: 'Personal names as an indicator of relations between native Irish and settlers in the Viking period', pp. 81, 86, n. 4. For this identification see *The History,* ed. & transl. Jones, pp. 44–5; Charles, *Old Norse Relations,* pp. 56–8; *Tracts,* p. 136; Maund, *Ireland, Wales and England,* p. 179. The Dubgall/Dubgilla mac Amlaíb, father of this Mathgamain, died a year later in 1014: Byrne *et al., A New History,* IX.139.
103 AU *s.a.* 1014; AB [1014].
104 See Smyth, *Scandinavian York and Dublin,* II.309.

mab Mathgavyn is generally regarded as the Ragnall (alias Gilla Comgaill)
Ua Eochada, king of Ulaid, who was slain by Tigern Ua Ruairc in Louth in
1131.[105] The family of Ua Eochada is said to have derived its name from
Eochaid mac Ardgail (*ob.* 1004), king of the Ulaid, and would thus have
produced those of Ua Duinn Shléibe and (possibly) Ua Mathgamna. It is
worth stressing that *Ranalld* is described as *mab* of Mathgamain in the
Historia, and thereby strictly one generation too early to have been an *ua*
Mathgamna. Gruffudd's other half-brother according to the *Historia* was
called *Ethumachgavyn* (Etawthawn, Ekamachawn, Ecu Mathawn). As
noted above the second element *-machgavyn* is evidently the same as
Mathgavyn, father of *Ranalld*. However, the remaining element *Echu-* is
obscure. If (as the Welsh text states) he was brother of Ranalld, then the
intervening word *mab* ('son') is to be expected, possibly abbreviated *m.* as
for *Ranalld*. The letter *-u-* may be a residue of this, perhaps resulting from
the omission of a 'minim' during copying. This would resolve the name to
'Eth m. Machgavyn': the Irish original may have been the personal-name
Aed. Alternatively the *mab* may be missing altogether, in which case the
-u- may represent Irish *ua* (we have seen the royal surname Ua Mathgamna
among the Ulaid) or be part of the personal-name *Ethu*. The latter would
suggest the name Eochu, often confused with the name Eochaid in the
sources.[106] We are thereby faced with a series of possible original forms
of the composite name *Echumachgavyn*: Aed mac Mathgamna; Aed Ua
Mathgamna; Eochu/Eochaid mac Mathgamna; and, Eochu/Eochaid Ua
Mathgamna. Of course, if this figure was the full brother of *Ranalld*, then
we ought to prefer *mac* over *ua*. Identification of a suitable ruler of the Ulaid
of the early twelfth century has been hampered by an onomastic confusion
among the Irish chronicles and regnal lists at this point; and Byrne has stated
that the task of unravelling them 'is perhaps unsoluble'.[107] An Aed Ua
Mathgamna is recorded being slain by the Fir Fernmaige in 1124 in the
Annals of the Four Masters. Another (?) Aed Ua Mathgamna is said to have
fought and fallen beside Niall mac Duinn Shléibe Uí Eochada in 1127
according to the Annals of Tigernach and *Chronicon Scotorum*.[108] Other
chronicles, however, call the antagonists of 1127 Eochaid Ua Mathgamna
and Aed (or Niall) mac Duinn Shléibe [=Ua Eochada].[109] Byrne identified
this Eochaid Ua Mathgamna (alias *Garrchú*) with the Eochaid mac Aeda of
the regnal list in Rawlinson B.502. According to the latter source, there was
also a Eochaid mac Duinn Shléibe who had a brother Aed/Niall. From these

---

105 ALC [1131]; Bartrum, ed. *Tracts*, p. 136; Byrne, 'Clann Ollaman', pp. 92–3; *Historia*,
ed. Evans, p. clxxix.
106 On this point see Bergin, 'Varia II'.
107 Byrne, 'Clann Ollaman', p. 92.
108 AT [1127]; *CS s.a.* 1123.
109 AU; AFM; Byrne, 'Clann Ollaman', p. 92.

sources we could have an Aed or Eochaid as Ua Mathgamna or (if he was brother to Ragnall Ua Eochada) Ua Eochada.[110] If, however, Ua Mathgamna and Ua Eochada were separate surnames, then either Aed/Eochaid was not Ua Mathgamna or *Ranalld* was not the same as Ragnall Ua Eochada, or the two men mentioned in the *Historia* were not after all brothers. The number of eligible identifications, compounded by the confusion in the chronicles and the silence of the genealogies, does indeed support Byrne's pessimism. The fact that in other cases, where the sources are fuller and more consistent, the *Historia* mentions figures who are historically identifiable but whose parentage according to the Welsh text is demonstrably incorrect, suggests that we should not expect perfect correlation of names and genealogical position in this case. The parallelling of the names Mathgamain, Ragnall, and Aed/Eochaid may be as far as we can go in unravelling this scheme.

SOURCES AND MODELS

From the foregoing discussion of the genealogy of Gruffudd ap Cynan it ought to be apparent that the author of the original text was not working in a genealogical vacuum, composing the text spontaneously, but that he had a series of probable sources (written and perhaps oral, genealogical and annalistic) upon which he could draw. Again the two sides of the genealogy are unequal in this relationship to the sources. For the Welsh side, we know of the production and recording of genealogies in Wales as early as the first third of the ninth century. The earliest extant collection (our HG) dates from the middle decades of the following century. The Venedotian ancestry of Gruffudd down to Beli Mawr is clearly based on material related to HG § 1, though with some differences. As we have seen genealogical preface to the *Historia*, if composed as early as the mid-twelfth century, is the earliest witness to the names above Beli to Adam. The fact that Geoffrey of Monmouth's *Historia Regum Britannie* was the source for much of the nomenclature of this section of the genealogy has however compelled caution. The source or sources of the names immediately before and after the Galfridian matter cannot yet be traced with absolute satisfaction.

The Hiberno-Scandinavian section of Gruffudd's genealogy presents different problems. We do have Irish (and Icelandic) genealogical and annalistic accounts of most of the members of this section, but there is no verbal parallel to suggest that any surviving Irish document was the source.

---

110 But, according to the tract *Banshenchas* Aed mac Duinn Shleibe Uí Eochada was son of Sadb ingen Cennetig Uí Briain: Dobbs, 'The Ban-Shenchus', p. 194. He could not also have been a son of Rhanillt, but, as we have seen, the genealogy in the *Historia* does contain historically-identifiable figures whose parentage was entirely different from that given in the Welsh text.

The particularly jumbled account of the deeds of Harald Fairhair and his brothers as well as the erroneous incorporation of Harald in the first place may suggest the oral accounts of twelfth-century Dubliners aware of their distant Norse heritage. It is equally likely that such details and the dubious description of the power of Gruffudd's grandfather Olaf may have had more to do with the aims of the author in drawing up the genealogy than with the relative ignorance of his sources (oral or otherwise). However, the author was not wholly anachronistic in his deployment of the Hiberno-Scandinavians. Despite the many errors discussed above (mostly consisting of faulty genealogical relationships between otherwise identifiable figures), he has not simply thrown together a handful of Irish rulers without some consideration (assuming he threw them together in the first place, which is not certain). When the genealogy is emended, there is an overall chronological consistency which even contemporary Irish fabricators of pseudo-history were not always capable of achieving.[111]

As a royal biography, the *Historia* is a unique document in mediaeval Wales: whereas Gruffudd's alleged Irish and Scandinavian kinsmen would have been familiar with native texts (containing significant genealogical sections) about the deeds of kings and other rulers, his Welsh relatives would not. One possible comparable genre is that of hagiography, which serves to glorify the lives of certain holy men retrospectively and thereby illustrate their fitness to fulfil the saintly vocation. Such texts do survive from mediaeval Wales (the earliest extant *Uitae* dating from the twelfth century but not necessarily without precedent) and many contain genealogical introductions whose primary function seems to have been to demonstrate the specifically royal origins of the saints in question.[112] The *Uitae* themselves are probably modelled (via innumerable hagiographic intermediaries) ultimately on the life of Jesus as outlined in the Gospels which in turn illustrate his fitness for the messianic vocation. This point is not without significance for Gruffudd ap Cynan, since the *Historia*, having related the secular ancestry of its subject proceeds to discuss briefly *y vonhed herwyd Duw* ('his pedigree in relation to God'), concluding *urth henne Gruffud oed vab y Gynan, mab Adaf mab Duw* ('therefore Gruffudd was the son of Adam son of God'). Such a telescoped descent has biblical parallels.[113] Without wishing to push interpretation of such material too far, it is interesting to speculate whether the Latin original for the introductory statement

---

111 See, for instance, Ó Corráin's analysis of the text *Caithréim Cellacháin Chaisil*, in which various Irish dynasts are rendered as contemporaries of Cellachán mac Buadacháin (*ob.* 954) when they can clearly be demonstated not to have been: Ó Corráin, '*Caithréim Cellacháin Chaisil*'. In this case the author was an Irishman, no doubt with access to Irish genealogical and annalistic sources, and writing for an Irish audience.

112 For the saints' genealogies from the Lives see Bartrum, ed., *Tracts*, pp. 22–31.

113 Matt. 1.1: Jesus son of David son of Abraham.

en dydyeu Edward Vrenhin Lloegyr a Therdelach Vrenhin Ywerdon a ganet Gruffud Vrenhin Gwyned en Ywerdon en Dinas Dylyn ('*in the days of* Edward king of England and of Tairdelbach king of Ireland, Gruffudd king of Gwynedd was born *in Ireland in Dublin*')

would have echoed the biblical

cum ergo natus esset Iesus in Bethlehem Juda in diebus Herodis regis . . . ('Now when Jesus was born *in Bethlehem of Judea in the days of* Herod the king . . .').[114]

The *Historia* concludes in a similarly biblical vein in comparing Gruffudd, on his deathbed, to the Patriarch Jacob in Egypt blessing his sons and declaring what kind of men they would be in the future (*pa ryw wyr vyddunt rhagllaw*).[115] Jacob (alias 'Israel') was founding-ancestor of the Israelites, and the genealogical significance of this passsage should not go unnoticed therefore. Finally, Gruffudd's death is said to be bewailed like the Jews' lamentation for Joshua son of Nun.[116] Lacking any (extant) secular Welsh parallel, it is not impossible that the Gospel lives of Jesus or the hagiographic intermediaries may have acted as a model for the *Historia*, perhaps including the use of genealogies.

FUNCTION OF THE GENEALOGY

The purpose of the genealogy of Gruffudd ap Cynan is, in effect, stated at the outset of the *Historia*:[117]

Ac urth henne, bonhedicaf gur oed y Gruffud hunnu o vrenhinyaul genedel a llinuoed goruchel, megys y tysts ac a bonhed y reeni

And therefore, that Gruffudd was a most high-born man by reason of his royal kindred and most distinguished lineage, as the pedigree of his parents testifies and relates.

As should be apparent from the foregoing discussion, one of the more recurrent themes of the genealogy is that of the royal status of Gruffudd's direct and collateral kinsmen: where possible a figure is called *brenhin* and the area over which he ruled is stated. This stress on kingship is the same for both members of the genealogy who are historically identifiable and those, such as Harald Fairhair, whose position in the genealogy (at least as described in the *Historia*) is demonstrably unhistorical. The Welsh side of

---

114 Matt. 2:1. My italics.
115 *Historia*, ed. Evans, p. 32; *A Mediaeval Prince*, ed. & transl. Evans, p. 83. The biblical episode alluded to is Genesis 49.
116 *Historia*, ed. Evans, p. 33; *A Mediaeval Prince*, ed. & transl. Evans, p. 83.
117 *Historia*, ed. Evans, p. 1.

the scheme is less marked by anomalies in this regard as its earlier, historical part does correspond to the Venedotian royal line; but it is worth reiterating that the claim that Cynan ab Iago was *brenhin* is probably false and the use of that title for Cunedda otherwise called *Gwledig* is perhaps suspicious. On the Hiberno-Scandinavian side, however, false royal claims abound, both in terms of the very title and of the extent of personal rule. For example, Olaf Sihtricsson (*Avloed Vrenhin*), who is Gruffudd's nearest male ancestor in this part of the genealogy, is credited with a rule encompassing Dublin and a fifth part of Ireland, as well as the Isle of Man and other islands, Denmark, Galloway, the Rhinns, Anglesey, and Gwynedd. But, as we have seen, modern scholars doubt that he ever ruled Dublin and therefore would give the other territories even less credence. The pattern continues: five out of Olaf's six direct male ancestors are said in the *Historia* to have been kings. This fact can be verified (for Dublin) for most of them, but the link to Harald Fairhair is wrong. Harald is similarly credited with rule over all of Ireland and the Islands of Denmark, in addition to founding Scandinavian power in Ireland in the first place. Of his brothers, Alyn was 'the most holy and renowned king of all Denmark' (which should read 'Norway', if he is St Olaf) while Rodolf is ancestor of the Norman kings of England (which is possibly correct if he is Rollo). The greater part of Ireland is represented in the genealogy (with only Connacht and the Northern Uí Néill of the major kingdoms being omitted) although not all the relevant kings are shown to be direct ancestors of Gruffudd. Again, Olaf is described as king of Dublin and a fifth part of Ireland; Dúnlang mac Tuathail was king of another Fifth, Leinster; Brian Bóruma was king of Munster, said to be *dwy rann* or 'two parts' (fifths?); Mael Sechlainn was king of Meath; and finally Ragnall mac Mathgamna is said to have acquired a further *dwy rann Ywerdon*. If the *rann* represents a Fifth, then we have a surfeit!

If anyone ever doubted Gruffudd ap Cynan's royal credentials, then (as the author of the *Historia* stated) a glance at his genealogy would show them otherwise. Indeed, in the light of this virtual plethora of royalty, Thomas Charles-Edwards has argued that the purpose of the genealogy is to prove Gruffudd's 'right to rule' the kingdom of Gwynedd, and was not merely a piece of over-enthusiastic genealogical panegyric.[118] This is acheived by means of a 'kinship of status', rather than a 'kinship of inheritance' as Gruffudd as *wyr Iago* would not have been eligible according to the proscriptions of *Llyfr Iorwerth*.[119] It is perhaps worth remembering that the original *Historia* was composed after the death of its subject: the genealogy need not represent Gruffudd's own claim to the kingship but, perhaps, that of his son Owain Gwynedd seeking to consolidate the dynasty.

---

[118] Charles-Edwards, *Early Irish and Welsh Kinship*, pp. 220–4.

[119] Thus, *ibid.*, p. 223: 'if a man was of clearly royal status he would not be excluded from a claim to succession on the grounds that his royal descent was too remote'.

The fact therefore that this genealogical introduction to the *Historia* was not compiled out of an objective interest in family history, but served to support the claims to Gwynedd of Gruffudd or (more likely) his immediate descendants must affect the way we regard the genealogical material itself. As we have seen, the overall scheme is acheived by means of a number of devices: stressing the kingly status of individual members of the genealogy, even overstating it; wholly false agnatic genealogical links (such as Harald Fairhair); and the use of a union into an Irish dynasty by the Dublin line. For each device, some instances can be verified in independent sources while others cannot or can be shown to be false. The cases where no external verification is available need not be discounted as similarly false, but the possibility that they are cannot be ignored either.

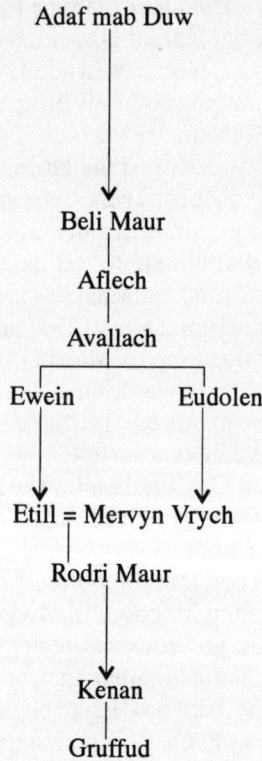

```
                    Adaf mab Duw
                         |
                         |
                         v
                    Beli Maur
                         |
                      Aflech
                         |
                     Avallach
                  _____|_____
                 |               |
               Ewein          Eudolen
                 |               |
                 v               v
            Etill = Mervyn Vrych
                    |
               Rodri Maur
                    |
                    |
                    v
                  Kenan
                    |
                 Gruffud
```

Figure 1:
Summary of the Paternal Ancestry of Gruffudd ap Cynan
according to the *Historia*

The Genealogy of Gruffudd ap Cynan

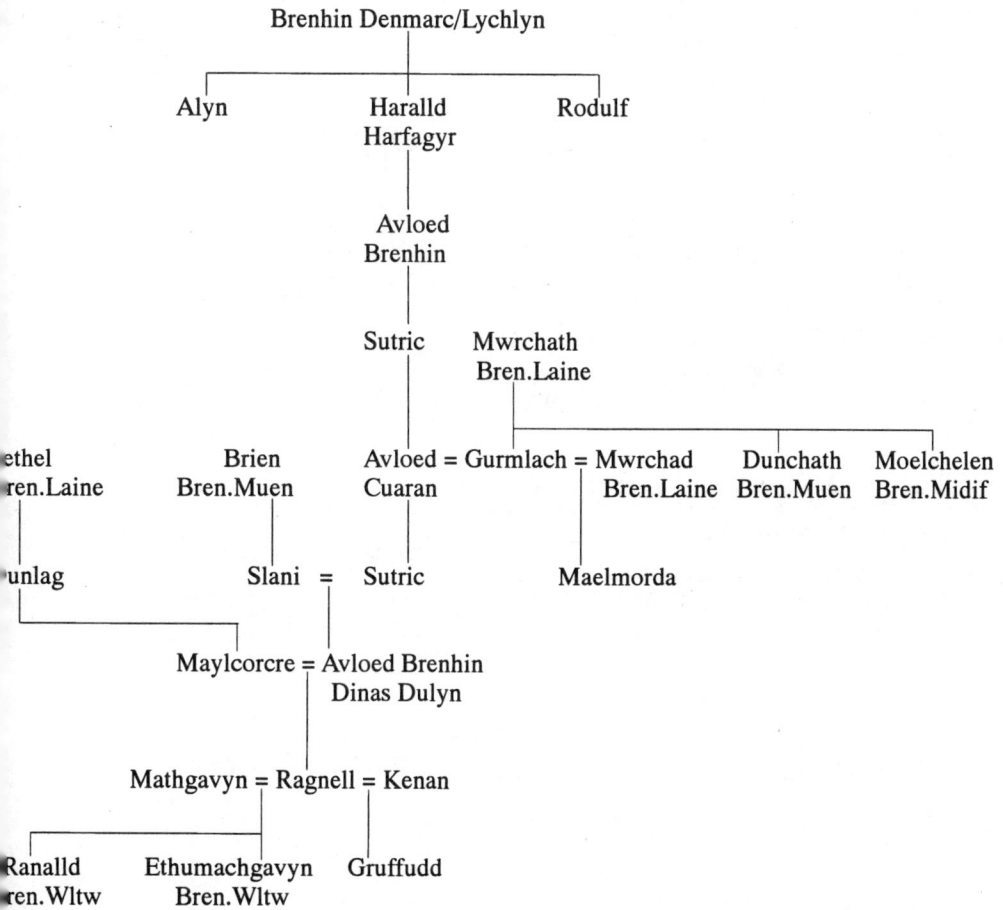

Brenhin Denmarc/Lychlyn

Alyn   Haralld   Rodulf
Harfagyr

Avloed
Brenhin

Sutric   Mwrchath
Bren.Laine

ethel   Brien   Avloed = Gurmlach = Mwrchad   Dunchath   Moelchelen
ren.Laine   Bren.Muen   Cuaran   Bren.Laine Bren.Muen   Bren.Midif

unlag   Slani = Sutric   Maelmorda

Maylcorcre = Avloed Brenhin
Dinas Dulyn

Mathgavyn = Ragnell = Kenan

Ranalld   Ethumachgavyn   Gruffudd
ren.Wltw   Bren.Wltw

Figure 2:
Maternal Ancestry of Gruffudd ap Cynan according to the *Historia*

Sihtric Caech
(927)

Murchad
(972)

Tuathal
(958)

[1]Olaf Cuarán = [2]Mael Sechlainn = Gormfhlaith = [3]Brian
(981)   (1022)   (1030)   (1014)

Mael Mórda
(1014)

Dúnlaing
(1014)

Sihtric Silkenbeard = *Sláine*
(1042)

Donnchad   *Sláine*
(1064)

Mael Corcraig = Olaf
               (1034)

Mathgamain = Ragnhild = Cynan

Ragnall   Aed/Eochu   Gruffudd
(?1131)   (?1124/7)   (1137)

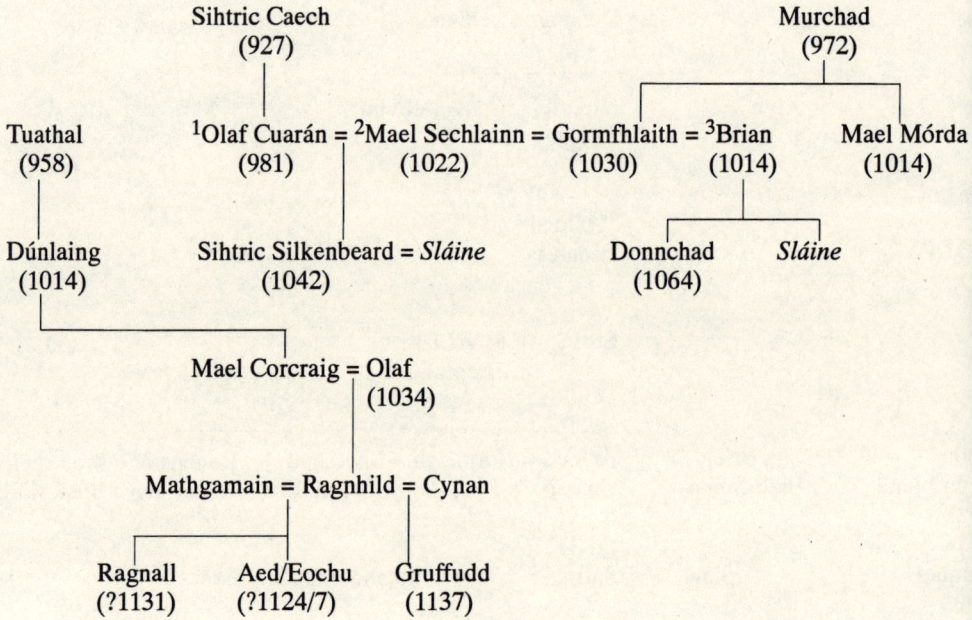

Figure 3:
Maternal Ancestry of Gruffudd ap Cynan emended from independent sources

IV

'GRUFFUDD, GRANDSON OF IAGO': *HISTORIA GRUFFUD VAB KENAN* AND THE CONSTRUCTION OF LEGITIMACY

K. L. Maund

Who was Gruffudd ap Cynan? The question is one which his contemporaries, at least, seem to have asked themselves: the compiler of the C-text of the *Annales Cambriae* certainly did so on first mentioning Gruffudd – *Grifud autem nepos Iacob*.[1] The event recorded is Gruffudd's first known action, and, it appears, his identity required a little explanation. The usual Welsh definition, by reference to a patronym, was unsatisfactory: it was necessary to go back to his grandfather in order to produce for him a place in the order of things.

This same concern underlies almost the entirety of Gruffudd's mediaeval biography, *Historia Gruffud vab Kenan*.[2] The primary concern of the latter seem to be not what deeds Gruffudd had performed, and why, but this same question: who was he? A recent analysis by T. M. Charles-Edwards has revealed a complex legal, framework underlying the *Historia*'s case for Gruffudd.[3] The purpose of the present paper is not to go over the same ground but to examine the way in which the issue of identity works within the text itself and to attempt to discover why should a complex manifesto of legitimacy was necessary by the time the *Historia* was written.

The word 'king', *brenhin*, occurs thirty-nine times in the opening part of the *Historia*, down to the end of the pedigrees. It is applied to Gruffudd himself, to his alleged distant ancestors, and to his more immediate relatives. It occurs with far more frequency in connection with the maternal, Hiberno-Scandinavian, side of his ancestry than with his paternal, Welsh,

---

1 'Gruffudd, grandson of Iago, besieged Anglesey'. *AC* (C), [1075]. The text given by Lloyd, 'Wales and the Coming of the Normans', pp. 166–79, is to be preferred to that of Williams ab Ithel, ed. *Annales Cambriae*.

2 *Historia*, ed. Evans. English translations may be found in *A Mediaeval Prince*, ed. & transl. Evans, and *The History*, ed. & transl. Jones.

3 Charles-Edwards, *Early Irish and Welsh Kinship*, pp. 220–24, 294–96.

kin.[4] The effect is relentless: son of a king; grandson of kings; brother, cousin, and great-grandson of kings; and, of course, a king himself. He and his relatives are, moreover, surrounded by the trappings of kingship, both actual and spiritual. Through his father he is related to the famous line of Troy, and beyond, to God Himself.[5] More recently, his ancestors build and own castles, command 'royal fleets' (*vrenhinyaul longes*), show prowess as warriors and saints, rule territories encompassing lands in several countries, and even possess bizarre, supernatural abilities.[6] Nor was the opportunity wasted to draw parallels with figures of legend: the author compared the activities of Gruffudd's so-called distant kinsman *Rodulf vrenhin* in Normandy with those of Romulus and Remus.[7]

Within a few paragraphs, the biographer neatly established the credentials of his subject. He ended by giving Gruffudd a sacred connexion: like all men – all good Christian men, anyway – Gruffudd is a son of God; and, to provide the mystical dimension, he is also a king whose coming has been foretold in prophecy.[8]

We are in the realm of the heroic (the historical carelessness of the text is further evidence of that), but there is a point to it. The biographer was obviously concerned to highlight and justify the regality of his subject, as as has long been recognised.[9] But it appears from the balance within this section of the text that he has another purpose also.

Legitimacy is the great theme of *Historia Gruffud vab Kenan*. Over and over again the biographer returns to this point. But in order to establish the legitimate claims of Gruffudd, the biographer had also to destroy or otherwise remove the claims of any rivals. I have discussed elsewhere the author's negative portrayal of Trahaearn ap Caradog;[10] however, he favoured other Welsh rulers with similar treatment. Cynwrig ap Rhiwallon,

---

4 *Ibid.*, p. 222, seems to consider this to be accidental. I hope to show that this may not be the full explanation.
5 *Historia*, ed. Evans, pp. 1–2; *A Mediaeval Prince*, ed. & transl. Evans, pp. 53–4.
6 For instance, Gruffudd's ancestor, Esyllt ferch Cynan comes *o gastell Dindaethue*, *ibid.*, p. 1. His grandfather King Olaf is said to rule not only Dublin, a fifth of Ireland, and Man, but also the islands of the Rhinns, Denmark and Galloway, and to have built a castle on Anglesey (*Historia*, ed. Evans, p. 2; *A Mediaeval Prince*, ed. & transl. Evans, p. 53). His more remote ancestors, Harald Harfagr and his brothers, conquer and subdue Ireland and part of France, building cities and castles (*Historia*, ed. Evans, p. 2; *A Mediaeval Prince*, ed. & transl. Evans, pp. 54–5). One of them, moreover, is venerated as a saint (*Historia*, ed. Evans, pp. 3–4; *A Mediaeval Prince*, ed. & transl. Evans, pp. 55–6). One of Gruffudd's putative half-brothers is not only a successful conqueror in Ireland, but has the ability to leap further than anyone else in that land and owns a horse with similar abilities (*Historia*, ed. Evans, p. 5; *A Mediaeval Prince*, ed. & transl. Evans p. 57.
7 *Historia*, ed. Evans, p. 4; *A Mediaeval Prince*, ed. & transl. Evans, p. 56.
8 *Historia*, ed. Evans, p. 5; *A Mediaeval Prince*, ed. & transl. Evans, p. 58.
9 Charles-Edwards, *Early Irish and Welsh Kinship*, pp. 220–24. But see also Davies, *Conquest*, p. 57.
10 Maund, 'Trahaearn'.

who may have had some control over parts of Gwynedd in the later 1070s, he described as a 'petty king' (*vrenhinyn*), as an 'oppressor' (*treisswr*).[11] Cynwrig was occupying Gruffudd's patrimony (*tref ei dad*) when Gruffudd first cames to Wales but was slain rapidly on Gruffudd's behalf by Gruffudd's new Welsh supporters.[12] His role in the text is simply to provide an immediate victory for Gruffudd, one for which, were we to rely solely upon the *Brutiau*, we should have no evidence at all.[13] The technique is quite sophisticated: Gruffudd has already been shown attracting the loyalty of the men of Gwynedd, and his first success is presented as due to their action.

To return, however, to the treatment of other Welsh rulers within the *Historia*, the greatest scorn was reserved for Trahaearn and his allies. Other rulers – rivals or otherwise – were treated more circumspectly. Rhys ap Tewdwr of Deheubarth, to whom Gruffudd was a (possibly incidental) ally at the battle of Mynydd Carn,[14] is not portrayed as lacking merit, but the biographer was at pains to stress his subordination to Gruffudd. Although Rhys is referred to as a king, he is made to address Gruffudd as 'king of the kings of Wales' (*brenhin brenhined Kemry*).[15] He is shown as promising homage to Gruffudd, as notably lacking Gruffudd's courage and prowess in the battle itself.[16] Similarly, the Powysian leader, Cadwgan ap Bleddyn, so prominent in the Welsh chronicle-accounts of the rebellion of the 1090s, is placed in a subordinate position to Gruffudd. Cadwgan, we are told, resorted to Gruffudd for advice and help, *ca* 1098, and, in the same passage, he is referred to as Gruffudd's son-in-law.[17] The intent is obvious, even heavy-handed; within the confines of the *Historia*, at least, no room is left for any doubt over Gruffudd's superiority to his Welsh contemporaries.

The treatment of Norman earls and others is more circumspect, as Charles-Edwards has noticed.[18] This is particularly so in the earlier part of the text, and it is in this earlier part that one may find the reason for this. To an extent, certainly, this circumspection must reflect the biographer's own contemporary situation: whenever in the twelfth century he was writing, he was writing in a Wales hedged by powerful, and perhaps touchy, Anglo-Norman lords. Something of the same attitude no doubt underlies his accounts of Gruffudd's Welsh rivals. The descendants of the maligned and despised Trahaearn had virtually destroyed themselves in dynastic feuding

---

11 *Historia*, ed. Evans p. 8; *A Mediaeval Prince*, ed. & transl. Evans, pp. 59, 60.

12 *Historia*, ed. Evans, pp. 7–8; *A Mediaeval Prince*, ed. & transl. Evans, pp. 59–60.

13 None of them explicitly associate Gruffudd, or his presence in Wales, with this death. See *ByT* (Pen. 20) [1073 = 1075]; *ByT* (RB) [1075]; *ByS* [1073=1075].

14 See Maund, *Ireland, Wales and England*, p. 80.

15 *Historia*, ed. Evans, p. 13; *A Mediaeval Prince*, ed. & transl. Evans, p. 66.

16 *Historia*, ed. Evans, pp. 14–16; *A Mediaeval Prince*, ed. & transl. Evans, pp. 67–8.

17 *Historia*, ed. Evans, pp. 23–4; *A Mediaeval Prince*, ed. & transl. Evans, p. 76. On Cadwgan's role in the rebellion, see Maund, *Ireland, Wales and England*, pp. 148–53.

18 Charles-Edwards, *Early Irish and Welsh Kinship*, p. 295.

in the early part of the twelfth century. The line of Cynwrig ap Rhiwallon had always been obscure. On the other hand the descendants of Rhys ap Tewdwr, and the relatives of Cadwgan ab Bleddyn were forces to be reckoned with, and not lightly to be dismissed or abused, even in panegyric of their opponents. However, it seems to me that the ambivalent attitude to the Normans in particular reflects more than simple political expediency.

Throughout the text, the biographer is at pains to emphasize a connexion between Gruffudd and his Norman neighbours. This connexion is certainly political: another aspect of Gruffudd's respectability and legitimacy is manifested in the good relations which he is said to have enjoyed with other rulers. He is the only Welsh ruler shown as being on such a footing. Other native kings – minor kings, *brenhinedd bychein* – come to his court, once he is established, for advice, protection, and assistance.[19] He, on the other hand, enjoys 'neighbourly relations' with those kings whose domains lie close to his: with Henry, king of England, with *Mwrchath*, king of Ireland; and with the king of the isles of Denmark.[20] The English king, moreover, is portrayed as being more anxious to negotiate than to fight with Gruffudd, a circumstance which seems not only to point up Gruffudd's prowess as a warrior but to hint that, in the political sphere, he is (within the *Historia*, at least) a major player, to be respected and handled with care.[21] His relations with the earls of Chester are presented more ambivalently. The biographer could not escape the historical actuality that, in the early years of his career, Gruffudd was probably subject to the goodwill of those same earls. The issue of dependence, however, is evaded: on his final return from Ireland (in 1099), Gruffudd made peace with Earl Hugh, and was granted lands. But the author of the *Historia* carefully did not say by whom these lands were granted, while later in the text he went into considerable detail in describing the grants made to Gruffudd by Henry I: Llyn, and Eifionydd, and Arlechwedd, given with 'peace and affection'.[22] The biographer's treatment of the incursions made by the earl and his followers into Gwynedd is similarly ambivalent. Gruffudd's captivity, during the 1080s,

---

19 *Historia*, ed. Evans, p. 31; *A Mediaeval Prince*, ed. & transl. Evans, p. 82.

20 *Historia*, ed. Evans, p. 30; *A Mediaeval Prince*, ed. & transl. Evans, p. 81. On Mwrchath, see Maund *Ireland, Wales and England*, pp. 178–81.

21 *Historia*, ed. Evans, p. 29; *A Mediaeval Prince*, ed. & transl. Evans, pp. 80–1. It is interesting to note that, at the end of this section, on Henry I's expeditions into Wales, the biographer finds it necessary to reintroduce Trahaearn briefly. The latter's death had occurred years and pages previously: his occurrence here is apparently to provide Gruffudd once again with an enemy. The earls of Chester and the men of Powys, we are told, were unable to oppose Gruffudd, but the terms used of them are mild. Once again, it is Trahaearn for whom the really disparaging language is reserved. Consider, too, the fate of William Rufus (*Historia*, ed. Evans, pp. 22–5; *A Mediaeval Prince*, ed. & transl. Evans, pp. 74–5) whose expedition ended in loss and turmoil in the face of Gruffudd's strategies.

22 *Historia*, ed. Evans, pp. 28–9; *A Mediaeval Prince*, ed. & transl. Evans, pp. 79–80.

had permitted Earl Hugh to make considerable gains in North Wales, and certainly the men of the Norman force are shown in the *Historia* as causing great harm there, while Hugh himself is made to play the role of Saul to Gruffudd's David.[23] But, compared with the harsh words levelled at Trahaearn, Hugh escapes lightly.[24] The real enemies, for the biographer, are not the Normans, but those Welsh dynasties whom he perceived, or described, as having in some way threatened or harmed Gruffudd's claims in the North.

But the connection which the biographer draws between Gruffudd and the Norman lords is more complex than this. The author of the *Historia* was not simply setting out to avoid causing offence; it is engaged in a careful and complicated attempt to identify Gruffudd with those same Normans, and in particular with their kings.

To analyse this connexion, it is necessary to return to the pedigree-section of the text. As I have already observed, at least part of the purpose of the 'regality' of these pedigrees is to lend royalty to Gruffudd himself.[25] But this, I suggest, is far from being their sole purpose, and, moreover, the emphasis on the Irish and Scandinavian connexions is more than just the product of chance.[26] The biographer here sought to show that Gruffudd was the equal of the neighbouring kings in Ireland and England (and, by the implication of other sections of his text, the superior of his contemporaries elsewhere in Wales).[27] Furthermore, Gruffudd is the kinsman of these neighbours, and, most importantly of all, of the Norman kings in particular; he derived, indeed, from an apparently senior line within their putative dynasty. The biographer presented Gruffudd's descent from Harald Harfagr, and that of William the Conqueror and his sons from Harald's so-called brother Rodulf, very close together in the text. Indeed, the succession of pedigrees is interrupted at the same point for a description of the exploits of Harald and his brothers.[28] Harald invades and conquers Ireland, builds cities, placing his kinsmen in them, and rules all Ireland, along with the isles of Denmark, a claim transmitted by him to his descendant Olaf, Gruffudd's grandfather. The implication is clear: Gruffudd and his

[23] *Historia*, ed. Evans, pp. 18–19; *A Mediaeval Prince*, ed. & transl. Evans, pp. 70, 71. Later, William Rufus wears the same mantle, *Historia*, ed. Evans, p. 23; *A Mediaeval Prince*, ed. & transl. Evans, p. 75.

[24] *Historia*, ed. Evans, p. 23; *A Mediaeval Prince*, ed. & transl. Evans, p. 75, where he is described as 'the root of all the evil'. However, there is none of the relentless character-assassination used upon Trahaearn.

[25] Charles-Edwards, *Early Irish and Welsh Kinship*, pp. 220–24.

[26] *Ibid.*, p. 222.

[27] Rhys ap Tewdwr's submission (*Historia*, ed. Evans, pp. 13–14; *A Mediaeval Prince*, ed. & transl. Evans, pp. 66–7), as was discussed above; but also the comments near the end of the text regarding Gruffudd's patronage of 'other minor kings', *Historia*, ed. Evans, p. 31; *A Mediaeval Prince*, ed. & transl. Evans, p. 82.

[28] *Historia*, ed. Evans, pp. 2–4; *A Mediaeval Prince*, ed. & transl. Evans, pp. 54–6.

Norman contemporaries, William Rufus, Henry I, and Stephen, are kinsmen, products of a similar process of colonisation and conquest; and Gruffudd is descended from the elder line.[29] The latter point is made all the clearer, I suggest, by the penultimate line of this section of the *Historia*, where we are told that 'From him [Rodulf] came the Norman kings who subdued England in battle, namely King William, and his two sons who succeeded him, William of the Long Sword and Henry and Stephen his nephew, who were contemporaries of *King Gruffudd*'.[30] The part of the pedigrees dealing with Gruffudd's Scandinavian connexions is certainly the longest individual section, and I cannot credit that this is simply the result of an accident in the balance of material available to the biographer – nor even to his desire to tell a good story.

This might go part of the way to explaining the circumspect treatment of the Normans in the *Historia*: it should be noted in this context that William Rufus's unsuccessful expedition, in particular, is presented in quasi-Biblical terms, with Gruffudd acting as David to William's Saul.[31] Gruffudd, like David, has right on his side, and William, like Saul, is behaving unfairly, but the relationship remains one of respect. This compares interestingly with the account of Gruffudd's victory over Trahaearn ap Caradog in the battle of Gwaed Erw: the latter is recounted not in terms of righteous strength kept unleashed (as is the case with the descriptions of Gruffudd's reaction to the expeditions of William and of Henry I), but rather the explicit language of victory is employed.[32] Against Trahaearn, Gruffudd is like Agamemnon,

---

[29] The confusion surrounding the foundation of Waterford by Harald is particularly interesting. The biographer has established initially that Harald has two brothers, Alyn and Rodulf, *Historia*, ed. Evans, p. 3; *A Mediaeval Prince*, ed. & transl. Evans, p. 55. Alyn dies in battle (apparently in Denmark), and becomes a saint. Rodulf goes to France, where he founds the duchy of Normandy and fathers its dynasty, *Historia*, ed. Evans, p. 4; *A Mediaeval Prince*, ed. & transl. Evans, p. 56. However, Harald has meanwhile established Waterford, and – placed as ruler therein 'one of his brothers' (*Ac vn o'e vroder a Possodes yn vn o'r dinassoed a adeilassei*), whose descendants, we are told, rule there to this day. This point has usually been taken to show that the *Historia* was composed before the Norman conquest of Waterford in 1171. However, it has to be said that a case could be made here, within the terms of the *Historia*, itself, for the Normans themselves representing continuity of rule in that town by kinsmen of Harald. This might make a late composition date for the *Historia*, more possible (Maund, *Ireland, Wales and England*, pp. 172–74). Against late composition, however, should be attested the apparent ignorance of the biographer of the rise to power in Ireland of the Ui Conchobhar kings of Connacht – the pedigree-section of the *Historia* connects Gruffudd to the dynasties of Leinster, Munster, Meath, and Ulster, but makes no mention of Connacht. For further discussion of the date of the *Historia*, see Jones, below, pp. 149–56.

[30] *A Mediaeval Prince*, ed. & transl. Evans, p. 56.

[31] *Historia*, ed. Evans, p. 23; *A Mediaeval Prince*, ed. & transl. Evans, p. 75. The same analogy is applied to Gruffudd and Hugh of Chester; see note 23.

[32] *Historia*, ed. Evans, pp. 29–30; *A Mediaeval Prince*, ed. & transl. Evans, pp. 80–1.

like Judas Maccabeus fighting a faithless king (*brenhin anfydlavn*), like Julius Caesar, like Arthur, avengers all.[33]

Historia Gruffud vab Kenan is, above all else, concerned with establishing Gruffudd's position – as a king, as a rightful, legitimate king, as a powerful king, as a king equal to other kings. The historical events underlying his story – for story it is – are subordinate to the panegyric and promotionary purpose of the text. In the end, the Gruffudd of the *Historia* becomes little more than a symbol in the biographer's hands, progressing from being a royal and able youth with a claim to uphold, to become through adversity and conquest, an established ruler whose reign provides seemingly inevitable peace, prosperity, and security. Indeed, the biographer takes us one step further even than this, depicting Gruffudd's retirement from secular affairs in order to obtain, in his last days, the appropriate religious crown of spiritual retreat and holy death (with the effect that the pedigree-section and the biography-section of the text achieve an odd symmetry: both end by drawing Gruffudd closer to God).[34]

One is left, as ever when dealing with the *Historia*, with the question: why was the biography written? Was it to legitimate a king whose claim to rule was legally uncertain, owing to his dynastic position, as Charles-Edwards has suggested?[35] To a degree, that must be so: but that argument not only begs the question of the form of the laws of inheritance and succession operative in late eleventh-century Wales, but must also raise the query as to why the biographer would exhume a possibly sensitive issue (in the twelfth century, at least) after the death of the king in question. Gruffudd might have been too far removed in generational terms from a kingly ancestor, but his son Owain Gwynedd was not and would need no such defence. There are no hints in the Welsh chronicles that Gruffudd's kingship was more questioned during his lifetime than that of any of his contemporaries. The argument seems once again to lead round to the early career of Llywelyn ab Iorwerth, as I have suggested elsewhere:[36] he too was the grandson, but not the son, of a king, and was thus theoretically excluded from inheriting the kingship;[37] like Gruffudd, he was raised away from Gwynedd, and faced rivals there who had excluded his father from a share of the patrimony. Against this one must measure the problems inherent in trying to date the

---

[33] *Historia*, ed. Evans, pp. 8–9; *A Mediaeval Prince*, ed. & transl. Evans, pp. 60–1. Compare also the language used of Gruffudd's prowess in the battle of Bron-yr-Erw (*Historia*, ed. Evans, pp. 11–12; *A Mediaeval Prince*, ed. & transl. Evans, pp. 62–3): Gruffudd is defeated only through others' fears.

[34] His retreat and death, *Historia*, ed. Evans, pp. 31–34; *A Mediaeval Prince*, ed. & transl. Evans, pp. 82–3. Cf. the final pedigree, *Historia*, ed. Evans, p. 5; *A Mediaeval Prince*, ed. & transl. Evans, p. 57.

[35] Charles-Edwards, *Early Irish and Welsh Kinship*, pp. 220–24.

[36] Maund, *Ireland, Wales and England*, pp. 172–74.

[37] Charles-Edwards, *Early Irish and Welsh Kinship*, pp. 220–24.

composition of the *Historia*. Yet, for some reason, the biographer was engaged in almost a re-invention of the line of the North Welsh kings descended from Rhodri Mawr. He established the connexion of its twelfth-century representatives with Rhodri, yes, but he placed far less stress on that than on their connexions outside Wales, and in particular with the ruling Norman dynasty. He promoted Gruffud's dynasty to superiority over other Welsh rivals – most explicitly over the line of Deheubarth: it is hard to avoid remembering in this context the importance and prestige enjoyed in the late twelfth century by the South Welsh ruler, Rhys ap Gruffudd, in comparison with the less comfortable position of the sons of Owain Gwynedd. Such a figure was not to be ignored by any Northern dynast, especially not by a young and hopeful one. And, over and over again, the biographer emphasised that, by courtesy of Gruffudd ap Cynan himself, the North Welsh line was more than Welsh, that its representatives had every reason to consider themselves the equals of their neighbours to east and west. The problem remains, perhaps, ultimately insoluble. But the impression cannot be avoided: in composing *Historia Gruffud vab Kenan*, the biographer has left for us an almost perfect paradigm for the legitimate righteousness of a dynastic outsider.

V

NORSE HISTORICAL TRADITIONS AND THE *HISTORIA GRUFFUD VAB KENAN*: MAGNÚS BERFŒTTR AND HARALDR HÁRFAGRI

Judith Jesch

INTRODUCTION

A Norse point of view on the death of Hugh de Montgomery, Earl of Shrewsbury, off Anglesey in 1098 is provided by the poet Bjǫrn krepp-hendi:[1]

Lífspelli réð laufa	The sword-tree [warrior] caused
lundr í Ǫngulssundi,	the death of Hugh the Valiant in
broddr fló, þars slǫg snuddu,	Ǫngul-sound, where weapons
snúðigt, Huga ens prúða.	rushed, arrow flew quickly.

Bjǫrn was a court poet in the service of Magnús berfœttr, king of Norway, and the 'sword-tree' was of course his patron. Magnús had other poets who celebrated this deed, for instance Þorkell hamarskáld:[2]

Dunði broddr á brynju.	Arrow drummed on mail-coat.
Bragningr skaut af magni.	The chieftain shot forcefully. The

Acknowledgement
Special thanks are due to Claus Krag, for first encouraging me to think about Haraldr hárfagri in 1985, and for much stimulating correspondence and conversation across the historical/ philological *Ginnungagap* since then.

[1] *Den norsk-islandske skjaldedigtning* (ed. Jónsson, IA.436, IB.406). For convenience, I give this comprehensive collection as the basic reference for all skaldic verse cited. Although the skaldic poems cited in this paper are all in need of re-editing, I have not made any major changes to them for this paper, except that my text is usually closer to the versions in the *Íslenzk fornrit* editions of the various sagas containing the poems, where these exist. The prose contexts of and the problems of establishing texts for skaldic verses are discussed below. All translations of skaldic verse are my own and aim to replicate the contents of the verse rather than their style, though I try to suggest kennings where they are used, without attempting to reproduce all of their layers of meaning.

[2] *Ibid.*, IA.438, IB.408.

Sveigði allvaldr Egða
alm. Stǫkk blóð á hjalma.
Strengs fló hagl í hringa,
hné ferð, en lét verða
Hǫrða gramr í harðri
hjarlsókn banat jarli.

mighty ruler of the people of
Agder bent his bow. Blood
sprayed on helmets. Bowstring-
hail [arrows] flew into ring-mail,
the troop fell, and the prince of the
people of Hordaland caused the
earl to be slain in a hard fight for
land.

A third such court poet, who actually seems to have been present at the battle, was Gísl Illugason:[3]

Hǫðum hildi
með Haralds frænda
Ǫnguls við ey
innanverða,
þars af reiði
ríklundaðir,
konungr ok jarlar,
kapp sitt brutu.

We fought a battle with Harald's
kinsman to the landward side of
Anglesey, where the powerful
ones, king and earls, angrily
pressed their courage.

Margan hǫfðu
Magnús liðar
bjǫrtum oddi
baugvang skorinn.
Varð hertoga
hlíf at springa
kapps vel skrifuð
fyr konungs darri.

Magnús's men had cut many a
shield with bright point. The
duke's [i.e. Hugh's] protection,
very well decorated, had to split
before the king's dart.

Bǫðkennir skaut
bǫðum hǫndum.
Allr vá hilmis
herr prúðliga.
Stukku af almi,
þeims jǫfurr sveigði,
hvítmýlingar,
áðr Hugi felli.

The fighter shot with both hands.
All of the leader's band struck val-
iantly. White arrows sprayed from
the bow which the king bent, before Hugh fell.

Although embellished with formulaic battle-descriptions, each of these poems contains the clear statement that the Norwegian king caused the death of the Norman earl in a sea-battle off Anglesey. The implications that these Norse points of view might have for the whole history of the area have been relatively little explored and deserve further consideration.

Previous commentators on the *Historia Gruffud vab Kenan* have recognised Norse elements in the text and have tried to unravel their relation to

---

3 *Ibid.*, IA.442, IB.411–12.

Gruffudd's life with the aid of Scandinavian sources. However, the days are long gone (if they ever existed) when any one scholar could be equally confident in the languages and the vast literatures of both the Celtic and the Norse worlds. To a Norse specialist, it is clear that the scholars who have worked on the *Historia* have not been able to do the impossible by fully mastering the Norse language and its literature as well. Thus, they have in the main restricted their mining for nuggets of information to one text, Snorri Sturluson's *Heimskringla* (with occasional references to other texts, gleaned largely from secondary works), and their use of this text has generally been dependent on translated versions. In this paper I hope to demonstrate the insufficiency of citing *Heimskringla* without consideration of the sources Snorri used in writing it and the historiographical tradition in which he wrote, and to provide a fuller account of the Norse texts which have relevance to the Norse references in the *Historia*. How a fuller understanding of the Norse texts might affect the interpretation of the *Historia*, I must leave to others to decide, but I hope at least to suggest some new questions they might ask, and a new context in which it might be considered. In particular, I would like to stimulate a reconsideration of the origins of the Norse elements in the *Historia*, and of the route or routes by which they found their way into it.

The *Historia* contains two clusters of information on which Norse texts may shed some light: the alleged descent of Gruffudd from one *Harald harfagyr* (who may or may not be identical with the Norwegian king Haraldr hárfagri), to which I return below, and the apparently fortuitous raid of the Norwegian king Magnús berfœttr on Anglesey in 1098, with which I began. The events of 1098 are widely recorded in insular as well as Norse sources,[4] so the latter tend to be referred to by scholars only where they might amplify or confirm the other accounts,[5] while Gruffudd's alleged descent from Haraldr hárfagri is generally dismissed as spurious, without any convincing explanation of its relationship to Norse historical traditions of this king. In the following, however, I wish to consider the Norse texts on their own terms, without prejudging their relationship to the insular material. This will involve me first in some general discussion of the historical status and literary context of both skaldic poetry and prose historiography, before I return to the question of what light these Norse texts might shed on the *Historia Gruffud vab Kenan*.

---

4 Power, 'Magnus Barelegs', is a useful survey, although she gives remarkably little prominence to the skaldic verses that are the core of my account.

5 E.g. Jones, *History*, pp. 80–1; Charles, *Old Norse Relations*, p. 89, and Evans, *Historia*, pp. cxciii–iv. I am grateful to my former student Bethan Hughes for translating parts of Evans' introduction for me.

KING MAGNÚS AND HIS POETS

The stanzas cited above are not isolated poetic utterances but were originally part of longer encomia composed by professional court poets (ON *skáld*) for their royal patron. Such poems could be panegyrics for the patron while he was still alive, and it is probable that Bjǫrn's poem was of this type, while both Þorkell's and Gísl's poems were clearly *erfikvæði*, or eulogies composed after the king's death.[6]

The stanzas still preserved of Bjǫrn krepphendi's *Magnússdrápa* celebrate the following aspects of King Magnús's career:[7] (1) a military expedition to Halland and elsewhere, (2) suppression of a rebellion in northern Norway and Trøndelag, (3) an expedition to the British Isles with: (a) the burning of Lewis, (b) the harrying of Skye and Tiree, (c) the burning of North Uist, (d) an attack on Sandey (probably Iona) and the burning of Islay, (e) the expulsion of the people of Mull, (f) attacks on the population of Kintyre and Man, (g) the capture of Lǫgmaðr, son of Guðrøðr, on Man, and (h) the battle off Anglesey.[8] The main thrust of the poem is captured in two lines from stanza three, which was probably designed as a refrain: *Vítt rýðr jǫrn á ýtum/Óleifs mǫgr en fǫgru* ('the son of Óláfr [i.e. Magnús] reddens the gleaming weapons on people in many places'). The rest of the extant poem gives details of these unfortunate people. Some of them are the undifferentiated populations of the various districts in which he harried, the widows of Viskadalr in Halland, the armies of Trøndelag, the farmers of North Uist, the maidens of the southern Hebrides, and the people of both Mull and Man. Others are more specific but unnamed, such as two chieftains killed in Trøndelag. Three significant adversaries overcome by Magnús are named and characterised: Þórir who was hanged for treachery in Trøndelag, Lǫgmaðr the son of Guðrøðr, king of Man, and Hugh 'the Valiant'. Finally, Magnús's complete mastery of his enemies, both internal and external, is emphasised by the kennings used to describe him. As well as the more usual warrior- and king-kennings, the kennings applied to Magnús emphasise the geographical areas he has won mastery over. While such kennings are conventional, there does seem to be a particular concentration of them in this poem: Magnús is *Vǫrsa dróttinn* 'lord of the people of Voss', *Hǫrða ræsir* 'chief of the people of Hordaland', *buðlungr Þrœnda* 'prince of the people of Trøndelag', *Sygna harri* 'leader of the people of Sogn', *Grenlands dróttinn* 'lord of Grenland', *lofðungr Þrœnda* 'prince of the people of

---

6 Fidjestøl, *Fyrstediktet*, pp. 195–7.

7 *Den norsk-islandske skjaldedigtning* (ed. Jónsson, IA.434–7, IB.404–6). A *drápa* was a long panegyric with a refrain.

8 I follow Fidjestøl, *Fyrstediktet*, pp. 150–2, 173, for the ordering of the stanzas in this poem and the interpretation of *Sandey*.

Trøndelag', and *Egða gramr* 'prince of the people of Agder', all of these being districts in Norway. He is also *Skota støkkvir* 'evicter of the Scots' and *Jóta fellir* 'feller of the Jutes'. After noting the death of Hugh, the poem concludes triumphantly with the following half-stanza:

Qll hefr Jóta fellir	The feller of Jutes has been torch-
eylǫnd farit brandi,	ing all the islands, the land has
vítt liggr dyggs und dróttum	widely been subjugated to the
dǫglings grund, um stundir.	forces of the brave leader.

The poet frequently (six times in nine stanzas) has recourse to the adverb *vítt* 'far, widely', and the battle off Anglesey underscores how far Magnús actually got on this expedition.

Þorkell hamarskáld's five-stanza *Magnússdrápa*,[9] which is probably not preserved in its entirety, refers to the following episodes: (1) Þórir's rebellion, (2) two stanzas referring to the expedition to the British Isles and the killing of the Norman earl, (3) an expedition to Sweden, and (4) a final stanza which may refer to Magnús's second expedition to the west, when he was killed in Ireland in 1103. The stanza referring to the battle of Anglesey echoes Bjǫrn's poem in paralleling Magnús's lordship at home in Norway (he is again *allvaldr Egða* 'mighty ruler of the people of Agder' and *Hǫrða gramr* 'prince of the people of Hordaland') with his success in the *hjarlsókn* 'battle for land' in Anglesey.

Gísl Illugason's poem is not given a title in any medieval source,[10] but is usually referred to as his *Erfikvæði* ('memorial poem') for Magnús berfœttr. It differs from Bjǫrn's and Þorkell's panegyrics in being in a different (and simpler) metre (*fornyrðislag* rather than *dróttkvætt*) and in being fairly fully preserved. Its twenty stanzas cover most of its hero's career, recounting the following episodes: (1) Magnús's youthful attempts to win glory (stanza one), (2) his suppression of rebels in Norway, and his protection of merchants from thieves (stanzas 2–8), (3) his expedition to the west, in particular the capture of the 'prince of North Uist' on Skye and the flight of the Scots, and the capture of Lǫgmaðr, resulting in Magnús's acquiring 'four ancestral lands' (stanzas 9–10), (4) the three stanzas on the battle of Anglesey quoted above followed by three stanzas describing the sea-journey home (stanzas 11–16), (5) Magnús's expedition to Sweden (stanzas 17–18), and (6) two final stanzas in which the poet describes how he was an eyewitness to and participant in Magnús's victories (stanzas 19–20). Like Bjǫrn and Þorkell, Gísl emphasises the king's land-claims. The very first stanza has him roused to battle when certain warriors wish to steal land from him, and in the second stanza he sails north to claim his land from the

---

9   *Den norsk-islandske skjaldedigtning* (ed. Jónsson, IA.438–9, IB.407–8).
10 *Ibid.*, IA.440–44, IB.409–13. In my interpretation of st.10, I follow the *Morkinskinna* text of this poem, as printed in IA, rather than Finnur Jónsson's reconstruction in IB.

rebellious Egill. This internal success is matched by success in subjugating foreign lands: the 'four ancestral lands' already noted, and in stanza seventeen the fact that he won fifteen districts (in Sweden) with his sword. Again, kennings emphasise Magnús's power both in Norway and abroad, he is *Haða dróttinn* 'lord of the people of Hadeland', *Dana skelfir* 'terrifier of the Danes', and *Upplanda gramr* 'prince of Uppland'.

THE PANEGYRIC TRADITION

The foregoing analysis has already indicated some similarities between the three poems in praise of Magnús, and there are others. An exhaustive examination of the parallels between these poems must wait for another occasion, but here I will note some examples from those stanzas dealing with Magnús's first expedition to the British Isles. I will then go on to discuss parallels between these three poems and the work of other Norse poets associated with the British Isles in the eleventh and twelfth centuries.

In addition to the repetition of names, dictated by the content of the poems, and the shared fondness for a particular type of kenning describing Magnús, already mentioned, additional verbal echoes between the three poems are worthy of note. Both Þorkell (stanzas three and four) and Bjǫrn (stanza seven) call Magnús *allvaldr* (literally, 'all-ruler') at the height of his successful western expedition. Gísl's stanza describing the fall of Hugh echoes the vocabulary and assonances of Þorkell's stanza describing the same event (both quoted in full above).[11] In a half-stanza (stanza two) describing Magnús's journey west and introducing the stanza describing the battle, Þorkell calls the Norwegian king *hugprúðr* ('valiant-minded'), hinting at Hugh's name (and therefore his death) and ironically appropriating his nickname 'the Valiant' for Magnús:

Vestr lét varga nistir,	The valiant-minded feeder of
vann hilmir frið bannat,	wolves [warrior] quickened the
hrǫnn brutu hlýr en stinnu,	journey west, the leader was able
hugprúðr fǫru snúðat.	to prevent peace, the waves broke
	on the rigid prow.

The rhyme of *prúð-* 'valiant, splendid' and *snúð-* 'quick-' is also found in Bjǫrn's stanza 9a describing Hugh's death, while the adverb *prúðliga* (referring to Magnús's army) is used in Gísl's stanza thirteen (both cited above).[12]

Along with the other similarities in the work of these three poets, such verbal echoes suggest word-games played by poets composing for the same

---

11 Above, pp. 115–16.
12 Above, pp. 115–16.

patron in the same context, and indicate the kind of poetic milieu there must have been in Magnús's retinue. Gísl makes clear that he was a participant in Magnús's first western expedition, the other two do not. However, the fact that they were well acquainted with both war and poetry among Norse leaders active in the British Isles is indicated by the echoes of earlier skaldic poets in their work, particularly Arnórr jarlaskáld, poet of the earls of Orkney, of Haraldr harðráði and of Magnús the Good.[13]

Arnórr was one of the more prolific of Norse poets, although it is true that he was active in the eleventh century, the period from which a large proportion of surviving skaldic verse is preserved, and our perceptions may be distorted by the vagaries of preservation. It is also easier to trace the influence of a poet who is represented by many surviving verses, and harder to assess the significance of any such influence that has been noted. Nonetheless, such poetic links are important to an understanding of the development of skaldic verse and thus of its historical significance. Poets throughout the early Norse period knew and referred to the work of their predecessors and Arnórr seems to have been influential on the poets employed by Magnús berfœttr.

Stanza 16b in Arnórr's *Þorfinnsdrápa*, a panegyric on the earl of Orkney,[14] describes Þorfinnr's raiding in England thus:

Hyrr óx, hallir þurru,	Fire increased, buildings dimin-
herdrótt rak þar flótta,	ished, the war-band chased the
eim hratt, en laust ljóma	fleeing ones there, the enemy of
limdolgr, náar himni.	branches [fire] spewed smoke,
	and the glow reached nearer the
	sky.

This is echoed in both Bjǫrn's and Gísl's poems about Magnús, although in different contexts. Gísl's stanza five recounts Magnús's harrying of northern Norway:

Hyrr sveimaði,	Fire swirled, buildings dimin-
hallir þurru,	ished, the high flame crossed their
gekk hár logi	districts.
of herǫð þeira.	

Bjǫrn's stanza five shows Magnús harrying in the Hebrides:

Lék of Ljóðhús fíkjum	Throughout Lewis, the sorrow of
limsorg náar himni.	branches [fire] played lustily

---

13 On Arnórr, see Fidjestøl, 'Arnórr jarlaskáld'.
14 *Den norsk-islandske skjaldedigtning* (ed. Jónsson, IA.346–7, IB.319).

Judith Jesch

Vítt vas ferð á flótta   nearer the sky. Everywhere the
fús. Gaus eldr ór húsum.   troop was eager to flee. Fire
                                gushed from the houses.

In his memorial ode (*Erfidrápa*) on King Haraldr harðráði, Arnórr
describes (stanza twelve) the king's landing in England just before the
fateful battle of Stamford Bridge in 1066:[15]

Uppgǫngu bauð yngvi   The splendid prince, who never in
ítr með helming lítinn,   his life feared danger, suggested a
sás á sinni ævi   landing with a small troop.
sásk aldrigi háska.

The first two lines of this half-stanza are almost exactly reproduced in
Þorkell's stanza five:[16]

Uppgǫngu réð yngvi   The splendid prince decided on a
ítr með helming lítinn,   landing with a small troop, I think
áræði hykk áðan   Eysteinn's father then had confi-
Eysteins fǫður treystask.   dence in his courage.

These two stanzas by Arnórr are those which have had the clearest echoes
in the work of Magnús berfœttr's poets, but there are further examples. Thus
stanza 7b of *Þorfinnsdrápa* has left its mark on all three:[17]

Stall drapa, strengir gullu,   The prince's heart was not fright-
stál beit, en rann sveiti,   ened, (bow)strings called, steel bit
broddr fló, bifðusk oddar   and blood ran, (arrow)point flew,
bjartir, þengils hjarta.   bright (spear)points quivered.

We find the flying arrow-point (*broddr fló*) in stanza nine of Bjǫrn's poem,
and the bright spear-points (*oddar bjartir*) in stanza twelve of Gísl's poem,
both referring to the battle of Anglesey (and both cited above).[18] Stanza three
of Þorkell's poem (also cited above) has only isolated words echoing
Arnórr (*broddr, strengr, fló*),[19] but the listing of the different weapons and
their activities in battle in Þorkell's poem must also owe something to
Arnórr.[20]

15 *Ibid.*, IA.351, IB.324.
16 Arnórr also uses a similar construction in stanza 16 of his *Magnússdrápa* for Magnús
   the Good (*ibid.*, IA.342, IB.315).
17 *Ibid.*, IA.345, IB.317.
18 Above, pp. 115–16.
19 Above, pp. 115–16.
20 Other echoes include the collocation *frán egg* from Arnórr V,9 and VI,1 repeated in Gísl's
   stanza 17, the use of *siklingr* and *floti* in the same line in Arnórr II,9 and Gísl's stanza 3,
   and the echo of the first line of Arnórr II,12 in Bjǫrn's stanza 5.

124

Clearly there is a danger in making too much of such verbal echoes when we are dealing with a highly conventional form of poetry practised among a fairly restricted social group. While poets knew, and borrowed freely from, each others' work, they often made their own use of what they borrowed: there are plenty of examples where borrowed expressions are used in a wholly different context. Therefore it is significant, not only that our three poets borrowed from Arnórr, but also that both lender and borrowers were celebrating rulers who were based in, or frequently active in, different parts of the British Isles in the eleventh century. It is also relevant that Arnórr had a long-standing connection with Orkney, where his poetry may have been remembered more carefully than elsewhere. As well as celebrating two of the earls of Orkney, Arnórr's poetry for Haraldr harðráði had an Orcadian connection, for the last leg of Haraldr's journey to Stamford Bridge started in Orkney, where his wife waited for him and the remnants of his army returned after the battle. A century later, Rǫgnvaldr, earl of Orkney, was well known both as a poet and as one who had a scholarly interest in metrics. These facts suggest a lively interest in poetry in Norse Orkney, not all of it preserved. Chronologically, Magnús's poets come between Arnórr and Rǫgnvaldr, and we know that the king's expeditions to the west always began and ended in Orkney. Although it must remain an unprovable assertion, the evidence strongly suggests that Magnús berfœttr's poets consciously composed within a branch of the Norse poetic tradition that was associated with the British Isles in general, and was based in the flourishing cultural centre of Orkney from the early eleventh century. We can further test this assertion by seeing whether there are echoes from Bjǫrn's, Þorkell's and Gísl's poems in the work of later poets with Orcadian associations.

Ívarr Ingimundarson is listed in *Skáldatal* (a list of court poets) as one of the poets of Magnús berfœttr, although none of his work for this king survives. What does survive is a poem in praise of Magnús's son, Sigurðr jórsalafari.[21] According to the sagas, Sigurðr was left behind as a boy to rule Orkney during his father's first western expedition and only went back to Norway after Magnús's death on his second western expedition. Ívarr's poem has quite a number of reminiscences of Gísl's, but since they are largely of single words in different contexts, rather than of whole lines, or sequences of ideas, it is perhaps wiser not to make too much of them.[22]

As a ruler, Earl Rǫgnvaldr of Orkney might have expected to have poems composed in his honour but none survives. Instead, Rǫgnvaldr was an accomplished poet himself. He was particularly adept at the occasional stanza (*lausavísa*), and is also credited by some with introducing love poetry

---

[21] *Den norsk-islandske skjaldedigtning* (ed. Jónsson, IA.495–502, IB.467–75).
[22] Even more difficult to evaluate are the extensive verbal correspondences between the Eddic poem *Helgakviða Hundingsbana I* and Gísl's *Erfikvæði*, since any conclusions hinge on the date of the Eddic poem.

to the Norse world. In a typical stanza he interweaves his military prowess against the heathens of Spain with the praise of Ermingerðr, countess of Narbonne:[23]

Vǫn ák, út á Spáni	I expect a rendezvous with the
var skjótt rekinn flótti,	woman. Out in Spain, the fleeing
flýði margr af mœði	ones were quickly chased, many a
menlundr, konu fundar.	neck-ring-tree [man] fled from
	exhaustion.

The second line of this exactly reproduces the second line of Bjǫrn krepphendi's *Magnússdrápa*, while *mœði* occurs in stanza six of that poem, also in a context which mentions women (although in Bjǫrn's case, these are the Hebridean maidens whom the warrior causes to weep). As well as his *lausavísur*, Rǫgnvaldr is known for having composed, together with the Icelander Hallr Þórarinsson, the first Norse *clavis metrica*, known as *Háttalykill*.[24] In its surviving form, this poem contains forty-one pairs of stanzas composed to exemplify as many metres. Metrically, the poem is an amalgam of native traditions and continental influences, while the deeds of ancient Norse heroes and more recent Norwegian kings provide the excuse for the content of the poem. The two poets were schooled in both Latin book-learning and the skaldic tradition, and the poem is a tissue of echoes from earlier skaldic verse.[25] Thus four different stanzas echo stanza three of Þorkell hamarskáld's *Magnússdrápa* (describing the battle off Anglesey and cited above):[26] stanza 36b has the rhyme *alms . . . hjalma*, in close proximity to the word *hagl*, stanza 39b also has the word *almr*, with *hné ferð* in the previous line, while stanzas 38a and 40a echo the first line of Þorkell's stanza with, respectively, *dunðu dǫrr á brynjur* and *dunði bitr á brynjur/brandr*. The last line of 40a, . . . *hné drótt at velli*, has some similarity to line six in Þorkell's stanza. There may also be a metrical link: stanza 40a exemplifies a metre called *álagsháttr*, in which the even-numbered lines begin with a monosyllabic word which belongs, in sense, to the previous line, while the rest of the line is a self-contained clause.[27] Although Þorkell's stanza does not conform to this metre throughout, his lines 3–4 are a good example of it.[28] Since it is likely that *Háttalykill* as preserved today is

---

23 *Den norsk-islandske skjaldedigtning* (ed. Jónsson, IA.509, IB.483).
24 *Ibid.*, IA.512–28, IB.487–508. This text should be supplemented by Helgason and Holtsmark, *Háttalykill*.
25 Helgason and Holtsmark, *Háttalykill*, pp. 135–6.
26 Above, pp. 115–16.
27 See also Snorri Sturluson, *Háttatal* (ed. Faulkes, pp. 15–16).
28 *Álagsháttr* can be seen as an intensification of the form Snorri calls *hjástælt* (*ibid.*, pp. xxi, 10, 76; and Kuhn, *Dróttkvætt*, pp. 179–82) and it may be that Þorkell's stanza is better described thus. The same tendency to *hjástælt* can be found in Bjǫrn's stanzas (Fidjestøl, *Fyrstediktet*, p. 151).

incomplete, it is probably just an interesting coincidence that it ends with a stanza about Magnús berfœttr.

VIKING VERSE

Careful readers will have noticed that the foregoing discussion has been based on the assumption that the texts of Bjǫrn's, Þorkell's and Gísl's poems (not to mention those of the other poets mentioned), as found in Finnur Jónsson's edition of skaldic poetry, represent as nearly as possible the actual poems composed and performed orally by Magnús's poets around or soon after the year 1100. But can we assume that the Icelandic manuscripts of the thirteenth century or later (which form the basis of Finnur's edition) accurately record the oral compositions of a century or more earlier? Can we in fact use skaldic verse as a contemporary source for the Viking Age?

Unlike the anonymous Eddic poems, which record mythological, legendary and gnomic matter, and most of which survive in a manuscript anthology from the thirteenth century, the poems which are assigned to named poets and which we term 'skaldic' are rarely preserved for their own sake, but are recorded in a variety of prose contexts with a variety of functions. Thus we have the occasional verses which embellish the Sagas of Icelanders, many of which may not be as old as they pretend to be, or composed by the person named as their poet. More convincingly historical are the verses which form the backbone of the Kings' Sagas and which are frequently, though not always, cited as authorities for their accounts by the authors of these sagas. Finally, there are the verses cited as examples by Snorri Sturluson in his *Edda*, particularly the section called *Skáldskaparmál*, an exposition of poetic diction.

Embedded in these prose works, then, we have a vast corpus of verse in a variety of metres, but mainly *dróttkvætt*, purporting to be by a large number of poets, most of whom can be located in a particular chronological and historical context. If we take this chronology at face value, we have a corpus ranging in date from about A.D. 800 up to the time of the writing of the prose works in which it is preserved, i.e. from around 1200 onwards. (Skaldic verse continued to be composed in the thirteenth century and later, but such texts do not concern us here.) Such a corpus of poetry, composed and preserved in the oral tradition until it came to be written down, would, if correctly dated, be of unique value for studying early Scandinavia, for which our only contemporary written sources are runic inscriptions. Thus the arguments for assigning this poetry (or most of it) to the dates suggested by the attributions in the texts need a brief review. In particular, there are two main questions to consider: (1) are the attributions correct, and (2) if they are, how well do the written texts of the thirteenth century represent verses composed and transmitted orally, in some cases possibly over several centuries?

The answers to both of these questions presuppose a lot of work on the whole corpus of skaldic poetry which has hardly been done, and they must therefore be tentative. However, some points have been clarified, in at least a preliminary way. Thus, it is possible to make a distinction between verse that was thought to be historical by the historians and saga-authors of the thirteenth century, and verse which they did not treat as having historical authority, without necessarily implying that it was entirely fictional.[29] The basis for such a distinction lies partly in explicit statements by writers such as Snorri Sturluson on the historical value of old poems, and partly in the way such poems were actually used in their texts.[30] While it would be possible to contest the details of such a judgement, a generalisation that does have value as a starting point for the study of skaldic verse is that while some of the poems in the Sagas of Icelanders may be as old as they claim to be, they are unprovably so, and any historical study should concentrate on the skaldic verse in the Kings' Sagas and Snorri's *Edda*.[31]

Assuming, then, that enough of the attributions in the Kings' Sagas and Snorri's *Edda* are correct to validate generalisations about the corpus, how can we tell that the recorded versions give a fair impression of these originally oral compositions? Again, the answer is that we can never be sure, but it is very likely. Skaldic verse is characterised by complex metrical rules applied within a small poetic space: any changes to the text may violate one or another of these metrical rules. This does not mean that the text is immutably fixed, only that, as Snorri himself recognised, *kvæðin þykkja mér sízt ór staði færð, ef þau eru rétt kveðin ok skynsamliga upp tekin* ('the poems seem to me least likely to be corrupted [i.e. compared to other evidence, both oral and prose], as long as they are correctly composed and carefully interpreted').[32] While this is not a cast-iron guarantee, it does mean that our best chance of reconstructing Viking Age verse lies with skaldic verse rather than, for instance, Eddic verse with its looser structures.

Without denying the possibility that not all skaldic verses are what they seem, it is clear that they provide a useful, and surprisingly neglected, source for the study of the Viking Age, and beyond. It should also be remembered that the difficulties of the verse and its preservation are not evenly distributed. While it would be a brave scholar who tried to make statements about

29 See Einarsson, 'Role of verse'.
30 Snorri Sturluson, *Heimskringla* (ed. Aðalbjarnarson, I.7, II.422). For a study of different attitudes to historical authority, see my 'History'.
31 See in particular Fidjestøl, *Fyrstediktet* and 'New edition'; Foote, 'Wrecks' and 'Things'; Kuhn, *Dróttkvætt*, pp. 258–63; and my own 'Skaldic verse'.
32 Snorri Sturluson, *Heimskringla* (ed. Aðalbjarnarson, I.7; all translations from Old Norse prose texts are my own). Kuhn, *Dróttkvætt*, p. 253, also assumes that quite a lot of verse is quite well preserved.

the ninth, or even the tenth, century on the basis of verse purporting to be from that period, by the eleventh century the verse is copious and generally well-preserved. And while one might feel a general skepticism about how long poetry can be remembered unchanged in the oral tradition before it is fixed in writing, the need for such skepticism lessens as the purported date of composition nears that of the recording. Extant versions of poems from around 1100, such as those under consideration in this paper, are thus most likely to be fair representations of their originals.

EDITING VIKING VERSE

However, an essential prerequisite to the use of such poems as sources for the late Viking Age is an understanding of their textual transmission and therefore of the extent to which it is possible to reconstruct them from their recorded forms. While some small progress has been made in establishing a model for distinguishing the reliably ancient verse preserved in thirteenth-century Icelandic prose texts, there has been less progress in setting out the principles for reconstructing such verse from the available sources. Finnur Jónsson published a corpus in 1912–1915, with both diplomatic and edited texts of all known skaldic verse dated to the period 800–1400, organised chronologically by poet. Since many of the longer praise poems are pre-served in more or less dismembered form, as individual stanzas scattered among their prose contexts, Finnur also had to reconstruct these longer poems, assign unidentified stanzas to named poets and occasionally choose between poets where there were two or more attributions for a stanza. Thus, while the 'B' volumes of the corpus, containing Finnur's edited (and often emended) texts with Danish translations at the bottom of the page, are obviously artificial constructs, even the 'A' volumes, the diplomatic texts taken from the manuscripts, show heavy editorial selection and reconstruc-tion of poems and the work of individual poets.[33] In the 'A' volumes, Finnur chose a 'best text' for each stanza and provided variants from other manu-scripts and texts in the apparatus (though this is by no means complete, nor always consistent). Thus, any one of the longer poems in his edition can have been put together from individual stanzas preserved in a variety of texts and manuscripts. In the 'B' texts, Finnur does not always follow the 'best text' of his 'A' version, but appears to choose freely and eclectically from the variants, and to emend on occasion. Although his procedure is not spelled out anywhere, it is clear that he used metrical and stylistic criteria as well as following the presumed stemmatic relationships of the manu-scripts. The corpus is thus a curious combination of editorial approaches:

---

[33] For Kuhn's sharp criticism of both Finnur Jónsson and Kock, first published in 1934, see his *Kleine Schriften* I, pp. 439–46.

underlying the choice of 'best texts' is a set of assumptions about the manuscript relationships of the prose texts in which skaldic verse is preserved (Finnur was also an editor of several of these), but the reconstruction of individual poems and of the work of individual poets is an exercise in textual criticism that attempts to go back beyond these prose sources to the 'original' poetic compositions. It is exactly this relationship between prose context and verse source that is the key to the editing of skaldic verse and which needs much more discussion (not to mention theoretical underpinning).[34]

Many of Finnur's editorial decisions were criticised by Axel Kock in his monumental *Notationes norroenae*, but Kock's approach can best be described as *textimmanent*: any variant can be grist to Kock's mill as long as it fits in with his metrical and stylistic criteria. Kock's approach is fairly systematic, based on close knowledge of the whole corpus, but in the end his texts are even more idealised than Finnur's, and he accepts all of the latter's reconstructions of poems and identifications of poets despite his criticisms of the details of the edited texts.

Bjarne Fidjestøl has attempted a critical revaluation of Finnur's criteria for reconstructing the praise poems for kings and chieftains (what he calls 'fyrstedikt'),[35] based on specific statements in the prose texts which help identify the constituent stanzas of a poem, and the order of stanzas in the prose texts which can help reconstruct their order in the original poem. Fidjestøl's emphasis on the prose contexts means that his book is only the first stage in a revaluation of the corpus, and it concentrates on the poems as larger units rather than on the problems of reconstructing individual stanzas.

Russell Poole,[36] on the other hand, has approached the reconstruction of individual poems from internal criteria rather than from the external witness of the prose context. He identifies stylistic devices such as the use of the present tense, or concatenation, and uses them to group stanzas and to create, in some cases, previously unrecognised poems. However, without some methodological discussion about the appropriate methods for reconstructing skaldic poems independently of their prose contexts, there is the danger of a circular argument here.

Individual skaldic stanzas have also been edited as a part of the prose texts in which they are preserved. Here, one might think the question of reconstruction was of less significance, since the job of the editor is

34 The discussions in Fidjestøl *et al.* (edd.), *Tekstkritisk teori og praksis*, show a revival of interest in the theory of editing, but none of them addresses the particular problem of editing 'layered' texts, such as the Kings' Sagas containing skaldic verse which may have an independent textual history. Jón Helgason, 'Planer', assumed that the stemma of the prose text was the most important factor.
35 Fidjestøl, *Fyrstediktet*.
36 Poole, *Viking Poems*.

presumably to arrive at the text of the poem as included in the prose source, rather than at its hypothetical 'original'. And indeed, we find some editors try to avoid using variants from other text traditions in their reconstructions of the verses in their prose texts, but this is not always possible. So we find that they turn to metrical, grammatical, lexical, stylistic, or other criteria to reconstruct the verse texts, and such criteria may indicate the choice of a variant from another prose text containing the verse in question.

THE SAGA CONTEXTS

The purpose of this excursus on the rather arcane problems of editing skaldic verse has been to make two points: (1) that it is possible to reconstruct Viking Age sources from the mediaeval Icelandic texts which preserve them and, however, (2) that these sources can never be studied entirely apart from their mediaeval prose contexts. A third point would then follow, (3) that reference to the mediaeval prose sources alone neglects the important evidence provided by the Viking Age poetry. Thus, we must now consider the contexts in which this poetry was written down and preserved for the future.

While there is still no scholarly consensus about the details of the development of historical prose in the North, the general outlines are well known and have been made accessible in English,[37] so they do not need to be repeated here. It will suffice to identify (in a grossly oversimplified manner) the most important stages in the writing of Norwegian history: (1) in the twelfth century, synoptic histories of the kings of Norway were written in both Latin and Old Norse, in both Iceland and Norway; (2) interest in the first Scandinavian saint, King Óláfr, spurred the writing of individual royal biographies, some originally in Latin, but now surviving principally in vernacular sagas; (3) the preceding types of historical enquiry influenced the three great comprehensive histories of the kings of Norway of the early to mid-thirteenth century, the anonymous *Morkinskinna* and *Fagrskinna*, and Snorri Sturluson's *Heimskringla*; (4) in the fourteenth century, there was a period of consolidation when the great compilations like *Flateyjarbók* were produced, conflating previous versions of historical (and some fictional) sagas. Although the stages are distinct enough, it can be difficult to trace the development of the material through these stages. With all these texts covering roughly the same ground, their relationships are almost impossible to untangle, but it is clear that there were complex genetic relationships between most of these texts.[38] It is also very difficult in all this material to distinguish clearly between *manuscript* and *work*: many of the

---

[37] e.g. Turville-Petre, *Origins*; Andersson, 'Kings' Sagas' (with copious bibliography); and, succinctly, Whaley, 'Kings' Sagas'.

[38] Andersson, 'King's Sagas', attempts to explain this complex problem. See also Louis-

mediaeval manuscripts seem to be influenced by texts other than their immediate exemplar, and show a greater or lesser degree of scribal interference. Questions of production and audience are also relevant: while it is clear that the majority of historical writing was practised by Icelanders, they were equally clearly writing as much for a Norwegian as an Icelandic audience, and they may also have made use of Norwegian sources. What is clear, however, is that there is a gradual accretion of material: the earliest texts are fairly skimpy, whereas the compilers of a manuscript like *Flateyjarbók* aimed at all-inclusiveness. It is not always possible to identify the sources for this accretion of material, but it is likely that even in the early thirteenth century when Snorri was working on *Heimskringla*, material could come from the oral tradition (although this includes the possibility of material that had once been written being transmitted orally). Also, we must reckon with lost written sources, some of them perhaps in the form of notes, or *schedae*, rather than fully-fledged manuscript texts. It is really only possible to cut this Gordian knot by assuming a vast body of material, in both written and oral form, known widely and in many versions, which was realised in different ways in different texts at different times, with each new written text adding to the potential body of material that could influence future texts. While there is still some progress to be made from source studies, it is unlikely that we will ever be able to reconstruct the development of Norse history writing in full.

Although individual sources cannot always easily be pinpointed, it is possible to identify the types of sources used in the different stages. In particular, Snorri gives us quite a lot of information about his predecessors and models, both in the Prologue to *Heimskringla*, and with references to specific named texts (few of which can be identified with extant sagas) throughout it.[39] But even Snorri does not name works (such as the compilation we now know as *Morkinskinna*) which were evidently not only known to but heavily used by him. However, Snorri is quite clear about the significance of skaldic verse to his historical enterprise, and he shares with the authors of *Fagrskinna* and *Morkinskinna* the use, on an unprecedented scale, of skaldic verse as both authority and evidence for his narrative. Snorri's explicit theorising, in his Prologues to both *Heimskringla* and the separate *Óláfs saga helga*,[40] about the value of skaldic verse as evidence gives us an important clue to his attitude: in addition to his view that skaldic verse was reliable because it was resistant to corruption, as noted above,[41]

Jensen, *Kongesagastudier*, for a more detailed study of the manuscript, as well as textual, tradition.

[39] For a summary of Snorri's sources, see Whaley, *Heimskringla*, ch. 4.

[40] There is some doubt over how much of the prologue to the separate saga can be attributed to Snorri, but the *Heimskringla* prologue certainly reflects his historiographical views, see Sverrir Tómasson, *Formálar*, pp. 213–22, 374–83.

[41] Above, p. 126.

Snorri was also willing to take on trust the statements of skaldic poems about the 'journeys and battles' of 'chieftains and their sons', because of their public nature: 'no one would dare to tell to his [i.e. the chieftain's] face those deeds which everyone who was listening, as well as he himself, would know to be nonsense and lies'.[42] He also refers to 'previous scholars', who would, 'when they wanted to know the truth, take for true the words of those men who had themselves seen the events, and were nearby at the time', and emphasises the particular reliability of poets who had participated in battles.[43] This desire to reconstruct the truth from the available evidence, however, affects the ways in which skaldic verse is presented in all these three works, though in none more so than *Heimskringla*. Longer poems are dismembered and individual stanzas made to work at different points in the narrative, and the stanzas themselves are subject to interpretation and misinterpretation.[44] Thus, we must be aware that we are reading skaldic stanzas in a particular way, influenced by the interpretations of the saga-writers. But this can rub the other way, too, at least where there are alternative versions for comparison. Thus, as we have seen, Bjarne Fidjestøl was able to argue that Snorri's ordering of Bjǫrn krepphendi's stanzas was a result of his own interpretation of events,[45] and to suggest an order closer to the original, based in part on comparisons with *Morkinskinna*.

MAGNÚS BERFŒTTR IN THE SAGAS

This effect, whereby we tend to read skaldic verse through the eyes of the prose writers of the thirteenth century, coupled with the fact that the informational content of most skaldic verse is not very great, makes it difficult to disentangle what might be genuine (and contemporary) information about Magnús's expeditions to the west from the historical and interpretive framework of thirteenth-century authors such as Snorri, and many scholars do not make the attempt.[46] A more positive approach is to use the interpretations of saga-writers such as Snorri to our advantage. Although they, too, approached their sources as so much historical chaff to be winnowed, they were nevertheless closer to their skaldic sources than we are, they may have known poems in their entirety, before they were dismembered to lend authority to prose narratives, they may have known further stanzas that are now lost, and they may have had access to additional information associated with the poems but which is not

---

[42] Snorri Sturluson, *Heimskringla*, Prologus (ed. Aðalbjarnarson, I.5).
[43] *Ibid.*, II.422.
[44] For some examples of Snorri's misinterpretations of skaldic stanzas, see von See, 'Skaldenstrophe'.
[45] Fidjestøl, *Fyrstediktet*, pp. 150–2.
[46] e.g. Power, 'Magnus Barelegs'.

actually incorporated into the poetic text itself.[47] Earlier in this essay, I tried to look beyond the meagre information about Magnús's expedition found in the poems of Bjǫrn, Þorkell and Gísl, to elucidate the social and cultural structures within which the poems were composed and transmitted, and I did this by relating the poems to each other and to the rest of the skaldic corpus. Similarly, it should be possible to look in the prose contexts of the preserved poems for such thought-structures that probably came from, and certainly illuminate, the historical traditions (including of course the skaldic poems) behind the prose texts. In this way, we can come to a better understanding of both complexes of Norse material in the *Historia Gruffud vab Kenan*, the genealogy from Haraldr hárfagri and Magnús berfœttr's intervention in Anglesey. I hope, in fact, to show that these two historical traditions are linked.

The Norse prose accounts of the life and death of Magnús berfœttr differ, often quite considerably, in ways that can be explained in terms of contemporary or national concerns, and there is little point in rehearsing such differences of approach yet again.[48] More interesting (and more relevant to this discussion) is a similarity between the texts which has, as far as I can tell, so far gone unremarked. This is the explicit comparison and association of Magnús with his grandfather, Haraldr harðráði ('the severe'). Despite their differences in some other respects, all the Norse prose histories mention this link.

Two of the earliest texts compare Magnús with his grandfather in character, while emphasising their dissimilarity to the intermediate generation (Haraldr's son and Magnús's father, Óláfr kyrri). Thus, Theodoricus says:[49]

Hic Magnus patri multum dissimilis moribus, avo suo Haraldo magis fuit conformis.

[This Magnús was very unlike his father in character, and resembled more his grandfather Haraldr.][50]

The closely related Norwegian synoptic history, *Ágrip*,[51] says that he was

maðr herskár ok rǫskr ok starfsamr ok líkari í ǫllu Haraldi fǫðurfeðr sínum í skaplyndi heldur en fǫður sínum. Allir váru þeir miklir menn ok fríðir sýnum.

---

47 Without necessarily accepting Beyschlag's concept of 'Begleitprosa', I would agree with Fidjestøl ('Sogekvæde', p. 61) that skaldic verses must have been accompanied by some kind of information which located them in history.
48 See Power, 'Magnus Barelegs'.
49 Theodoricus, *De Antiquitate Regum Norwagiensium*, XXX (ed. Storm, p. 59).
50 Warm thanks are due to David and Ian McDougall for allowing me to quote from their forthcoming translation of Theodoricus.
51 *Ágrip*, XLVII (ed. Einarsson, p. 45).

[a man martial, vigorous and industrious, and altogether more like his father's father Haraldr in his character than his father. They were all tall men and handsome to look at.]

The physical similarity between all three generations is expanded on by *Morkinskinna*:[52]

Hann var manna fríðastr sjónum, þegar frá var tekinn Óláfr faðir hans, ok manna hæstr var hann. Var mark gọrt um þessa þrjá langfeðga, Harald konung, Óláf konung ok Magnús konung berfœtt, á Maríukyrkju norðr í Kaupangi, þeiri er Haraldr konungr lét gera. Var klappaðr kross á steinveggnum við dyrrnar þar er Haraldi konungi var hœgt at kyssa á, ok annarr Óláfi konungi, þriði Magnúsi konungi, ok var sá neðarst mjọk miklu, ok allra jafnlangt í milli. Magnús konungr var manna kurteisastr.

[He was the best-looking man, apart from his father Óláfr, and he was the tallest of men. A mark was made for these three generations (King Haraldr, King Óláfr and King Magnús berfœttr) on St Mary's church, in the north in Trondheim, which King Haraldr had had built. A cross was cut into the stone wall by the door where King Haraldr was able to kiss it, and another for King Óláfr, and a third for King Magnús, but this last one was by far the lowest down, and there was an equal distance between each of them. King Magnús was the courtliest of men.]

Fagrskinna has an almost identical text,[53] with the exception of the reference to Óláfr in the first sentence. In *Heimskringla*, Snorri remarks on the similarities in both character and physique, but at separate points in the text (in neither case does he follow his predecessors in doing this at the obvious point, when Magnús is introduced). In chapter seven, the following description comes just after Magnús has secured his kingdom by putting down the rebellion in northern Norway, and just before his first western expedition:[54]

Hann var maðr rọskr ok herskár ok starfsamr ok líkari í ọllu Haraldi, fọðurfọður sínum, í skaplyndi heldr en feðr sínum.

[He was a man vigorous and martial and industrious, and altogether more like his father's father Haraldr in character than his father.]

In chapter sixteen, in the period between his two expeditions, Snorri repeats the anecdote about the three men's height:[55]

Hann var manna hæstr. Mark var gọrt um hæð hans á Maríukirkju í Kaupangi, þeiri

---

52 *Morkinskinna* (ed. Jónsson, p. 291). I cite this text in normalised form.
53 *Fagrskinna*, LXXIX (ed. Einarsson, pp. 301–2). This text is sometimes called *Nóregs konunga tal*, but should not be confused with the poem of the same name discussed below, pp. 138–9.
54 Snorri Sturluson, *Heimskringla* (ed. Aðalbjarnarson, III.218).
55 *Ibid.*, III.230.

er Haraldr konungr hafði gera látit. Þar á norðrdurum váru klappaðir á steinveg-
ginum krossar þrír, einn Haralds hæð, annarr Óláfs hæð, þriði Magnúss hæð, ok þat
markat, hvar þeim var hœgst kyssa á, ofast Haralds kross, en lægst Magnúss kross,
en Óláfs mark jafnnær báðum.

[He was the tallest of men. A mark was made of his height on St Mary's church in
Trondheim, which King Haraldr had caused to be built. There by the north door
three crosses were cut into the stone wall, one at Haraldr's height, one at Óláfr's
height, the third at Magnús's height, thereby marking where each of them was able
to kiss, Haraldr's cross highest, Magnús's lowest, and Óláfr's equidistant between
them.]

The comparison between Magnús and his grandfather can go beyond the
merely physical. As was well known, Haraldr died in England at the battle
of Stamford Bridge, and some writers saw a parallel with his grandson's
death in Ireland nearly forty years later. Theodoricus follows his explicit
comparison of the two men with the following comment:

Et quia paulo superius fecimus mentionem, eundem Haraldum de equo corruisse et
in illo casu mortem ejus præfiguratam fuisse . . .

[And since I mentioned a little earlier that this same Haraldr had tumbled from his
horse and that his death was prefigured in that fall . . .]

which anticipates his comparison of their deaths in chapter thirty-two, when
describing Magnús's death in Ireland:[56]

incautius exercitum ducere coepit, eodem modo deceptus, quo et avus ejus Haraldus
in Anglia.

[he began to lead his army with less caution, and fell into the same trap as his
grandfather Haraldr in England.][57]

Ágrip makes the same point about Irish treachery:[58]

Dirfðisk hann af því ok gerðisk síðan óvarari, með því at í fyrstu gekk hónum með
vildum sem Haraldi fǫðurfeðr hans, er hann fell á Englandi, drógu hann til lífláts
ok in sǫmu svík . . .

[He grew bold from that and then became less cautious, in that at first things went
in his favour, as for his father's father Haraldr, when he fell in England, and the
same treachery drew him to death . . .]

Morkinskinna puts the accusation of treachery into the mouth of one of

---

56 Theodoricus, *De Antiquitate Regum Norwagiensium*, XXX and XXXII (ed. Storm, pp.
   59, 63).
57 See note 50.
58 *Ágrip*, L (ed. Einarsson, p. 46).

Magnús's followers, replying to the king's speech of encouragement before his final battle:[59]

'Er land þetta fjǫlmennt en fólkit svíkalt . . . Fór svá um frænda yðvarn Harald konung at fyrst var honum allt upp gefit í Englandi þar sem hann kom við, en þó lauk svá at hann létsk þar sjálfr.'

['This country is populous and the people treacherous . . . It happened to your kinsman King Haraldr that at first everywhere he came to in England submitted to him, yet it ended with his own death there.']

Neither *Heimskringla* nor *Fagrskinna* make these accusations of treachery, nor do they use Magnús's death to draw comparisons with Haraldr.

The connection between their expeditions to the west is made in a slightly different way in *Orkneyinga saga*, which has Hákon Pálsson, the earl of Orkney, trying to use King Magnús to help him regain power there. The saga recounts his argument in indirect speech as follows:[60]

segir ok, ef hann fengi ríki í Suðreyjum, at þaðan væri hœgt at herja á Írland ok Skotland, ok ef hann kœmi undir sik Vestrlǫndum, at þaðan væri gott at eflask með styrk Norðmanna á móti Englismǫnnum

[he also said that if he got power in the Hebrides, then it would be possible to harry Ireland and Scotland from there, and if he subjugated the western parts of the British Isles, it would be easy to raise troops from there to join the Norwegian force in attacking the English]

and then breaks into direct speech for the punchline:

'ok hefna svá Haralds Sigurðarsonar, fǫðurfǫður þíns'.

[and thus avenge Haraldr Sigurðarson, your father's father'.]

This speech convinces Magnús, although he disconcerts Hákon somewhat by pointing out that he will also be making a claim on his lands in Orkney. It is also of interest that Hákon begins his speech by referring Magnús to the deeds of an even earlier king of Norway:[61]

---

59 *Morkinskinna* (ed. Jónsson, p. 333).
60 *Orkneyinga saga*, XXXVIII (ed. Guðmundsson, pp. 93–4).
61 *Ibid.* This harks back to *Orkneyinga saga* IV (ed. Guðmundsson, pp. 7–8) which tells how Haraldr hárfagri *lagði undir sik Hjaltland ok Orkneyjar ok Suðreyjar; hann fór allt vestr í Mǫn ok eyddi Manarbyggðina. Hann átti þar margar orrostur ok eignaðisk lǫnd svá langt vestr, at engi Nóregskonungr hefir lengra síðan* ('subjugated Shetland and Orkney and the Hebrides; he went all the way west to Man and devastated the settlements of Man. He had many battles there and appropriated land further west than any Norwegian king since').

þat væri hǫfðingsbragð at hafa leiðangr úti ok herja vestr um haf ok leggja undir sik Eyjar, sem gerði Haraldr inn hárfagri . . .

[it would be a chieftainly deed to take out the levy and harry across the sea in the west, and subjugate the islands, as did Haraldr hárfagri . . .]

but to this point I shall return in a moment.

GENEALOGICAL CONCERNS

Although each text interprets it in a slightly different way, they are all clearly drawing on a historical tradition which makes a link between Magnús and his grandfather Haraldr. Whether this link is expressed in terms of their character, appearance or death, each individual interpretation of this tradition is less important than the fact that the link is made. Snorri, as usual, takes the greatest liberties with his sources and moves the passages linking Magnús and Haraldr away from their natural place(s), either at the introduction (i.e. birth) of Magnús, or at his death, and places them elsewhere in the text for effect. He has the height anecdote just before Magnús's fatal expedition to Ireland, thus contriving to suggest a comparison between the two men's deaths, without having to make this explicit as Theodoricus does.

The important point that emerges from all of the texts is the linking of the two men in a dynastic succession. Similarity of appearance and character guarantees a genetic link, which is strengthened by the emphasis on the intermediate position of Óláfr in the height anecdote. The genealogical link is also important to the *Orkneyinga saga* version, with its emphasis on revenge, primarily the prerogative of direct male descendants. This emphasis on Magnús's link with Haraldr can be traced back beyond the saga texts and is at least as old as Gísl Illugason's poem. In this he is twice called *Haralds frændi* 'Haraldr's kinsman', in stanza eleven, the first of the three Anglesey stanzas, and in the concluding stanza twenty. Some genealogical interest is found in all three poems: in stanza three (the refrain?) of Bjǫrn's poem, Magnús is called *Óleifs mǫgr* 'son of Óláfr', and he is mentioned several times as a father himself, of Sigurðr (Gísl, stanza nineteen) and of Eysteinn (Þorkell, stanza five; Gísl, stanza twenty). As far as we know, there was never any doubt as to the parentage of Magnús. Admittedly his mother was a concubine (according to the sagas), but there seems to have been no suggestion that he was not the son of Óláfr and the grandson of Haraldr. So why this obsession with lineage? And what possible relevance can these dynastic concerns have to the Irish Sea region in the time of Gruffudd ap Cynan? The *Orkneyinga saga* link with Haraldr hárfagri provides a clue: the Norse texts suggest that it is not accidental that the two Norwegian kings mentioned in the *Historia Gruffud vab Kenan* are Haraldr hárfagri and

Magnús berfœttr, and the link between them is the other Haraldr, called *harðráði*, who died at Stamford Bridge in 1066.[62]

THE TWO HARALDS IN THE NORSE TRADITION

It is a commonplace in both mediaeval and modern histories that the Norwegian kingdom was unified and the royal dynasty founded by Haraldr hárfagri (*ob*. 933/945), and that all subsequent kings were descended from him, regarding Norway as their *óðal*, their hereditary possession. The development of the Norwegian monarchy within this framework is a prominent theme in *Heimskringla*, and modern historians have naturally taken this scheme over from their mediaeval predecessors, arguing for its importance as a controlling idea for the monarchy itself, if not as a fact. Recently, however, Claus Krag has convincingly argued that this overly-systematic interpretation of Norwegian history is largely a later construct.[63] There are two points that are of relevance to us here: (1) how could the Norwegian dynasty be linked genealogically to Haraldr hárfagri? and (2) when did this happen?

As Krag points out, there is a clear break in the line of descent from Haraldr Hálfdanarson hárfagri at the time of his namesake, Haraldr Sigurðarson harðráði. Contemporary evidence (from skaldic verse, but also from a Byzantine source) suggests that Haraldr harðráði's main claim to the Norwegian throne was in respect of his status as half-brother to St Óláfr.[64] They shared a mother, so Haraldr could hardly be in the same male line of descent from the ancient kings of Norway as Óláfr. It is true that in the sagas Haraldr's father Sigurðr is given a genealogy that eventually traces him back to Haraldr hárfagri, but as the crucial link is through the colourful Lapp girl Snæfríðr, this has all the appearance of being spurious, an attempt by the mediaeval historians of Norway to create a dynasty.

Thus, it would be fairer to see St Óláfr as the true founder of the Norwegian dynasty that was on the throne in the thirteenth century when Snorri was writing. For his half-brother Haraldr, this kinship was sufficient grounds for a claim on the throne, especially as Óláfr's son Magnús the Good had died without a son. And as Haraldr's nickname (*harðráði* = 'the

---

62 The two Haralds, Hálfdanarson and Sigurðarson, have been known to generations of English-language historians as Harald 'Fairhair' and Harald 'Hardrada' respectively. As the former epithet is a misleading translation and the latter a bastard Anglicisation of the original epithet in an oblique case, I prefer to keep to the Old Norse terms. Neither is easy to translate, but I would recommend that historians who wish to do so use 'the Finehaired' and 'the Severe'.

63 Krag, 'Norge som odel'.

64 See also Adam of Bremen, *Gesta Hammaburgensis Ecclesiae Pontificum*, III.xiii (ed. Trillmich, p. 340).

Severe') suggests, he was a forceful enough ruler not to need too much genealogical underpinning. However, at some point after his reign, the genealogies were tidied up, and Haraldr harðráði and all the other Norwegian kings were presented as the descendants of Haraldr hárfagri. Krag traces this process to the 'learned historians' of Iceland (and Norway) in the twelfth and thirteenth centuries.[65] But an outside view, from the British Isles, may also shed some light on the question.[66]

It is well known that insular historians could not tell their Haralds apart: they seem to have been generally acquainted with Haraldr harðráði because of his exploits in England in 1066, but for some unaccountable reason kept calling him something that is recognisably a version of the Norse epithet *hárfagri*. Haraldr hárfagri's connections with the British Isles remain dubious at best,[67] and even if they were genuine, it is unlikely that he was still remembered in the British Isles in the eleventh and twelfth centuries. Thus the most likely explanation for this insular confusion is that it happened at a time when there was genealogical and historical activity linking the two Haralds.[68] Exactly how an awareness of this was picked up by the Anglo-Norman writers I must leave for others to work out, but I think it is possible to clarify the Norse end of this process. The linking of the two Haralds in *Orkneyinga saga* suggests Orkney as a point where Norse historical traditions could cross over into insular ones.[69]

One of the earliest Norse historians whose name we know, but none of whose work survives, was the Icelander, Sæmundr fróði ('the Learned', 1056–1133), famous for his researches into the history of the kings of Norway. We can get some idea of the scope of his work, however, from the *Nóregs konungatal*,[70] a poem composed around 1190 in honour of the Icelandic chieftain Jón Loptsson (1124–1197), which enumerates the kings of Norway starting with Haraldr hárfagri's father, Hálfdan the Black, and ending with Sverrir (ruled 1184–1202). The king who receives most emphasis is Magnús berfœttr, significant because his illegitimate daughter Þóra was the mother of Jón, who was also a grandson of Sæmundr. This connection with Sæmundr suggest that the anonymous poet made use of

[65] For further detail, see Stefán Karlsson, 'Ættbogi', pp. 697–8.
[66] Norse specialists tend to assume the correctness of the Norse traditions and thus, either that Haraldr Sigurðarson 'inherited his nickname from his illustrious ancestor' (Turville-Petre, *Haraldr the Hard-Ruler*, p. 3), or that the nickname is erroneously attached to him in 'English and French accounts' (Whaley, 'Nicknames', p. 122).
[67] Sawyer, 'Harald Fairhair'.
[68] Sawyer, *ibid.*, also links the saga tradition about the first Harald's expeditions to the British Isles with Magnús Barelegs' expeditions.
[69] The significance of Orkney as a channel for Norse-Celtic contact was pointed out by Michael Chesnutt in 1968 ('An unsolved problem', esp. p. 129), and I tried to explore Orkney's role as an intermediary between Norse and English culture in 'England and *Orkneyinga saga*', but much work could still be done along these lines.
[70] *Den norsk-islandske skjaldedigtning* (ed. Jónsson, IA.579–90, IB.575–90).

Sæmundr's work on the Norwegian kings and, indeed, he is referred to in stanza forty:

Nú hefk talt	Now I have enumerated ten land-
tíu landreka,	rulers, of whom each was [de-
þás hverr vas	scended] from Haraldr; I
frá Haraldi;	recounted their lives just as
intak svá	Sæmundr the Learned said.
ævi þeira	
sem Sæmundr	
sagði enn fróði.	

This is usually taken to indicate that Sæmundr's history ended at this point (the previous stanza describes the funeral of Magnús the Good, who died in 1047). The clear break in the poem is indicated not just by the source reference, and the intervention of the narrative voice, but by a brief 'flash-back' in stanza forty-two, before the poet continues the account of the lives of the kings:

Þat's mér sagt,	It has been said to me that there
at Sigurðr hrísi	was once a son of Haraldr called
Haralds sonr	Sigurðr hrísi; Halfdan was the
héti forðum;	heir of Hrísi, and Sigurðr sýrr the
vas Halfdan	son of Halfdan.
Hrísa arfi,	
en Sigurðr sýrr	
sonr Halfdanar.	

Sigurðr sýrr was of course the father of Haraldr harðráði, and the stanza neatly links the preceding reference to Haraldr hárfagri as the ancestor of Norwegian kings to the following stanza which continues the enumeration of kings with Haraldr harðráði.[71] The dynastic perspective returns in stanza seventy-two, which makes the contemporary king Sverrir the ruler of 'all that realm which has been owned by the descendants of Haraldr son of Halfdan'. The remaining eleven stanzas detail the descent of the Oddaverjar ('the people from Oddi', the farm owned by both Sæmundr and Jón) from Magnús berfœttr.

Nóregs konungatal shows the kind of historical activity practised in the wake of Sæmundr at one of Iceland's main cultural centres, Oddi, where Snorri Sturluson spent his early years under the aegis of Jón Loptsson. As the home of a family which had close connections with Orkney, Oddi provided the link whereby Orcadian historical traditions, such as those which formed the basis of *Orkneyinga saga*, found their way into Icelandic

---

[71] We find the same basic genealogy in the work of Sæmundr's slightly younger contemporary, Ari fróði Þorgilsson: *Íslendingabók*, IX (ed. Benediktsson, p. 20).

literature.[72] The impulses probably went in both directions: we have already seen how Rǫgnvaldr cooperated with the Icelander Hallr Þórarinsson in composing *Háttalykill* in the middle of the twelfth century. And *Háttalykill* shows that historical research was not confined to Iceland, for it too is an enumeration of kings. The emphasis is slightly different, though, for *Háttalykill* begins with a collection of legendary kings from well before the 'historical' time of Haraldr hárfagri (as Snorri was also to do in *Heimskringla*). Haraldr hárfagri is introduced in stanza thirty, and the incomplete poem ends with Magnús berfœttr in stanza forty-one.

Háttalykill shows how historical research went hand in hand with an interest in old poetry,[73] and that both types of activity happened in Orkney. The Oddi connection ensured that there was cross-fertilisation between these activities in Orkney and in Iceland. *Nóregs konungatal* shows that one of the aims of historical research in the twelfth century was to link Haraldr harðráði with the main line of the Norwegian dynasty, descended from Haraldr hárfagri. That Magnús berfœttr modelled himself on his grandfather, also an accomplished warrior who raided in the west, is suggested both by the fact that his skalds echoed the work of Haraldr's skald Arnórr, and by the references in Gísl's poem to Magnús as *Haralds frœndi*. The strong link between Magnús and Haraldr harðráði,[74] made by the historians of the twelfth century, got entangled with the contemporary efforts to link *harðráði* with *hárfagri*.

However the Norse material alone will not account for the confusion of the two Haralds in insular historiography. The apparently earliest reference to Haraldr harðráði Sigurðarson as *Hárfagera* occurs in MS. D of the Anglo-Saxon Chronicle, in the annal for 1066. The date of this reference is crucial (see below), but the history of D is complex and the individual sections difficult to date.[75]

John of Worcester also calls Harald of Norway *Harvagra* in a passage to do with the events of 1066 in which he seems to be following a text most like MS. C of the Chronicle.[76] He also used this cognomen on two other occasions, in the annals for 1048 and 1098.[77] The former reference is clearly derived from an account like that of MS. D of the Chronicle (which tells us

---

[72] Sveinsson, *Sagnaritun*.
[73] Fidjestøl, 'Sogekvæde', p. 63, uses *Háttalykill* as his main example of a genre of 'historical skaldic poetry' which characterised the twelfth century, and which represents one aspect of the emergence of a historical consciousness in that century.
[74] The strength of this link is reflected in the confusion of Charles, *Old Norse Relations*, pp. 48, 72, who calls 'Magnus Barefoot' the 'son of Harald Hardrada', no doubt confusing him with Haraldr's son Magnús, who ruled Norway while his father was in England, and who briefly shared the kingdom with his brother Óláfr after their father's death.
[75] See Whitelock, *Peterborough Chronicle*, pp. 28–32.
[76] *Florentii Wigorniensis monachi chronicon ex chronicis* (ed. Thorpe, I.226).
[77] *Ibid.*, I.200, II.42.

that Harald was a paternal uncle of Magnus), expanding this by telling that Harald was the son of Sigurd and the sister's son of St Olaf.[78] The genealogical bent is continued in the account of the events of 1098, where John tells us that Magnus Barelegs was the son of Olaf, son of *Haroldi harvagri*. Orderic Vitalis, in referring to the events of 1066,[79] also calls Harald *Harafagh*.

Both John of Worcester and Orderic show that Haraldr was thought to be called 'hárfagri' in the early twelfth century.[80] MS. D of the Anglo-Saxon Chronicle may suggest that he was already known by this name at the time of his death, or very soon after. However, if David Dumville is right 'that D's annals for the period 1023–56, and again for 1065–6, seem little more than a conflation, of the texts represented to us by C and E, made after, perhaps well after, the Conquest',[81] then this suggestion loses much of its force. Thus we may not wish to build too much on the evidence of MS. D, although it will probably still remain as the earliest evidence of the cognomen *hárfagri* applied to Haraldr Sigurðarson.

At this point, we should return to the testimony of skaldic verse, where it is noteworthy that there are no indubitably early instances of *hárfagri* applied to the first Haraldr (Hálfdanarson). Characteristically, the epithet is used of him in both *Háttalykill* and *Nóregs konungatal*, products as we have seen of twelfth-century historiography. It is also used of him in a stanza attributed to a female poet, Jórunn.[82] Fidjestøl has argued that her verses are not contemporary comments on the events they describe, but a historical poem based on some earlier version of those events.[83] The poem is thus extremely difficult to date, and Fidjestøl contents himself with noting that this genre of historical poetry is not otherwise attested before about 1100. The fourth reference to the first Haraldr as *hárfagri* in skaldic verse is in a variant to the text of Þorbjǫrn hornklofi's *Haraldskvæði*, a praise poem in

---

[78] It is interesting that John calls Haraldr's father *rex Norreganorum*, and I think the only other insular source to do so is the late and (for these purposes) derivative *Cronica Regum Mannie & Insularum* (ed. Broderick, f. 32r). This may also reflect genealogical activities to legitimate Haraldr's ancestry.

[79] *Ecclesiastical History* III (ed. Chibnall, II.142). There may be a reminiscence of his Norwegian nickname when, later in the same passage (*ibid.*, II.144) Harald is called *tirannus*. According to Chibnall, I.46, this section of the *History* was written between 1114 and 1124.

[80] It should be noted that Adam of Bremen, *Gesta Hammaburgensis*, III.xvii (ed. Trillmich, p. 346), writing not later than 1075, does not call Haraldr Sigurðarson anything like *hárfagri*, although he does reflect the Scandinavian tradition in saying that he *crudelitate sua omnes tyrannorum excessit furores*. Earle and Plummer, *Two of the Saxon Chronicles*, II.256, give a list of the texts which call Haraldr Sigurðarson some version of *hárfagri*.

[81] Dumville, 'Annalistic writing', p. 33. Dumville favours the period 1080–1100 for this conflation.

[82] *Den norsk-islandske skjaldedigtning* (ed. Jónsson, IA.60, IB.53).

[83] Fidjestøl, *Fyrstediktet*, pp. 180–1.

eddic style. The reconstruction of this poem is a complex business,[84] and the term *hárfagri* occurs in a stanza that is preserved only in *Fagrskinna*, and in only one of the two main manuscripts of that text. Some editors dismiss the reading *hárfagra* in this stanza, preferring the variant *afarauðga* ('exceedingly wealthy') which improves the metre.[85] Thus neither Jórunn nor Þorbjǫrn is very convincing as an early reference, and it would take some special pleading to argue that the cognomen *hárfagri* was indubitably attached to the first Haraldr before about 1100.

The Norse evidence could thus be consistent with either of two explanations: (1) that *hárfagri* was originally the cognomen of Haraldr Sigurðarson and that it was transferred to Haraldr Hálfdanarson at the time when historical research was establishing the latter as the ancestor of the former or (2) that *hárfagri* was always the cognomen of Haraldr Hálfdanarson, but was mistakenly transferred to Haraldr Sigurðarson in insular sources, influenced by the historical research attempting to establish the former as the ancestor of the latter. Whichever of these explanations might be correct, and I myself incline to (1), the conclusion to be drawn from them is the same: at some point between the death of Haraldr Sigurðarson in 1066 and the early twelfth century, his genealogy was a matter of interest in the British Isles as well as in Scandinavia.

NORSE TRADITIONS IN THE HISTORIA GRUFFUD VAB KENAN

This scenario could explain the references to *Harfagyr* in the *Historia*.[86] Van Hamel suggested long ago that *Alyn* in the *Historia* should be identified with St Óláfr.[87] This identification, though not without its problems, suggests a way of linking the *Historia* to the Norse texts without having to assume a long oral tradition among the vikings of Ireland, remembering the exploits of Haraldr hárfagri in the ninth century. Van Hamel does not make the connection between Haraldr hárfagri and Haraldr harðráði, and the ambiguities of the text allow him to conclude that 'Alyn was not Harald's brother but his father's'.[88] We do not need to follow him in this, and a case can be made for *Harald Harfagyr* and *Alyn* being Haraldr harðráði and his half-brother St Óláfr respectively. As Van Hamel pointed out, *Alyn*'s sanctity and manner of death correspond with those of St Óláfr, and the name of his

---

[84] Helgason (ed.), *Skjaldevers*, pp. 10–15.
[85] E.g. Jónsson (ed.), *Den norsk-islandske skjaldedigtning* IB.22, and Einarsson (ed.), *Ágrip ... Fagrskinna*, p. 59; Helgason (ed.), *Skjaldevers*, p. 15 retains the reading *hárfagra*.
[86] Jones, *The History*, pp. 104, 106; Evans, *Historia*, pp. 2, 3; Evans, *A Mediaeval Prince*, pp. 55, 56.
[87] Van Hamel, 'Norse history', p. 341.
[88] *Ibid.*, p. 337.

slayer, *Thur*, can be equated with St Óláfr's killer (and witness to his first miracle) in the Norse tradition, Þórir hundr.[89]

The passage introducing the story of Alyn's death begins by saying that *Harald Harfagyr* and his two brothers were the sons of the king of *Llychlyn* (Norway?), but this immediately follows a reference to a king *Harfagyr*, son of the king of Denmark (*Denmarc*).[90] The different ways of referring to *Harfagyr*, and the different countries his father was supposed to have ruled, suggest (to me at least) the meshing of two different sources at this point. In the light of what has been said above, I would like to suggest the possibility that this is a somewhat garbled account of the (half-)brothers Haraldr harðráði (here called *hárfagri* as in all insular sources) and St Óláfr, embedded within a historian's reconstruction of the first Haraldr hárfagri's viking voyages to western parts of the British Isles, of the type found in Norse works.[91] Thus, as I discuss below, Snorri attempted a similar reconstruction of Haraldr hárfagri's western raids in chapter twenty-two of the latter's saga,[92] and he, too, goes on to describe Gǫngu-Hrólfr (i.e. Rollo) and his settlement in Normandy almost immediately afterwards. Like the author of the *Historia*, Snorri thought that Rollo was a Norwegian, not a Dane, but not that he was the brother of Haraldr hárfagri. And Snorri makes the same point about Normandy being so called because it was populated by Norwegians.[93]

In the extant Norse historical tradition, Snorri and *Orkneyinga saga* (an earlier version of which he used as a source) are the only texts to refer to the first Haraldr hárfagri's raids in the west. If, with Sawyer, we would like to speculate that this theme became important in the context of attempts to legitimate Magnús's activities in the British Isles by reference to similar activities on the part of his ancestor, the first Haraldr, then Orkney is as good a place as any for the location of such historical research, as has already been outlined above. In fact, it is possible to speculate in more detail about the development of this historiographical tradition of Haraldr hárfagri's raids in the west.

Writing in the 1070s, Adam of Bremen notes only that Haraldr (Sigurðar-

[89] *Ibid.*, pp. 341–3. I cannot judge the plausibility of van Hamel's suggestion that Thur's cognomen *kiaul* means 'the Doglike' and translates the Norse *hundr*, but it would be an attractive solution.

[90] *The History*, ed. & transl. Jones, p. 104; *Historia*, ed. Evans, p. 2; *A Mediaeval Prince*, ed. & transl. Evans, p. 55.

[91] Thus I am suggesting that, unlike most other insular sources, the *Historia* shows evidence of the term *Harfagyr* being applied to the two different Haralds, although this need not mean the author was aware he was doing so. See also note 101, below.

[92] Snorri Sturluson, *Heimskringla* (ed. Aðalbjarnarson, I.120–22).

[93] Is it possible to see another shift of source in the passage in which the author of the *Historia* explains the 'men of *Nordwei*' as 'a race from *Llychlyn*' (*The History*, ed. & transl. Jones, p. 106; *Historia*, ed. Evans, p. 4; *A Mediaeval Prince*, ed. & transl. Evans p. 56).

son) subjugated the Orkney Islands (and Iceland).[94] Over a century later, the anonymous author of the *Historia Norwegiae* has Norwegian *piratae*, related to a certain *Rognwald*, subjugating large parts of the British Isles, including Caithness and Dublin, *in diebus Haraldi comati* (like Snorri and the author of the *Historia Gruffud vab Kenan*, he goes on immediately to mention the conquest of Normandy by *Rodulfus* or *Gongurolfr*).[95] From this, it would be but a short step for a Norse historian to conclude that the first Norwegian king to claim overlordship over the islands in the west must have been Haraldr hárfagri. Following a suggestion by Sigurður Nordal,[96] we can reconstruct the development of this historiographical tradition as follows. The earliest traceable account of Haraldr hárfagri's raids in the west was in the lost, original version of *Orkneyinga saga* (*ca* 1200), which told of his expedition of revenge against Torf-Einarr to Orkney. This formed the basis of Snorri's account in his saga of St Óláfr,[97] which has the islands subjugated to Haraldr as a result of this expedition. When Snorri expanded his *Óláfs saga* at either end to make *Heimskringla*'s more extensive history of all the kings of Norway, he developed this account further using legends about the activities of Rǫgnvaldr's relatives in the British Isles. Thus, we first have Haraldr subjugating parts of the British Isles in order to give them to Rǫgnvaldr as compensation for the death of his son Ívarr,[98] and then only later his expedition against Torf-Einarr, another son of Rǫgnvaldr.[99] This expanded account of Snorri's in turn found its way into the extant *Orkneyinga saga*.

Thus, the *Historia*'s account of *Harfagyr*'s early history in Ireland need not depend on 'traditions current among the Norse colonists in Ireland'[100] and Gruffudd's alleged descent from that illustrious king suspiciously apes the eagerness of his contemporaries in Norway to trace their descent from a king of the same name.[101] What the *Historia* does depend on can only be answered when we have a clearer idea of the date at which it was written. But if K.L. Maund is right in arguing for a late twelfth-century date (or even later),[102] then the author would have been in a position to benefit, directly

---

94 Adam of Bremen, *Gesta Hammaburgensis Ecclesiae Pontificum*, III.xvii (ed. Trillmich, p. 346).

95 Storm, ed., *Historia Norwegiae*, pp. 89–90.

96 Nordal, 'Orkneyingasaga', pp. 44–5.

97 Snorri Sturluson, *Heimskringla* (ed. Aðalbjarnarson, II.158–9).

98 Snorri Sturluson, *Heimskringla* (ed. Aðalbjarnarson, I.120–22).

99 *Ibid.*, I.133–4.

100 Van Hamel, 'Norse history', p. 337.

101 The Welsh genealogical tract *Achau Brenhinoedd a Thywysogion Cymru*, 6a (ed. Bartrum, p. 99) has two *Harallt Harfagyr*s among Gruffydd's ancestors, clearly corresponding to Haraldr harðráði and Haraldr hárfagri respectively, and parallels Scandinavian texts in noting that the latter overran *Llychllyn*, expelled all its kings and became high king over it himself.

102 Maund, *Ireland, Wales, and England*, pp. 172–3.

or indirectly, from Norse historical research in the twelfth century. This research developed the ancestry of Haraldr Sigurðarson back as far as his namesake Haraldr Hálfdanarson, in the process developing accounts of the earlier Haraldr's reign (and in particular his raids on the British Isles), and in the process, the epithet *hárfagri* was transferred from one to the other (with the contradictory Norse and insular traditions of who this nickname belonged to representing in fossilised form the two stages of this process). I have already suggested that Orkney would have been a likely point for the dissemination of such research to more southerly parts of the British Isles in general, and to the Irish Sea region in particular. The raids of Magnús berfœttr reflect a chain of connection from Orkney down to Anglesey, and the same route could have served for cultural exchanges. It has been a commonplace to view the Irish Sea littorals as one cultural area, but in this view there has been a tendency to overemphasise the east-west connections at the expense of the equally important (from a Norse point of view) north-south axis. And while there is little evidence of Norse historical or saga traditions spreading from Ireland, there is plenty of evidence for Orkney as a cultural centre in just the right period.[103]

If we can believe the *Life of St Gwynllyw*,[104] then Gruffudd himself went to Orkney. Charles would even see Gruffudd as a channel for Scandinavian influence on the revival of Welsh culture from his reign onwards, and this possibility cannot be entirely ruled out.[105] However, in my view, Orkney in the second half of the twelfth century makes the most likely source for the Norse traditions that are preserved, somewhat garbled, in the *Historia Gruffud vab Kenan*. And it may be that we need the Isle of Man as a staging-point for this contact. Broderick emphasises links between the House of Gwynedd and Man in the late twelfth century,[106] and Man's links with Orkney significantly go back to 1066 and the time of the first impact of Haraldr harðráði (or was it hárfagri?) on these islands.[107]

---

[103] *Orkneyinga saga* LXVIII–IX, LXXXII, C and CVI (ed. Guðmundsson, pp. 178–81, 186n., 272, 284) suggests that there was plenty of contact with Wales and the southern Irish Sea region as far as the Scilly Isles in the twelfth century. For Orkney in general, see the contributions in Crawford (ed.), *St Magnus Cathedral*, and Batey *et al.* (edd.), *The Viking Age in Caithness, Orkney and the North Atlantic*.

[104] Vita Sancti Gundleii XII (ed. Wade-Evans, p. 182).

[105] Charles, *Old Norse Relations*, pp. 75, 84.

[106] Broderick, 'Irish and Welsh', pp. 35–6.

[107] As indicated not only by the late *Cronica*, but also by numismatic evidence, see Cubbon and Dolley, 'Kirk Michael', esp. pp. 17–20.

VI

HISTORIA GRUFFUD VAB KENAN: THE FIRST AUDIENCE

Nerys Ann Jones

Historians of the kingdom of Gwynedd and of the Irish Sea area in general in the eleventh and twelfth centuries have long recognised *Historia Gruffud vab Kenan* as an unique and important text. In the modern period, questions concerning its value as a historical source have occasionally been raised and during the last hundred years the pendulum of opinion has swung from J. E. Lloyd's absolute trust in the *Historia* as a reliable and truthful witness of the events of Gruffudd's reign[1] to the scepticism expressed by K. L. Maund.[2] As yet, however, there has been no systematic analysis of the text with a view to addressing the questions of *tempus, locus, persona, et causa scribendi*. The two editors of the *Historia*, Arthur Jones[3] and D. Simon Evans,[4] seem to have been more interested in the subject of the biography than in the biographer. Indeed, in the introductions to their editions they devoted most of their energy to setting the life of Gruffudd ap Cynan, rather than the *Historia* itself, in its historical context. Nevertheless, they put forward some views as to the authorship, provenance, purpose and dating of the *Historia* and in this paper my intention is to reexamine their arguments. These questions are, of course, intimately connected with each other and with questions about the materials and models the author had for his work. It will not be possible to reexamine all aspects of the *Historia* here, but it is hoped that my discussion will serve as a starting point, at least, for further study of the text.

It has been the general view that the *Historia* in its existing form is an early thirteenth-century translation of a mid-twelfth-century Latin original. The earliest surviving manuscript to contain the text, Aberystwyth, National Library of Wales, MS. Peniarth 17, has been dated to the second half of the

---

[1] Lloyd, *A History*, II.379.
[2] Maund, *Ireland, Wales, and England*, pp. 78–9.
[3] *The History*, ed. & transl. Jones.
[4] *Historia*, ed. Evans; *A Mediaeval Prince*, ed. & transl. Evans.

thirteenth century and located in Gwynedd.[5] Neither the author of the
hypothetical Latin text nor the translator is named but valuable information
about each of them could be gleaned from a close examination of the
Historia and a comparison with contemporary sources. It was only the
hypothetical twelfth-century author who was investigated by Jones and
Evans, however; a study of the identity of the translator and his contribution
to the text remains to be undertaken.

In their introductions, both editors endeavoured to establish a number of
facts about the author. First, they were both certain that he was a Welshman
living in Gwynedd, and Evans also argued that he was Welsh-speaking and
literate in Welsh.[6] They substantiated their claim that the author was
ethnically Welsh by the fact that in the Welsh version the audience is
addressed as *[c]aredicaf vrodyr Kemry*,[7] translated by Evans as 'most
beloved brethren of Wales'.[8] On this evidence alone, however, the possibility that the author was of mixed or even non-Welsh blood cannot be ruled
out.[9] There is not much doubt, however, that he had spent some of his life
in Gwynedd. His intimate knowledge of the geography of north-west Wales,
as compared with the more general nature of his references to places in the
South is proof enough of his familiarity with Gwynedd. No conclusions
were drawn by either of the two editors from the author's detailed and
apparently accurate knowledge of the places connected with Gruffudd's
upbringing in Ireland or from the author's familiarity with legends concerning Gruffudd's Irish and Scandinavian ancestors.[10] That the author was
probably Welsh-speaking and literate in Welsh is clearly demonstrated by
the fact that he quoted and translated into Latin a Welsh *englyn* and also
explained Welsh place-names. Evans's further claim that the author was
familiar with the techniques and the simple, direct style of the *cyfarwydd*
(the native storyteller of Wales) and that this is reflected in the existing text
of the *Historia*,[11] is less convincing as it is based on the premise that the
Welsh text is a particularly close translation of the lost Latin original. That,
of course, cannot be proved and such slight knowledge as we have of the
art of translation in mediaeval Wales suggests that it is not likely.[12] The two

5 See Huws, *Llyfrau Cymraeg 1250–1400*, p. 19.
6 See *The History*, ed. & transl. Jones, p. 17, n. 1; *Historia*, ed. Evans, pp. ccxxix, ccxxx.
7 *Historia*, ed. Evans, p. 6.
8 *A Mediaeval Prince*, ed. & transl. Evans, p. 58.
9 It is true that *brodyr* could be taken to mean 'fellow countrymen' (see GPC 311) but
   Walter Map, who was half-Welsh, refers to the Welsh as his compatriots; Walter Map,
   De Nugis (ed. & transl. James *et al.*, p. 182).
10 For a thorough examination of the Irish material in the *Historia*, see Duffy 'Ireland and
   the Irish Sea Region', pp. 228–38.
11 *Historia*, ed. Evans, p. ccxxix.
12 See, for example, Lloyd-Morgan, 'Rhai agweddau'.

editors agreed that the *Historia* is the work of a cleric.[13] Evans listed numerous examples to show that the author was heavily influenced by the thought and learning of the Church and that he was concerned with the contribution of the bishops to the success of Gruffudd's rule and also with Gruffudd's role as a patron of churches in Gwynedd and beyond. Neither editor drew attention to the understanding of legal arguments demonstrated in the text nor to the author's obvious concern with the question of Gruffudd's legal right to rule Gwynedd.[14]

Finally, both editors speculated upon the possible relationship between the author and the court of Gwynedd in the twelfth century. Jones came to no clear conclusion. On the one hand he saw the *Historia* as 'a professional panegyric after the fashion of a court bard but subdued by clerical influence' and probably composed under the patronage of Gruffudd's sons.[15] On the other hand, the fact that there is hardly any mention of these sons, Owain Gwynedd and Cadwaladr, in the text prompted him to suggest that it must have been written independently of the influence of the court, perhaps at a time when their achievements during their father's lifetime had been forgotten. Evans argued that the propagandistic nature of the text suggested a biographer who was close to the centre of power in twelfth-century Gwynedd and went on to identify him as David, who was archdeacon in Bangor during the sixties of the twelfth century and possibly the son of archdeacon Simeon who is named in the *Historia* as being present at Gruffudd's deathbed.[16]

David, like his father before him, certainly appears to have been the ecclesiastical power behind the throne of Gwynedd, and in many ways he does seem to fit the bill. It is rather strange, however, that there is no suggestion in the text of the conflict between the kings of Gwynedd and the archbishops of Canterbury concerning the election of the bishop of Bangor in which both David and Simeon were heavily involved.[17] As J. Conway Davies observed, 'During the whole of his rule, Owain resisted the interference of the archbishop of Canterbury and the king of England in the ecclesiastical affairs of his principality. He was fighting for the ecclesiastical no less than the political independence of his principality.'[18] If the *Historia* is 'a manifesto designed to bolster the claims of Gwynedd' as Evans suggested,[19] one would expect the author, who is at such pains to stress the kingdom's superiority within Wales and its independence of the

13 *The History*, ed. & transl. Jones, p. 16, *Historia*, ed. Evans, p. ccxxviii.
14 This aspect has been discussed by Charles-Edwards, *Early Irish and Welsh Kinship*, pp. 294–5, and Maund, *Ireland, Wales, and England*, p. 173.
15 *The History*, ed. & transl. Jones, p. 18.
16 *Historia*, ed. Evans, pp. ccxlvi–ccxlvii.
17 See Davies, *Episcopal Acts*, II.415–37.
18 *Ibid.*, p. 436. The word 'principality' is of course anachronistic.
19 *A Mediaeval Prince*, ed. & transl. Evans, p. 18.

neighbouring kingdoms, to paint a picture of ecclesiastical independence too. The two bishops of Bangor in Gruffudd's day are given scant attention in the *Historia*. The unpopular Norman appointment, Bishop Hervé, who was probably forced to abandon his diocese during the revolt of 1094 to return only as an occasional visitor,[20] is depicted in the *Historia* as playing a leading role in securing peace between Gruffudd and Henry I sometime after 1099.[21] There must be some significance in this and also in the fact that no reference is made in the text to Hervé's bitter hostility towards the people of Gwynedd or to their success in getting rid of him which resulted in the bishopric being left vacant for nearly eleven years. There is no mention either of the appointment of Bishop David in 1120, probably seen as a great victory for the king, clergy, and laity of Gwynedd, as David was allegedly chosen by them rather than by the king of England and the archbishop of Canterbury.[22] Bishop David is merely named in the *Historia* as one of the clergy who anointed Gruffudd's body prior to his death.[23] This lack of reference to events which could have been used to portray Gruffudd as a champion of the church in Gwynedd raises doubts not only about Evans's theory on the authorship and origin of the *Historia* but also about the long-accepted view on the dating of the text.

Between them, Jones and Evans presented a total of ten reasons for placing the composition of the *Historia* sometime between the death of Gruffudd in 1137 and the death of his successor, Owain Gwynedd, in 1170. Some of these arguments may be dismissed out of hand as they are based on misinterpretations of the text. It was only a misreading of the sentence translated as, 'From him [Rodulf] came the Norman kings who subdued England in battle, namely king William and his two sons who succeeded him, William of the Long Sword, and Henry and Stephen his nephew, *who were contemporaries of king Gruffudd*'[24] which allowed them to claim that, since the list of English kings ends with Stephen, the *Historia* must have been composed during the reign of Henry II.[25] A similar misunderstanding led Jones to conclude that the phrase *a allei dyfot ar gof y'r etifedd wedy y ryeni*, 'which could be remembered by descendants after their forbears',[26] referring to the destruction which the Normans wrought in Anglesey in 1098, suggests that only one generation had passed since this had happened.[27]

A few of the arguments for a twelfth-century date are based on unproven assumptions about the nature of the text. Jones's assertion that there are no

[20] Davies, *Episcopal Acts*, II.95.
[21] *Historia*, ed. Evans, p. 28; *A Mediaeval Prince*, ed. & transl. Evans, p. 79.
[22] Davies, *Episcopal Acts*, II.550–1.
[23] *A Mediaeval Prince*, ed. & transl. Evans, p. 83.
[24] *A Mediaeval Prince*, ed. & transl. Evans, p. 56 (my italics).
[25] *The History*, ed. & transl. Jones, p. 18; *Historia*, ed. Evans, p. ccxlix.
[26] *Historia*, ed. Evans, p. 25; *A Mediaeval Prince*, ed. & transl. Evans, pp. 46, 77.
[27] *The History*, ed. & transl. Jones, pp. 18–19.

anachronisms or 'casual irrelevancies' in the *Historia* to suggest a date much later than Gruffudd's own reign is clearly erroneous,[28] as K. L. Maund has shown with regard to the picture of kingship presented in the text.[29] Jones's further claim that the author's independence of any extant historical works indicates that it was written soon after Gruffudd's death is an argument from silence since the author's written sources, if he had any, are probably lost.[30] The question of the quality and quantity of the sources available to him and also the possibility that he might have deliberately shaped or coloured his materials were not considered by Jones. He therefore argued that the omission of important events in the careers of Gruffudd and his contemporaries must indicate that the *Historia* was written 'before the fame of Gruffydd's contemporary princes had spread beyond their own locality and incidents and legends touching Gruffydd himself had not become matters of common knowledge in Wales'.[31]

Both editors accepted without question the author's claim that he had received information about the physical appearance of both Gruffudd and his wife Angharad from 'Gruffudd's special acquaintances' and 'the country's wise men'.[32] Jones, on the one hand, used this as proof that the biography was composed soon after Gruffudd's death in 1137, at a time when there would have been 'many still living who . . . could offer the evidence of contemporaries or eye witnesses'.[33] Evans, on the other hand, argued that it implies that the author himself was not familiar with the appearance of either Gruffudd or his wife, and therefore the *Historia* must have been composed after the death of Angharad in 1162.[34] Even if the descriptions are accepted as genuine eye-witness reports, this last argument does not stand because the nature of the author's attribution of these descriptions to others indicates that he was not familiar with the physical appearance of Gruffudd and Angharad when they were in their heyday, many years before their deaths in old age. However, the extremely stylised nature of these passages, the fact that they follow the common rhetorical pattern of commencing with the head and working down to the feet, and that the same epithets are used for both husband and wife, do suggest that what we have here is a device employed by the biographer to add authority to the work.[35] The description of the text as *historia hen* in the opening rubric, if any weight is to be placed on it at all, may be explained as a similar

---

28 *Ibid.*, p. 17.
29 Maund, *Ireland, Wales, and England*, pp. 7–8.
30 *The History*, ed. & transl. Jones, pp. 24–5.
31 *Ibid.*, p. 18.
32 *Historia*, ed. Evans, pp. 17, 21; *A Mediaeval Prince*, ed. & transl. Evans, pp. 70, 74.
33 *The History*, ed. & transl. Jones, p. 25.
34 *Historia*, ed. Evans, pp. ccxliii–ccxliv.
35 On the fabrication of eye-witness reports, a common feature in many mediaeval saints' Lives, see Colgrave, 'Bede's miracle stories', pp. 224–5.

device,[36] and also the author's assertion that the second section of the *Historia* is based on *hen gyvarwydyt*. Evans, however, attached significance to these two statements and used them to date the text long after Gruffudd's death.[37]

The argument that the description of St Davids in the *Historia* as *archescopty Mynyv*, 'the archbishopric of Mynyw',[38] may be interpreted as a veiled reference to the twelfth-century campaign to have St Davids made a metropolis is presented but discounted for various reasons by the two editors.[39] This leaves only one argument for placing the hypothetical original Latin text of the *Historia* in the reign of Owain Gwynedd. This is based on a claim, made in the section on Gruffudd's pedigree, that Waterford was ruled by one of the brothers of Gruffudd's ancestor, Harald Hárfagri, and that 'his descendants have been kings of that city since then till today'.[40] The two editors were right to argue that it is unlikely that the author was unaware of the capture of Waterford by Strongbow in 1171 as it must have been common knowledge to any well-informed Welshman of the age.[41] However, it appears to me, on examination of the section about Harald Hárfagri and his brothers, that the sentence which contains this crucial reference may have been tampered with or may even be a later addition to the text. The allusion to an anonymous fourth brother who received Waterford from Harald disrupts the three-fold structure of this section and causes many inconsistencies within it.[42] The status of this reference is therefore uncertain.

---

[36] For other examples of this device, which is found in numerous pseudo-historical works, courtly romances, etc., compare the *liber uetustissimus* of Geoffrey of Monmouth and the claim in Rhygyfarch's Life of St David (ed. & transl. James, p. 48), 'I have gathered together . . . out of the very many . . . scattered in the oldest manuscripts of our country . . .'. Note that the reference to the text as 'old history' occurs in MS. Peniarth 17 only, and that a variety of terms are used in later copies of the lost variant form of the *Historia*, none of them betraying a relationship with the rubric at Peniarth 17 (see *Historia*, ed. Evans, pp. cclvii–cclxii). This raises questions as to the origin and significance of the phrase *historia hen*, not considered by Jones and Evans.

[37] *Historia*, ed. Evans, pp. ccliv, 35.

[38] *Historia*, ed. Evans, p. 13; *A Mediaeval Prince*, ed. & transl. Evans, p. 66.

[39] *The History*, ed. & transl. Jones, pp. 30–1; *Historia*, ed. Evans, pp. ccxlvii, 73.

[40] *A Mediaeval Prince*, ed. & transl. Evans, p. 56.

[41] *The History*, ed. & transl. Jones, p. 19; *Historia*, ed. Evans, p. ccxliv.

[42] *Historia*, ed. Evans, pp. 3–4; *A Mediaeval Prince*, ed. & transl. Evans, pp. 55–6. Note that the first sentence of this section refers to *Harald Harfagyr* and his two brothers. *Alyn* is named as one of these two brothers and the story of the first miracle he performed after his death is told. This is followed by an account of how the three brothers 'of him mentioned above' (which seems to refer to *Alyn*) embarked on an expedition in search of warfare, which brought them to Ireland. The author recounts Harald's conquest of Ireland, and it is in connection with this that the reference to Harald's fourth, anonymous, brother, occurs. The section ends with an account of *Rodulf*, 'the third brother', and his exploits in France.

It may be that this reference to the continuity of rule of the descendants of Harald in Waterford had a contemporary political significance which is lost to us today.[43] A greater understanding of the purpose of the *Historia* and of the identity of its original audience may help solve this puzzle as well as many others. As I mentioned above, Jones was unclear as to why and for whom the *Historia* was composed. Evans advocated that it was a piece of propaganda promoting the kingdom of Gwynedd, composed sometime during Owain Gwynedd's reign and aimed at both foreigners and Welshmen.[44] By comparing the content of the *Historia* with chronicles and other sources, he demonstrated convincingly that the author's intention was not to give a historically accurate account of Gruffudd's life but to praise him.[45] Evans noted that in the *Historia* Gruffudd is given honourable motives for all his actions and fails only through bad counsel or treachery. Unfortunate events in his career are omitted and any weaknesses in his claim to the throne of Gwynedd are glossed over or explained away. In order to give Gruffudd the highest profile possible, no mention is made of some of the leading figures of the period, and the status and role of others are reduced or their actions are attributed to Gruffudd.

One characteristic not noticed by Evans, however, is the way in which the author deliberately depicted many of Gruffudd's enemies and rivals, both Welsh and Norman, in the worst light possible. Take, for instance, the portrayal of Trahaearn ap Caradog as a usurper and a coward, shown by Maund to be at odds with the account provided in the extant chronicles.[46] An element of grotesque humour is introduced completely gratuitously into the description of his slaying. Fatally wounded, he is likened to a beast 'chewing with his teeth the fresh herbs and groping on top of his arms' and then 'Gwrcharki, the Irishman, made bacon of him as of a pig'.[47] It is difficult to allow that this would endear any of Trahaearn's descendants to the cause of Gwynedd.[48]

It has been argued by Evans and others that the author seems to be anxious not to anger the Normans in his audience. Yet Hugh, earl of Chester, is described as 'the root of all the evil like Antiochus of yore',[49] and the

43 See, for example, Maund's suggestion above, p. 114 n. 29.
44 *Historia*, ed. Evans, pp. ccxlii–ccxliii.
45 *Ibid.*, pp. ccxxxvi–ccxl.
46 Maund, 'Trahaearn'.
47 *Historia*, ed. Evans, p. 15; *A Mediaeval Prince*, ed. & transl. Evans, p. 68.
48 On the descendants of Trahaearn, see Morgan, 'The territorial divisions', p. 29. Note that one of Trahaearn's grand-daughters, Gwladus ferch Llywarch, was the wife of Owain Gwynedd, probably chosen by Owain as a bride in order to win over Llywarch, her father: see Roderick, 'Marriage', p. 13. This should, of course, be taken into account when dating the text.
49 *Historia*, ed. Evans, p. 22; *A Mediaeval Prince*, ed. & transl. Evans, p. 75.

Normans in general are labelled as treacherous and cowardly.[50] It is true that Robert of Rhuddlan is praised as 'a renowned, valiant baron of strength',[51] but at the same time the author has gone to great trouble to include the account of Gruffudd's defeat of Robert which he could easily have omitted.[52] It is clear that the author had no regard for the finer feelings of any descendants of Robert of Rhuddlan or Hugh of Chester. Nor had he any fear of offending the king of England and his supporters since the accounts of each of the three Welsh campaigns of William Rufus and Henry I are related as stories of pride before a fall. In his account, William, for example, entered Wales 'prepared to exterminate and destroy all the people completely so that there would not be alive as much as a dog', but he had to withdraw for fear of being ambushed by Gruffudd's men and he returned to Chester 'without inflicting any kind of loss on that journey to the people of the land'.[53] The author made a meal of the king's humiliation, stressing that he did not get any booty 'except for one cow' but that he lost many horsemen, esquires, servants, horses, and other possessions.[54] He then went on to emphasise that it was through Gruffudd's clemency alone that the king's life was spared: 'And had Gruffudd allowed his men to mingle with them in the woods, that would have been the last day for the king of England and his Frenchmen. He, however, spared them, as king David of yore spared Saul.'[55] Even if it were true, this is hardly the kind of material which 'would help the cause of Gwynedd and its prince at a sensitive time of crisis and anguish', as Evans claimed.[56]

It seems to me, then, that the *Historia* as we have it is much more likely to have been intended for a Venedotian audience only, and this is confirmed by the fact that on the only occasion when the author addressed his audience directly he called them 'beloved brethren of Wales'.[57] The question of the function of the *Historia* needs to be considered in the light of this, but much more research on all aspects of the text, especially its structure and sources, must be completed before a satisfactory answer can be reached.

---

[50] *Historia*, ed. Evans, pp. 25, 26; *A Mediaeval Prince*, ed. & transl. Evans, pp. 77, 78.

[51] *Historia*, ed. Evans, p. 7; *A Mediaeval Prince*, ed. & transl. Evans, p. 59.

[52] See *Historia*, ed. Evans, p. cl, where it is argued that the author had to tamper with the chronological order of events in order to include Gruffudd's attack on Rhuddlan which occurred, according to Orderic Vitalis, in 1088, during the period when, according to the *Historia*, Gruffudd was imprisoned.

[53] *Historia*, ed. Evans, p. 22; *A Mediaeval Prince*, ed. & transl. Evans, pp. 74, 75.

[54] *Historia*, ed. Evans, p. 22; *A Mediaeval Prince*, ed. & transl. Evans, p. 75.

[55] *Historia*, ed. Evans, p. 23; *A Mediaeval Prince*, ed. & transl. Evans, p. 75.

[56] *A Mediaeval Prince*, ed. & transl. Evans, p. 19.

[57] *Historia*, ed. Evans, p. 6; *A Mediaeval Prince*, ed. & transl. Evans, p. 58.

VII

THE SIXTEENTH-CENTURY LATIN TRANSLATION
OF *HISTORIA GRUFFUD VAB KENAN*

Ceri Davies

Our main source for the life of Gruffudd ap Cynan is the *Historia* which, in a Welsh form, is extant in thirteen manuscripts. The work is usually thought to have been originally written in Latin, probably in the 1160s, towards the end of the reign of Owain Gwynedd, Gruffudd's son. All copies of that Latin work have been lost, but not before it was translated into Welsh in a version which itself appears to have been subject to some further modifications. The manuscript-tradition of the *Historia* in Welsh has been studied in detail by D. Simon Evans in his edition, published in 1977.[1] Evans's text is based on the earliest surviving manuscript, Aberystwyth, National Library of Wales, MS. Peniarth 17, written in the thirteenth century. That manuscript is incomplete, and the text of the last ten pages has been supplied from MS. Peniarth 267, one of the many copies produced in the sixteenth and seventeenth centuries. These later copies are not direct descendants of MS. Peniarth 17. Rather they derive – either directly or indirectly – from a version probably to be dated to the fourteenth century and including the modifications referred to above. This ancestral manuscript came into the possession of the Wynn family of Gwedir and is usually referred to as 'The Book of Sir Richard Wynn'. It is now unfortunately lost, probably destroyed, and with it the clue to a number of questions relating to the text and transmission of the *Historia*.

An interesting coda to the history of the text is that the Welsh *Historia* was translated back into Latin in the third quarter of the sixteenth century. Awareness of the Welsh origins of the Tudors, coupled with the wider antiquarian pursuits of the period, led to a remarkable surge of interest, from the 1540s onwards, in Welsh history. This new Latin version of *Historia Gruffud vab Kenan* has survived in ten manuscript-copies.[2] Three of the

---

[1] *Historia*, ed. Evans, pp. ccli–cclxxiii, cclxxxii–cclxxxix. I am acutely aware of my dependence on Professor Evans's work throughout this essay and wish gratefully to acknowledge my debt to him.

[2] *Ibid.*, pp. cclxxiv–cclxxxii.

Latin copies are found alongside the Welsh text: they are London, British Library, MS. Cotton Vitellius C.ix; Aberystwyth, National Library of Wales, MS. Wynnstay 10; Aberystwyth, National Library of Wales, MS. Llanstephan 150. The last two, together with Cambridge, Trinity College, MS. 0.5.24 (1305), Oxford, Bodleian Library, MS. Jones 57 (*S.C.* 8965), and Aberystwyth, National Library of Wales, MS. Peniarth 276, may safely be ascribed to the seventeenth century. Cotton Vitellius C.ix, as also Aberystwyth, National Library of Wales, MS. 434 E, Cardiff, City Library, MS. 4.101, London, British Library, MS. Additional 19712, and Cardiff, City Library, MS. 3.11 may go back to the end of the sixteenth century. As Simon Evans has shown, only minor differences, the work of copyists and correctors, exist between the several copies. There are no major discrepancies, and all copies represent the work of one translator. Underlying the translation is the manuscript-tradition which stemmed from 'The Book of Sir Richard Wynn', but the translator may have had access also to the text of MS. Peniarth 17 or a descendant of it.

Who was the translator of the work? Sir John Wynn of Gwedir, at the beginning of his *History of the Gwydir Family*, claimed lineal descent for his family from Gruffudd ap Cynan, and referred thus to the account of Gruffudd's life.[3]

His troublesome life and famous acts are compiled by a most ancient friar or monk of Wales, and was found among the posterity of the said Gruffudd ap Cynan in the house of Gwydir in north Wales, and at the request of Maurice Wynn, esquire (who had the same in a most ancient book written, and was lineally descended from him) was translated into Latin by Nicholas Robinson, Bishop of Bangor, and are extant.

The 'most ancient book' is probably to be identified with 'The Book of Sir Richard Wynn': Richard Wynn was the son of Sir John, and grandson of Maurice, Wynn. Nicholas Robinson's role as Latin translator is confirmed by superscriptions and various catalogue-entries which are connected with the work. Thus, for example, on a page in Aberystwyth, National Library of Wales, MS. Llanstephan 150, the following information is given:[4]

Ystorya neu Fuchedd Gruffudd ap Kynan, Brenin Gwynedd: with the Latin translation by Nicholas Robinson Bp. of Bangor in the year 1566.

The learned bishop's connexion with the Latin translation seems clear enough. Not so clear is the date of the translation. 1566 was the year of Robinson's consecration as bishop of Bangor, and the reference here is

---

3   Wynn, *The History* (ed. Jones), p. 1.
4   See *Historia*, ed. Evans, p. cclxxxi.

probably to the year of his appointment, not necessarily to the year in which he produced his version of the *Historia*.[5]

That Nicholas Robinson (1530?–1585) should be connected with a work of this kind is not surprising. He was born and brought up in Conway, to a family of burgesses who were known to the Wynns of Gwedir. Sir John said as much, referring to him thus in his *Memoirs*:[6]

Nicholas Robinson D.D., born in the town of Conwy in Caernarfonshire. [He] was of honest parents and wealthy, whose father I knew, bailiff of the town, being chief officer.

Nicholas Robinson was educated at Queens' College, Cambridge, where he had a distinguished career, fully justifying Sir John Wynn's description of him as 'an excellent scholar'. Two features of his younger days have a particular bearing on his undertaking the work of translating the *Historia*. First, he enjoyed a considerable reputation as a latinist. During his time at Queens', Latin comedies by him were performed in the college, and when Queen Elizabeth visited Cambridge in the summer of 1564, Robinson was entrusted with the task of writing a Latin account of the occasion.[7] A similar account of the queen's visit to Oxford, in 1566, was composed by him. Secondly, he came to the notice and won the approval of Matthew Parker, archbishop of Canterbury, who appointed him as one of his chaplains. Parker, in addition to his obvious ecclesiastical duties, had profound anti-quarian interests, not least in the 'Protestant' account of early British Church-history which so won the approval of Welsh divines in the sixteenth century. Parker corresponded on the subject with Bishop Richard Davies and William Salesbury, and Robinson's own interest in Welsh history may have been sharpened by his association with Parker.[8] Appointment to the archdeaconry of Merioneth, and subsequently of Anglesey, together with his election as bishop of Bangor, meant that, in Arthur Jones's apt words, 'he lived in the heart of the country consecrated to the memory of the exploits of Gruffydd ap Cynan'.[9] In a letter to Archbishop Parker, dated 7 October, 1567, Robinson mentioned Gruffudd's *Historia*.[10]

It should be noted that Nicholas Robinson is not the only contender for the title of Latin translator of Gruffudd ap Cynan's Life. MS. Llanstephan

---

5 Compare Evans's comments in *Historia*, p. cclxxxi: 'Fe ddichon, yn wir, mai cyfeiriad sydd yma at ddyddiad cyfieithu'r *Historia*, eto teg cofio mai dyma flwyddyn cysegru Robinson yn esgob'.
6 Wynn, *The History* (ed. Jones), p. 60. On Nicholas Robinson, see A.O. Evans, 'Nicholas Robinson'.
7 See Binns, *Intellectual Culture*, p. 137.
8 See Williams, *Bywyd ac Amserau'r Esgob Richard Davies*, passim.
9 *The History*, ed. & transl. Jones, p. 12.
10 See *Historia*, ed. Evans, p. cclxxxi, n. 124.

150 not only contains the reference to Nicholas Robinson, quoted above, but also declares on its title-page:[11]

Vita Griffini Regis Venedotiae a Thelwello | juris perito in Latinum conversa.

This *Thelwellus iuris peritus* is Edward Thelwall (*ob*. 1610) of Plas-y-Ward, near Rhuthun. BL MS. Cotton Vitellius C.ix also contains ascription of the translation in the same words, although <*tiae a Thelwello*> is lost at the edge of a fire-damaged page. A catalogue, by William Maurice, of manuscripts in the library at Hengwrt also attributes one Latin translation of Gruffudd ap Cynan's Life to Thelwall, another to Nicholas Robinson. Robert Vaughan himself, in a catalogue of Hengwrt manuscripts (1659), referred to Thelwall's Latin translation of the Life.[12]

The nobility and learning of Edward Thelwall are amply attested. Thomas Wiliems of Trefriw includes him in a list of *gwyrda clodforus* ('honourable nobility') who gave him generous support in preparing his Latin-Welsh dictionary.[13] Particularly notable is the praise bestowed upon him in the autobiography of Edward, Lord Herbert of Cherbury:[14]

After I had attained the age of nine . . . my parents thought fit to send me to some place where I might learn the Welsh tongue, as believing it necessary to enable me to treat with those of my friends and tenants who understood no other language; whereupon I was recommended to Mr. Edward Thelwall, of Plas-y-Ward in Denbighshire. This gentleman I must remember with honour, as having of himself acquired the exact knowledge of Greek, Latin, French, Italian, and Spanish, and all other learning, having for that purpose neither gone beyond the seas, nor so much as had the benefit of any universities.

Thelwall's interest in the *Historia* is attested by references in a number of the Welsh copies of the work to *Llyfr Plas y Ward* (NLW MS. 3075 D; NLW MS. Panton 2; NLW MS. 53 B) and to *Exemplar Plaswardense* (NLW MS. Wynnstay 10; NLW MS. Panton 26). Furthermore, Edward Thelwall himself seems to have been very closely associated with, and possibly even wrote, one copy of the *Exemplar Plaswardense*. This is the so-called 'Thelwall Manuscript', now NLW MS. 13211.[15] There is, however, no evidence of substance to support the view that Edward Thelwall prepared a new Latin translation of the *Historia*. Probably nearer the mark is Simon Evans's suggestion that Thelwall's interest led him to make, or have made,

11 *Ibid.*, p. cclxxvi.
12 *Ibid.*, p. cclxxiv, n. 98, and p. cclxxv.
13 *Rhagymadroddion, 1547–1659*, ed. Hughes, p. 114.
14 *The Autobiography*, ed. Lee, p. 20.
15 See *Historia*, ed. Evans, p. cclxxxviii.

a copy of Nicholas Robinson's version.[16] He may have been responsible for small alterations and additions in the text – such minor differences appear between most copies – but they do not constitute a divergent translation or textual tradition. At some point, knowledge of Thelwall's interest in the *Historia* led to the ascription of the Latin version to him: Arthur Jones attributed that ascription to the antiquary Arthur Agard (1540–1615), Deputy Chamberlain in the Exchequer, who was responsible for BL MS. Cotton Vitellius C.ix, which contained both the Welsh text and the Latin version.[17] However, Nicholas Robinson almost certainly remains the author of the Latin work.

The Latin version which in places is most strikingly different from that of the other surviving manuscripts is that contained in Cardiff, City Library, MS. 4.101, 'The Booke of Sir John Wynn'. The Latin work (like the 'History of the Gwydir Family', also in the same manuscript) is written in Sir John's own hand. As Simon Evans has clearly demonstrated, John Wynn made changes and additions (which often correct or clarify the vulgate version) in the light of the Welsh text.[18] Wynn introduced also some variations in style. In the opening sentence, for example, he changed the *cum*-clause of the majority of manuscripts ('Cum in Anglia regnaret Edwardus et apud Hybernos Therdelachus') into an ablative absolute ('Regnante in Anglia Edwardo, in Hibernia Terdelecho, . . .'). But Arthur Jones's verdict must be correct:[19]

In this opening and in other places the text of Sir John Wynne's version gives an impression of being distinctly an independent one. But a careful collation of it with the other Latin texts quickly casts doubt upon the idea . . . Without doubt Sir John Wynne had before him both the Welsh version and the Latin translation, and in making his own Latin copy he merely altered passages in the Latin to suit his own pedantic fancy as to the construction of Latin clauses and to improve perhaps upon the text before him. The chief differences lie at the beginning and the end of the text, and the inference is that he quickly tired of making alterations and contented himself with a close copy.

The cultural significance of these various texts resides in the way in which they reflect the interest taken by Elizabethan Welshmen of rank in earlier Welsh history. It was also a matter of family-history. The Wynns of Gwedir, as we have seen, claimed descent from Gruffudd ap Cynan. Edward Thelwall became, in 1583, the fourth husband of 'the Mother of Wales', the notable Catrin of Berain, widow of Maurice Wynn, Sir John's father. At the same time, Simon, Edward Thelwall's son, married Jane Wynn, daughter

---

[16] *Ibid.*, p. cclxxxii: 'Hawdd credu iddo wneud copi o'r Lladin. Yn wir, fe wyddom iddo gopïo'r testun Cymraeg, a bod ei gopi yn gynsail i nifer o destunau'.
[17] *The History*, ed. & transl. Jones, p. 13.
[18] *Historia*, ed. Evans, pp. cclxxix–cclxxx.
[19] *The History*, ed. & transl. Jones, pp. 11–12.

of Catrin and Maurice Wynn, and half-sister to Sir John. It is hardly surprising that they turned for a Latin version of their ancestor's Life to Nicholas Robinson, 'an excellent scholar' and 'a very wise man' according to Sir John Wynn himself.[20]

What can be said of the nature and quality of Nicholas Robinson's Latin translation? I shall examine some sentences from the beginning of his version of the account of the battle of Mynydd Carn. In this section of the Welsh work, textual variations between manuscripts are few and insignificant, as Simon Evans's *apparatus criticus* shows. The Latin text used here is that of NLW MS. Peniarth 276, as printed by Robert Williams of Rhydycroesau,[21] but which I too have examined. I give first Simon Evans's Welsh text, followed by his English translation, and finally the Latin version.

A guedy kerdet dirvaur emdeith diwyrnaut, yg kylch gosper wynt a doethant y venyd, en e lle yd oed lluesteu y dywededigyon vrenhined uchof. Ac ena y dywaut Rys urth Ruffud vrenhin, 'Argluyd', hep ef, 'annodun y vrvyder hyt avory, canys gosper yu er aur honn, a'r dyd ysyd en trengi'. 'Annot di' hep y Gruffud dan igyon, 'os mynny. Mivi a'm bydin a ruthraf udunt hwy'. Ac y velly y bu. A dechrynv a orugant y brenhined eissyoes, val y guelsant y torvoed budugaul amravael a bedinoed Gruffud vrenhin a'e arwydyon yn eu herbyn, a gvyr Denmarc ac eu bwyeill deuvinyauc, a'r Guydyl gaflachauc ac eu peleu haearnaul kyllellauc, a'r Gwyndyt gleiuyauc tareanauc.[22]

After they had marched a full day's journey, towards evening they came to a mountain, where lay the camps of the kings mentioned above. Then Rhys told King Gruffudd: 'Lord,' said he, 'let us postpone the battle till tomorrow, because it is now evening, and the day is spent'. 'You postpone it,' said Gruffudd with a sigh, 'if that is what you want. I and my army will rush at them'. And so it happened. The kings were however terrified, as they saw the various triumphant forces and the armies of King Gruffudd and his ensigns opposing them, the men of Denmark with their two-edged axes, the Irish with their lances and their sharp-edged iron balls, and the men of Gwynedd armed with spears and shields.[23]

Longo jam itinere dimenso ad vesperam in montes perveniunt, ubi castra posuissent predicti reges. Tum Rhesus Griffinum sic est allocutus: 'Domine differamus proelium in crastinum, quod jam advesperascit, et lux defectura est'. 'Differ' inquit Griffinus 'quousque tibi placuerit, ego vero cum ea, quam paratam habeo, cohorte in eos impetum faciam'. Quod, ut dixerat, praestabat. Terrore ingenti conturbantur reges, stupentque dum copias Griffini feroces, constipata militum agmina, splendentia vexilla, Danos bipennibus armatos, Hibernos jacula ferreis cuspidibus cultellata ferentes, et hastatos scutatosque Venedotos contra se venire conspiciunt.

20 Wynn, *The History* (ed. Jones), pp. 60–1.
21 Williams, 'Life of Gruffudd ap Cynan'.
22 *Historia*, ed. Evans, p. 15.
23 *A Mediaeval Prince of Wales*, ed. & transl. Evans, p. 67.

One is immediately struck by the controlled liveliness of the translator's latinity. This is not hack-work! The opening sentence begins with the Classical use of the ablative absolute construction instead of a subordinate clause; *iter* is correctly used in its specific military sense, 'a day's march', *emdeith diwyrnaut*; there is the vivid use of the historic present (*perveniunt*); *castra ponere* is the correct idiom for 'to pitch camp' and is far more precise than is *yd oed lluesteu* in the Welsh text; the subjunctive *posuissent* implies awareness of the position of the enemy in the minds of Rhys ap Tewdwr and Gruffudd; the use of the perfect participle passive, *predicti*, is natural in Latin, and the awkward *dywededigyon* of the Welsh doubtless points to the use of *predicti* or the like in the original Latin work.

The exchange of words between Rhys and Gruffudd, expressed in direct speech, is equally effective. The Welsh version has *hep ef* and *hep y Gruffud* as the formulae for introducing the words of both leaders, doubtless representing Latin *inquit*. Robinson chose variety. The words of Rhys to Gruffudd are introduced by the verb *alloqui*. But the translator knew that, unlike *inquit, alloqui* must not be placed within the direct speech and that an introductory adverb or pronoun must anticipate the quoted words: hence his *sic* here. The words of Gruffudd, on the other hand, are introduced by means of *inquit*, correctly positioned within the direct quotation. The choice of language contains literary and scriptural echoes. *Differre in crastinum* is an expression used by Cicero (*De Oratore*, 2.367); *quod jam advesperascit* echoes Luke 24:29 (*Mane nobiscum, quoniam advesperascit, et inclinata est dies,* Vulgate); *deficere* is used especially in Classical Latin of failing light, while the future participle with *est* in *defectura est* conveys far more graphically the notion of the light being *about to* fail than does *[y] dyd ysyd en trengi*. Robinson appears to have omitted the Welsh *dan igyon* but he gave more colour to *os mynny* by his use of *quousque* rather than *si* with *placuerit*. The bracketing of the relative clause (*quam paratam habeo*) between the demonstrative *ea* and its noun *cohorte* reveals excellent command of Latin expression.

The beginning of the description of the battle is splendidly executed. The short *Quod, ut dixerat, praestabat*, while fuller than the Welsh *Ac y velly y bu*, makes for a quiet pause before the rhetorical colour of the final sentence. The use of the historic present in that sentence (*conturbantur, stupent, conspiciunt*) underscores the reality of the enemy's fear in a far more graphic way than does *a orugant* in the Welsh text. The position of *terrore*, coupled with the adjective *ingenti* and the verb *stupent* (neither of which has a direct equivalent in the Welsh text, whose *eissyoes* is represented by the conjunction *dum* controlling *conspiciunt*) prepares the ground for the list of Gruffudd's forces, as viewed by the enemy. The Latin has a precision about it which is lacking in the Welsh version, and a sense of climax is subtly gained by means of rhetorical *variatio*. Thus, for example, *y torvoed budugaul amravael a bedinoed Gruffud vrenhin* is conveyed in the chiastic arrangement of *copias Griffini feroces, constipata militum agmina* (noun, qualifying genitive, adjective> <adjective, qualifying genitive, noun). *Arwydyon* has been given added colour in *splendentia vexilla,* and there is a fine tricolon-crescendo in the presentation of the three named armies, the Danes, the Irish, and the men of Gwynedd. The sentence ends with a *clausula* of a type not infrequently met in the works of Cicero, *venire conspiciunt* (compare *impetum faciam* earlier), which brings the whole description to a satisfying conclusion.

Careful study of this one passage is enough, I think, firmly to establish the credentials of Nicholas Robinson as a highly proficient and effective writer of Latin. It is no wonder that he was chosen to compose official accounts of Queen Elizabeth's visits to the two universities, or that he was renowned as a Latin playwright during his days at Queens'. The Wynns of Gwedir also knew what they were doing when they commissioned him to prepare a Latin version of the *Historia.* He gave them a text which could confidently take its place among the neo-Latin writings of the day. Ironically enough, the loss of the twelfth-century version resulted in the production of a text which – at least from a literary and stylistic point of view – probably gave the educated heirs of Renaissance classicism greater satisfaction than the original work might have done.

VIII

MEILYR BRYDYDD AND GRUFFUDD AP CYNAN

J.E. Caerwyn Williams

I

We know more about Meilyr Brydydd than about most of the Welsh Court Poets because we are not wholly dependent on his poetry for our information. He was the father of the poet Gwalchmai, and grandfather of the poets Meilyr ap Gwalchmai and Einion ap Gwalchmai, and, in all probability, of another poet, Elidir Sais. Of these poet-grandsons, Einion ap Gwalchmai was apparently the most important in his day. His lineage on his mother's as well as on his father's side has been preserved under the heading 'Llwyth Aelan' in the genealogical tract 'Hen Lwythau Gwynedd a'r Mars' ('The Old Tribes of Gwynedd and the March').[1] We learn from this tract that Meilyr's wife was Tandreg, daughter of Rhys ap Seisyllt, and Meilyr himself was the son of:

Mabon ap Iarddur ap Mor ap Tegerin ap Aelan ap Greddyf ap Kwnws ddu ap Kellin enfyt ap Peredur teyrnoe ap Meilir eryr gwyr gorsedd ap Tydy ap Tyfodedd ap Gwylvyw ap Marchwyn ap Bran ap Pyll ap Kynyr ap Meilir Meilyriawn ap Gwron ap Kunedda wledig.

As we have Cunedda's lineage we can trace Meilyr Brydydd's lineage still further back!

Giraldus Cambrensis gives us the genealogies of the princes of north and south Wales, adding that the Welsh bards and the *datgeiniaid* or reciters kept the genealogies of these princes in their old authoritative books, and observing later on that even the meanest of the common people was mindful of his pedigree and recited it glibly not only as far back as his grandfathers, his great- and great-great-grandfathers but also to the sixth and even the seventh generation and far beyond.[2] In Wales as in Ireland we know that a

[1] See Bartrum, *Tracts*, 111–20.
[2] Giraldus Cambrensis, *Opera*, vi 167–8; Hoc etiam mihi notandum videtur, quod bardi Kambrenses, et cantores, seu recitatores, genealogiam habent praedictorum principum in libris eorum antiquis et authenticis, sed tamen Kambrice scriptam.

man enjoyed his status, his rights and his privileges by virtue of his 'nobility' or descent, so that his lineage was not a matter of mere interest but also of real import: on it depended his hereditary rights.

Giraldus Cambrensis knew that lineage counted for much among the nobility of western Europe. What surprised him was that the meanest among the Welsh knew his lineage and took pride in it. The fact that the genealogy of Meilyr Brydydd's family has been kept reflects not only its importance in its society – we know that Einion ap Gwalchmai[3] and we surmise that Gwalchmai served their princes in a capacity other than that of bard[4] – but also the importance of the bardic office itself, and it reminds us that in this period the poets performed with their poetry a necessary social function, that they were a part of the structure of their society.

As we have seen, Meilyr Brydydd's son was a poet. So also were two or three of his grandsons. It may be that Meilyr's father was also a poet, for poetry in those far-off days was a craft and, like other crafts, practised by certain families and handed down from generation to generation. Unfortunately the evidence for the existence of bardic families is not so ample in Wales as it is in Ireland but it is significant that some of the earliest poets known to us at the Venedotian court were related to each other and can be said to form a bardic family. It seems that with the passage of time bardic families ceased to play an important rôle in the transmission of the bardic craft with the consequence that the evidence of their survival is meagre. Cuhelyn Fardd was the son of Gwynfardd Dyfed and the eponym *bardd* suggests that both were poets.[5] Seisyll Bryffwrch reminds Cynddelw, his rival for the *pencerdd* chair in Powys, that he is not descended like himself from a bardic stock.[6] It is possible that Dafydd Benfras was the son of Llywarch ap Llywelyn (Prydydd y Moch).[7] Another possibility is that Einion ap Gwgon was the son of Gwgawn Brydydd. But this evidence for the survival of bardic families indicates that they were in decline rather than flourishing, and that they were yielding their place to the bardic schools for which they were the archetype.

Unfortunately the evidence for the existence of bardic schools in Wales is neither as plentiful nor as precise as the evidence in Ireland,[8] but there can be no doubt that such schools existed here. The Welsh law-tracts tell us

---

[3] See Stephenson, *Governance*, p. 210.

[4] *Ibid.*, 14.

[5] R. Geraint Gruffydd, 'A poem in praise of Cuhelyn Fardd', pp. 198–209.

[6] *Llawysgrif Hendregadredd* (henceforth, H), 181, 'a hyn kyndelw uawr kawr kyrt./ o honu ny heniw beirt'.

[7] Bleddyn Fardd (H. 183,13) refers to Dafydd Benfras as 'un mab llywarch', possibly Llywarch ap Llywelyn. Dafydd Wyn Wiliam, 'Dafydd Benfras a'i ddisgynyddion,' pp. 33–35, has advanced reasons for doubting this.

[8] On Irish bardic schools see Bergin, 'Bardic Poetry', pp. 162–3.

that a *pencerdd*, i.e., a poet who had won a chair in a poetic competition (ymryson), could take pupils and claim payment for teaching them.[9] Cynddelw, probably the most learned of the poets of the princes, refers to his pupils: *As gwtant yn dysc yn disgyblon* (H.131.18), 'Our pupils know our learning', and to his work in instructing them: *Ry dysgaf disgywen ueirtyon* (H.105.17) 'I (can) teach brilliant poets', while Llygad Gŵr compares himself to a teacher of distinction (*athro ethrylithawc*, H.64.5).

Obviously the craft of poetry was well-worth learning; there was inducement to learn and to teach it, as we can see from the history of Meilyr Brydydd and his family. As chief poet to Gruffudd ap Cynan, Meilyr Brydydd had a right to a holding of land from him. We cannot be certain that Trefeilyr, the name of a place in the parish of Trefdraeth, Anglesey, commemorates such a holding, but the fact that there is a Trewalchmai (Gwalchmai today) in the same part of Anglesey points in that direction. Moreover, it is significant that in a survey of the lands of Anglesey made in 1352 there are references to Gwely Einion ap Gwalchmai (Lledwigan Llys), Gwely Meilyr ap Gwalchmai (Trefdraeth Wastrodion), Gwely Wyrion Einion ap Gwalchmai (Trewalchmai), Gwely Dafydd ap Gwalchmai (Trewalchmai) and Gwely Elidir ap Gwalchmai (Trewalchmai).[10] Here *gwely* means 'a tract of tribal land held in joint ownership and called by the name of the stockfather of a particular progeny', and the fact that all these lands were in the same region as Trefeilyr suggests that their names commemorate a connection between them and Meilyr Brydydd's family. It is possible, of course, that the name 'Meilyr' in Trefeilyr refers to Meilyr ap Gwalchmai, especially since Gwely Meilyr ap Gwalchmai was also in Trefdraeth, but it is doubtful whether Meilyr ap Gwalchmai ever became as important as his grandfather and it seems safer to connect Trefeilyr with Meilyr Brydydd, the grandfather, than with the grandson.

Meilyr Brydydd's dates are determined by his poems, in particular by his elegy for Gruffudd ap Cynan who died in 1137. It is unlikely that Meilyr Brydydd survived long after his patron's death. It would appear that he sang his own death-bed song (*marwysgafn*) soon after that death, especially since in that song he expresses a wish to be buried on Bardsey Island where there was a monastery which he could have entered in his final days to make his burial there doubly sure. He would have been very old in 1137 if the prophecy sung 'in the hosting where Trahaearn son of Caradawg and Meilyr son of Rhiwallawn ap Kynfyn were killed', i.e., at the Battle of Mynydd

---

[9] Jenkins, 'Pencerdd a Bardd Teulu', pp. 19–46.

[10] For the lands held by Gwalchmai's progeny see 'The Extent of Anglesey', printed in Henry Ellis, (ed.) *Registrum Vulgariter Nuncupatum* 'The Record of Caernarvon' (1838), pp. 44–89, and again in an English translation by A.D. Carr, 'The Extent of Anglesey, 1352', pp. 158–272; see esp. pp. 161, 163, 165, 171, 243.

Carn in 1081, was actually sung by him as the Hendregadredd MS., p.7, claims.[11] Some authorities have accepted this manuscript attribution; others have rejected it on the grounds that as the author of a poem written in 1081 and of another in 1137 he would have a floruit extending over fifty years. But such a *floruit* is not utterly impossible. After all, such a long *floruit* must be given to his patron Gruffudd ap Cynan, and Llywarch ap Llywelyn (Prydydd y Moch) had a poetic career which lasted for at least forty-five years. This particular prophecy, to judge by some of its lines, was sung by a poet who despised the Irish at the time and could hardly be at home in Gruffudd ap Cynan's army made up, as it was, of a considerable number of Irishmen, and if it was indeed sung by Meilyr Brydydd it must have been sung while he was in the service of another prince. However, the prophecy is a vaticinium post eventum and could have been sung by Meilyr Brydydd before he was accepted into Gruffudd ap Cynan's service.

Our poet refers to himself as Meilyr Brydydd in his *marwysgafn* or death-bed song and it is as such that he is known to the Welsh poetic tradition, and scribe alpha, the main scribe of the Hendregadredd MS., ascribes the elegy for Gruffudd ap Cynan, the prophecy and the death-bed song to him.[12] The use of *prydydd* alone as cognomen rather than with the adjective *mawr* as in the case of Cynddelw Brydydd Mawr and Trahaearn Brydydd Mawr, or with the adjective *bychan* as in the case of y Prydydd Bychan, obviates the need to discuss whether the adjectives refer to the poet's physique or the quality of his poetry, but it confers distinction on Meilyr just as the use of the noun *bardd* conferred distinction on the two Llywelyn Fardd's so called. *Prydydd*, like *prifardd*, designated a poet of distinction. Cynddelw calls himself a *prydydd* and a *prifardd*, but he also calls himself a *pencerdd*, a 'master or chief poet', to Madog ap Maredudd, if we assume, as we must, that he was victorious in the contention between Seisyll Bryffwrch and himself, as well as *pencerdd* to Owain Cyfeiliog, Madog ap Maredudd's successor in south Powys. As we shall see, we have reason to believe that Meilyr Brydydd was *pencerdd*, 'master poet' to Gruffudd ap Cynan, and we cannot help wondering why he does not refer to himself as Gruffudd ap Cynan's *pencerdd*.

There is a tradition that Gruffudd ap Cynan brought musicians and poets with him from Ireland, and at first sight this does not seem unlikely since

---

[11] The prophecy was accepted as Meilyr Brydydd's by Loth, *La métrique galloise*, 1.146, by T. Gwynn Jones, *Trans. Hon. Soc. of Cymmrodorion*, 1913–14, p. 231, and by J.E. Lloyd, *A History* 11.531. It was rejected by Morris-Jones, *Cerdd Dafod*, p. xxiv, and Evans, *Historia*, p. cxxxiv, n. 116, is inclined to do the same. Giraldus Cambrensis, *Opera* vi (ed. Dimock), 57–61 refers to a certain Meilyr who lived in the neighbourhood of Caerleon (the City of the Legions) and could explain the occult and foretell the future. See R. Geraint Gruffydd, 'Meilyr Brydydd and Meilyr Awenydd', *Barn*, Hydref 1980, rhif 213, 313–16.

[12] Daniel Huws, 'Llawysgrif Hendregadredd', pp. 1–23.

we are told that he depended a great deal on Irish troops in his early attempts to gain the throne of Gwynedd, but it is important to remember that Irish poets, unlike their Welsh counterparts, did not fight alongside their patrons.

There is also a tradition that Gruffudd ap Cynan was responsible for some reforms in the practice of the arts of music and poetry. This tradition was so strong in the sixteenth century that the organizers of the Caerwys Eisteddfod of 1523 thought that the rules which they then formulated would be more readily accepted if they had the authority of Gruffudd ap Cynan's name behind them, and so they were proclaimed as 'The Statute of Gruffudd ap Cynan' (*Statud Gruffudd ap Cynan*).[13]

The tradition that the Venedotian prince brought musicians and poets with him from Ireland gains credibility if Gellan, the *telynor pencerdd* who was killed according to *Historia Gruffud vab Kenan* in one of the prince's battles, was an Irishman. Professor D. Simon Evans, the editor of the *Historia*, thought that Gellan could be an Irish name,[14] but Professor J. Lloyd-Jones connected it with the Welsh adjective *gell* which occurs also as a personal name,[15] and with *Gelhi, Gelhig*, and *Gellan* in the *Book of Llandâv*, and the Gellan mentioned may be the same person as Gellan, one of the sons of Gollwyn, to whom there is a reference earlier in the text. Even if the *Gellan* whose death is recorded was an Irishman, it would be easier to think of him as a musician than as a poet, since, as we have observed, it was not the practice of Irish poets to fight alongside their patrons. In any case, the description *telynor pencerdd* is ambiguous. It might mean that Gellan was a harpist to a *pencerdd* 'chief poet', or 'harpist master-craftsman'. Professor Evans translates *telynor pencerdd* as 'harpist and chief poet'.[16] As he seems to have been a combatant, Gellan could have been harpist to a *pencerdd* acting in this situation as *bardd teulu*, bard to the prince's troops. The Welsh Laws tell us that both the *bardd teulu* and the *pencerdd* were entitled to the gift of a harp. and we know that every Welsh nobleman of note in later times had a harpist in his service.

Of the scholars who have indirectly, if not directly, linked the revival of Welsh praise poetry in the twelfth century with Gruffudd ap Cynan, perhaps the most prominent was the late Professor T. Gwynn Jones. He concluded: 'that the tradition is well founded that Gruffudd ap Cynan introduced Irish minstrels and bards and that he is likely to have made some regulations for the government of the bards and musicians,'[17] and went on to write that 'Irish influence is traceable in the style and structure of the poems of this

---

[13] Thomas Parry, 'Statud Gruffudd ap Cynan', pp. 25–33.

[14] Evans, *Historia*, pp. c, cxii, ccxxxv, 22, 13n.

[15] Lloyd-Jones, *Geirfa Barddoniaeth Gymar Gymraeg, II* 539 s.n. *gell*.

[16] Evans, *A Mediaeval Prince*, p. 73. This book contains the text of the Welsh *Historia Gruffud vab Kenan* (admirably edited by D. Simon Evans with notes and introduction, and an English translation).

[17] *Trans. Hon. Soc. of Cymmrodorion*, 1913–14, p. 282.

period (s.c. the twelfth century)'. Unfortunately some of the examples of Irish influences that he instances, the use of the prefixes *dy-* and *ry* with infixed pronouns, and the use of the word *derwyddon* would not be accepted as such today, nor would the use of *ceangal* if by *ceangal* he meant *íarcomarc* or *dúnad*.[18]

The poetic embellishment *dúnad*, involving the last word or syllable of the final stanza repeating the first word or syllable of the poem, occurs in early and syllabic Irish verse, but it is also found in early Welsh verse, as for instance in the elegy for Owain ab Urien attributed to Taliesin. *Dúnad* in Irish verse and its counterpart *cyrchu* in Welsh verse must be regarded as independent developments or, if the embellishment was also found in continental Celtic verse, as parallel developments.

No doubt instances of one literature influencing another have occurred, and it is interesting to note that some scholars have argued that Irish influence is to be seen in the development of Norse skaldic poetry, although it should be said that the latest scholarship has returned a 'Not Proven' verdict.[19]

It was possible to give more credibility than was proper to the theory that Gruffudd ap Cynan was able to re-introduce or re-animate the tradition of Welsh praise poetry because traditionally Meilyr Brydydd was regarded as the first of the Welsh court poets. In accordance with that tradition the historian J.E. Lloyd described Meilyr as 'the harbinger of the new era, the earliest of the "Gogynfeirdd" of the Welsh poetic renaissance'.[20] The *Myvyrian Archaiology of Wales* opens its collection of the poetry of the *Gogynveirdd* with *Canuau Meilyr*[21] and centuries earlier the editor-scribe alpha of the Hendregadredd MS (NLW MS 6680B) had opened his collection with *Marwnad ruffut ab kynan meilyr brydyt ae can[t]*.[22] As we shall see, Meilyr in that marwnad testifies to the presence of poets other than himself in Gruffudd ap Cynan's domain, and two poems in the *Black Book of Carmarthen*, one a eulogy for Hywel ap Gronw ap Cadwgan, who was made Lord of Ystrad Tywi, Gŵyr and Cydweli, by Henry I, and was treachously murdered by his son's foster-father Gwgon ap Meurig in 1106,[23] and the other, a eulogy to Cuhelyn Fardd who must have been living in the first half of the twelfth century c.1100–1132,[24] show that there were praise poets in South Wales singing in the same tradition as Meilyr during his life-time.

---

18 On *íarcomarc* see Meyer, *Primer of Early Metrics*, p. 12; on *iarcomarc* and *dúnad* see Murphy, *Early Irish Metrics*, pp. 43–45.

19 See Lehmann, *The Development of Germanic Verse Form*, pp. 184–5.

20 Lloyd, *A History*, II. 531.

21 *The Myvyrian Archaiology of Wales*, p. 140.

22 Huws, 'Llawysgrif Hendregadredd', pp. 1–23.

23 Jarman, *Llyfr Du Caerfyrddin*, p. 50.

24 *Ibid.*, 4–5. See Gruffydd, 'A Poem in praise of Cuhelyn Fardd', pp. 198–209.

However, even without this evidence for the existence of praise poets in other parts of Wales, it would be difficult to believe that Gruffudd ap Cynan had started a new literary tradition by the introduction of Irish influences. If we look for affinities to the poetry of the *Gogynfeirdd*, we find them in the poetry of their predecessors, the *Cynfeirdd*. The Gogynfeirdd use the same metres, the same poetical embellishments, even the same language as their predecessors. Indeed, their work has been described as a re-working of that of the Cynfeirdd.[25]

But perhaps the most cogent argument against the invocation of Irish influence is that the Welsh poets were an order or a sodality as firmly entrenched in society as were their counterparts in Ireland, as much an institution and a part of the structure of society, quite as basic and as deeply rooted in the past. To use the words of J. Lloyd-Jones, 'They were part and parcel of the social structure which engendered them, and their position, privileges, and benefits are clearly defined in the laws.'[26] The supersession of the bardic institution in Wales would have meant a radical change in the country's social structure. Apart from the fact that Irish bards would have needed an Irish-speaking audience to function in Wales, it can be taken for granted that the Welsh bards would have resisted any attempt to curtail their own rights, not to mention any attempt to reform or displace them.

We need not, however, deny any influence to Gruffudd ap Cynan; indeed, it is easy to believe that his military, political and cultural influence did a great deal to re-animate the tradition of praise-poetry and to confirm the poets in their role as the propagandists and upholders of the aristocratic social order. Both contributions would have resulted from his efforts to raise the level of general culture enjoyed in his kingdom. As the son of a 'mixed marriage', between a Welsh nobleman and a Scandinavian princess, and as a man brought up in Ireland, Gruffudd ap Cynan would have felt the need to play the rôle of Charlemagne in the Continent, King Alfred in England, and Brian Ború in Ireland; in other words, to play the rôle of a culture king in a country that cannot have been very flourishing either economically or culturally in the immediate past.

And again, Gruffudd could not have kept either himself or his domain immune to the influence of the so-called twelfth-century Renaissance 'Everywhere in so-called western Europe during the twelfth century', we are told, 'in France, Germany, England, Italy and Spain, men's hearts and minds were waking to a new appreciation of the world, its colour, its vastness, its perils and its beauty. There was curiosity about the world in all its aspects, the world of men, the world of the spirit, the world of the cosmos and the world of nature'.[27] As Georges Duby has reminded us, this renais-

---

[25] Morgan, 'Dadansoddi'r Gogynfeirdd', BBCS xiii, 169–174; xv. 1–88.
[26] Lloyd-Jones, *The Court Poets of the Welsh Princes*, p. 4.
[27] Heer, *The Medieval Mind*, p. 101.

sance differed from its predecessors. Whereas in the past, attempts at renaissance were conceived as the rescue from degeneration and the restoration to their pristine glory of former achievements, now those achievements were taken up to exploit them 'as settlers exploited virgin lands, in order to take more from them'.[28] There was a conviction that former achievements were there not to be restored but to be improved, to be surpassed, if not, in some cases, to be superseded.

Whatever motives impelled its ruler, Gwynedd underwent changes for the better. The *Historia* tells us:

Then every kind of good increased in Gwynedd and the people began to build churches in every park therein, sow woods and plant them, cultivate orchards and gardens, and surround them with fences and ditches, construct walled buildings, and live on the fruits of the earth after the fashion of the men of Rome. Gruffudd also built large churches in his own major court, and held his courts and feasts always honourably. Furthermore, Gwynedd glittered then with lime-washed churches, like the firmament with stars.[29]

One would like to know more about Gruffudd ap Cynan's 'major courts', and the way he held court and arranged his feasts, but even with this knowledge and allowing for a degree of exaggeration on the part of the author of the *Historia*, one can easily imagine how Meilyr Brydydd and his fellow poets would relish these signs of unprecedented prosperity and would have felt that they had come into their own at last.

Meilyr Brydydd must have sung many a song in praise of Gruffudd ap Cynan. Indeed, in his death-bed song he tells us that he had received many a time from generous kings gold and silk cloth as payment for praising them. *Cefais-i liaws awr aur a phali / Gan freuawl rïau er eu hoffi* (H.8. 13–14). 'I received many a time gold and silk cloth / From generous kings for praising them.' Unfortunately it is difficult to decide the precise meaning of such terms as *rhi, teyrn,* and *brenin* as they were used by the poets. We know that Irish law-texts distinguish between *rí* or *rí túaithe,* the king of a *túath, ruirí,* the king who had lordship over more than one *rí túaithe* as well as over his own *túath,* and the *rí ruirech,* the king to whom both *rí túaithe* and *rí ruirech* were subject. The Welsh law-texts are nowhere so precise. And our annals are equally unhelpful. *Historia Gruffudd vab Kenan* tells us that when Gruffudd first sailed to Gwynedd he found there ruling 'unjustly and contrary to right Trahaearn son of Caradog and Cynwrig son of Rhiwallon, a petty king (*brenhinyn*) of Powys, over all Gwynedd, and they had divided it between them'.[30] Later on we are told that in Gruffudd's old

[28] Duby, 'The Culture of the Knightly Class, Audience and Patronage', in Benson and Constable (ed.), *Renaissance and Renewal in the Twelfth Century.*
[29] Evans, *A Mediaeval prince,* pp. 81–82.
[30] Evans, *op.cit.,* p. 59.

age 'The other minor kings (*A'r brenhinedd bychein ereill*) made for his court and protection, to seek his help and counsel as often as foreign peoples harassed them'.[31] We should like to know what Latin words the translator of the *Historia* had before his eyes when he wrote the Welsh words *brenhinyn* and *brenhinedd bychein*. If we knew, we would have some idea of what Meilyr Brydydd meant in lines 41–44 of his elegy where he refers to *brenhinedd* and *teyrnedd*.

The fact that Meilyr Brydydd's elegy is the only one of his songs to his patron that has been preserved, indicates that it was held in high regard by its recipient's family as well as by the poet's. It was composed some time after the king's death for there are several references to his burial (see lines 29, 31, 71, 83, 101).

As we have mentioned, Meilyr Brydydd is generally thought to have been Gruffudd ap Cynan's *pencerdd* although he does not refer to himself as such. His son, Gwalchmai, addressing Gruffudd ap Cynan's son, Owain Gwynedd, says:

> Arddwyrëws fy nhad ei fraisg frenhindad,
>   Ar awen amnad ei rad rhagfras;
> Arddwyreaf innau fan, cynhorawr ffosawd,
>   Ar barabl perwawd, ar draethawd dras. (H.14–15)

> My father extolled his mighty royal father,
> (He extolled) in an artful muse his very great gift,
> I too extol the chieftain, a leader in battle
> In the sweet expression of poetry in a song about lineage.

This suggests that Gwalchmai performed the same service to Owain Gwynedd as his father had done to Gruffudd ap Cynan, i.e., an official service, in his capacity as chief poet or *pencerdd*.

Meilyr Brydydd himself tells us that there were other poets at Gruffudd ap Cynan's court. He rebukes some of them. *Py dawant anant, na phrydant wawd?* (line 11) 'Why are the poets silent, that they do not fashion a song?' *Anant* is an old term for poets, which seems to have become obsolete sme time afterwards. It is cognate with Welsh *anadl* 'breath' and *enaid* 'spirit'.[32] It reminds us of Meilyr Brydydd's use of *awenydd* a derivative of *awen*, 'a poetic gift, genius or inspiration, the muse': *Gnawd gwarchan a gân eu hawenydd* (line 151), 'Customary is the song that their poet sings' (line 141). There is also in the elegy references to *mân feirdd* 'minor poets' and *cychwilfeirdd cyhuseidiawg* (line 85),? 'pompous wandering poets'. There are several references to the function of the poets as propagandists:

---

[31] *Ibid.*, p. 82.
[32] Williams, 'Anant: Ffriw', pp. 44–45.

> Gan gerddau cyhoedd oedd ardderchawg
> O Ysgewin barth hyd borth Efrawg (ll.55–6)

> In well-known songs he was (made) eminent
> From the region of Ysgewin to the port of York.

And there is one reference to the songs of the bards as judgments on their recipients: *Nid adfarn cerddau* . . . (line 13), 'Songs are not false judgments . . .'

Meilyr Brydydd had apparently served as Gruffudd ap Cynan's emissary more than once. *Eilwaith yd euthum yn negesawg* (line 77), 'A second time I went as an emissary'.

The poet does not make many references to Gruffudd ap Cynan's lineage; the only ones he mentions among his ancestors are Anarawd, Rhun and Rhodri (lines 23–24, 70) but he obviously knew the importance of a noble stock just as he knew the importance of comparing his hero to famous examplars such as Medrawd and Mechydd (lines 25. 97, 133).

Like his successors Meilyr Brydydd gives prominence to the generosity of his patron, a generosity extended to other poets as well as to himself. *Ni ddug neb ceiniad nâg ohonawd* (line 14), 'No songster went from him with a refusal'. He was,

> Hael a rannai yn ei rihydd,
> Ni chronnai na seirch na meirch gweilydd (ll. 93–4),

> A generous king who used to distribute gifts in his sovereignty,
> He hoarded neither arms nor unused horses.

He was especially generous to Meilyr Brydydd.

> . . . Neu'm gorug yn oludawg
> Yfais gan deyrn o gyrn eurawg (ll. 72–3),

> . . . he made me wealthy,
> I drank beside a king from golden drinking-horns.

> Dewisais innau (nid gau defnydd)
> Ar emys ei lys a'i luosydd (ll. 137–8),

> I for my part took my choice (no false issue)
> From among the war-horses of the yard of his court and his hosts.

Perhaps the most significant lines with regard to Meilyr Brydydd's special position in Gruffudd ap Cynan's court are –

> Yn llys Aberffraw er ffaw ffodiawg
> ẞûm o du gwledig yn lleithigawg (ll. 75–6),

> At the court of Aberffro for the fame of the fortunate one
> I sat on the couch beside the ruler,

and

> Ni thorraf â'm câr fy ngherennydd,
> Cerennydd ysydd herwydd Trinedd (ll. 156–7),

> I shall not break my (bond of) friendship with my friend,
> The (bond of) friendship which is according to the Trinity.

Cerennydd has rich connotations. Its usual meanings are 'kindred, kinship, relationship, descent, affinity; friendship, love, reconciliation; kinsman, relation'.[33]

As one would expect, great play is made of Gruffudd ap Cynan's bravery
and his success as a leader of warriors.

> Gwanai yng nghynnor eisor Medrawd
> Mal Urien urdden a'i amgyffrawd (ll. 25–6),

> Medrawd's peer in the forefront of the army used to make a breach
> Like the honourable Urien and/with his onslaught.

> Ergyrwayw brwydrin cyn rhewin rhawd
> Rhyn ruthrai dorfoedd oedd rybarawd. (ll.33–4)

> Hurler of spear in battle (was he) before the cataclysm to the host,
> Ferociously did he attack the hordes who were too ready (to test him).

As always in the poetry of the Gogynfeirdd there is an element of
exaggeration. In addition to proclaiming that Gruffudd ap Cynan is *pasgadur kynrain*, 'the nurturer of chieftains' (line 22) and *Prydein briawd* 'the
rightful possessor or ruler of Britain' (line 22) the poet claims:

> Kyfamug ei wir â mil farchawc;
> Clywyd y gyma hyd tra Bannawc (ll. 63–4),

> He fought for his right with a thousand knights;
> His battling was heard as far as beyond Bannock (mountain).

> Dybu o'i gyffred gwared bedydd (l. 136),

> From his attack came the salvation of the world.

His successes in battle made Gruffudd ap Cynan a wealthy monarch. His
pastures were full of herds (*yn breiddiawg*), he had a long-maned stud (*gre
fyngawc*), war-horses (*emys*), speckled steeds (*meirch amliw*) and cattle
more than one could want (*biw elfydd*) (lines 60, 67, 138, 118). His poet
boasts of his great possessions, *ei fawr feuydd* (line 153). There is a note of
pride in his reference: *Ni yn Eryri yn rheïawg* (line 59), 'We in Eryri
wallowing in riches'.

The Poets of the Princes, on the whole, tend not to indulge in details. The

---

[33] See Charles-Edwards, 'The date of the Four Branches of the Mabinogi', pp. 278–9, and
Hamp, 'Cerennydd', p. 683.

historian who reads their poems to find precise information regarding events, their dates and places, is disappointed. As the notes to Meilyr Brydydd's elegy show, it refers to several places where Gruffudd ap Cynan fought his foes and in this respect it is more informative than most of the elegies and praise poems. Dafydd Benfras's 'Cynnydd Llywelyn ap Gruffudd' (*Red Book Poetry* 1381 1–2) refers to some twenty successful assaults made by its subject but in this it is very much the exception that proves the rule. Perhaps it should be noted that even the *Historia Gruffudd van Kenan* is not as precise nor as elaborate as we could wish in its reference to Gruffudd ap Cynan's military exploits and its Latin author had less excuse for not giving more details as he was addressing a different audience in an international language, whereas Meilyr Brydydd like his successors was declaiming his verses to an audience well-acquainted with all the details of his patron's achievements and it may well have been that referring to those achievements in the most general terms would make less obvious and less embarrassing the absence of any references to the patron's failures, although such references in any case would not be in keeping with the main intention, that of extolling and exalting the recipient of the poem.

II

The following version of Meilyr Brydydd's Elegy for Gruffudd ap Cynan is in Modern Welsh orthography and is based on the edition prepared for Volume I in the series of the Works of the Gogynfeirdd prepared by the University of Wales Centre for Advanced Welsh and Celtic Studies under the General Editorship of Professor R. Geraint Gruffydd. The English translation has no literary pretensions. It simply paraphrases the literal meaning and in places it chooses one from among several possible interpretations.

MARWNAD RUFFUD AP CYNAN: MEILYR BRYDYDD A'I CANT

Rhên nef, mor rhyfedd Ei ryfeddawd,
Rhïau, Rhwyf elfydd, rhydd Ei folawd,
Rex rhadau wrno, rhy-n-bo-ni gardawd,
Rheg rhy-d-eirifam yn rhan Drindawd.
5 Pan ddyfo Dofydd yn nydd pennawd,
Peryf, pâr wrthfyn yn erbyn Brawd
Pan gaffwyf-i gan lain lân gyflogawd,
Can dyddaw angau angen drallawd.
Ac ail dra drymaf trengi meddwawd,
10 Llys lleufer ynys, gwrys gorfyndawd:
Py dawant anant, na phrydant wawd
I edwyn terwyn torf ei forawd?
Nid adfarn cerddau! Nid gan daerawd!

Ni ddug neb ceiniad nâg ohonawd.
15 Yn awen gyfrif cenif draethwawd
I ri a roai heb esgusawd.
Gruffudd glew dywal ar orfeddawd,
Gwir gwae ei werin, gwin eu gwirawd.
Gŵr a lywai lu cyn bu breuawd,
20 Blaidd byddin orthew yn nerw blyngawd!
Er perygl preiddwyr peri ffosawd,
Pasgadur cynrain, Prydain briawd;
Handoedd gad gyffro o Anarawd,
Ac ail o Run Hir, rhyfel ddurawd.
25 Gwanai yng nghynnor eisor Medrawd
Mal Urien urdden a'i amgyffrawd;
Gweled i ben llu, ni bu ddefawd,
Nur cadau, neuaddau o ystyllawd!
Cyn myned mab Cynan i dan dywawd
30 Ceffid yn ei gyntedd fedd a bragawd.
O olo Gruffudd yn rhudd feddrawd
Cwynif-i ddragon dwfn ddygn ddiwyrnawd.
Ergyrwayw brwydrin cyn rhewin rhawd,
Rhyn ruthrai dorfoedd oedd rhybarawd;
35 Rhy'i gaded Rhufain reg addfwyndawd,
Ni fynnai gamwr garu nebawd.
I gymeriaid lyw doddyw dyrnawd,
Difa draig wron, weinon wasgawd:
Gogwypo ei Dduw o'i ddiweddawd
40 Nad êl yn rhygoll o'i holl bechawd.

O gyfranc brenhinedd brain foddawg,

---

23 *Anarawd*, son of Rhodri Mawr; he died in 916. For further references to him in early Welsh poetry see Lloyd-Jones, *Geirfa Barddoniaeth Gynnar Gymraeg* (henceforth, G) 26, Lloyd, *A History*, i. 328, 326–30, *The Dictionary of Welsh Biography, s.n. Anarawd ap Rhodri*.

24 *Rhun Hir*, Rhun the Tall, son of Maelgwn Gwynedd. On him see Bromwich, *Trioedd*, pp. 502–2, Lloyd, *A History*, i. 168, suggests that the references to him as *Hir* 'Tall' indicate that he was tall in stature, like his father, and that the fact that in *Breudwyt Ronabwy* (ed. Richards) 20, he is linked with Arthur perhaps suggests that he took precedence over all the princes who were his contemporaries. See also Morris, *The Age of Arthur*, pp. 192, 206, 216 f., 240, 515.

25 *Medrawd*. See Bromwich, *Trioedd Ynys Prydein*, 207, 434–5. Medrawd was regarded as a paragon of bravery and courtesy in Welsh poetry until the time of Tudur Aled, the first Welsh poet, apparently, to refer to him as a traitor, the rôle he plays in Arthurian literature generally.

26 *Urien*, Urien Rheged, patron of the poet Taliesin. See Bromwich, *Trioedd*, pp. 516–20 Williams, *Canu Taliesin*, pp. xxiii–xxxvi, *Poems of Taliesin*, pp. xxxvi–iv, Lloyd, *A History*, i. 165

29 *Mab Cynan*, Gruffudd ap Cynan. The poet refers to Gruffudd ap Cynan as Gruffudd (see 1.31) and as the son of the Cynan (see 1.46).

35 *Rhufain*, an interesting reference to Rome, the seat of the Papacy.

Pan fai gyfluydd o wŷr gwychawg,
Atgoryn deyrnedd yn weinyddawg,
Pob pump, bob pedwar yn wâr weiniawg.
45 Gwylynt, golithrynt yn ogelawg
Rhag unmab Cynan, y cyndyniawg.
Yr arynaig lew law ddiferiawg,
Ni ludd ei erlid yn odidawg.
Ceimiad cas agarw, syberw serchawg,
50 Cyd galwed unig nid oedd ofnawg;
Ar bob rhai rheidiai yn eur-rodawg
Rhag byddin Emrais drais drahaawg.
Cadau ddidudydd, cleddyf ddurawg,
Cŵl clywed cystudd ar rudd mynawg;
55 Can gerddau cyhoedd oedd ardderchawg
O Ysgewin barth hyd borth Efrawg.
Dybu brenin Lloegr yn lluyddawg,
Cyd doeth ef nid aeth yn warthegawg:
Ni yn Eryri yn rheïawg,
60 Ni thorres i bawr a fu breiddiawg.
Gruffudd grym cyhoedd (nid oedd guddiawg)
A ddiffyrth ei wŷr yn orwythawg;
Cyfamug ei wir â mil farchawg;
Clywyd ei gyma hyd dra Bannawg!
65 Brenin brwydr efnys gwrŷs gwellyniawg,
Pen rhïau, parau anoleithiawg,
Perchen pefr ystre o'r re fyngawg,

---

52 *Emrais*, probably Emrys Wledig, rather than Emrys Myrddin (Ambrosius Merlinus) although it is difficult to assess the extent to which the Welsh poets differentiated between the two. See G 474–5, Bromwich, *Trioedd*, pp. 345–6.

56 *Ysgewin barth*, Portskewett, near Cas-gwent, in the south-east corner of Wales. Giraldus Cambrensis tells us that for its length Wales could be measured from Porth Wygyr in Anglesey to Porth Ysgewin in Gwent 'a portu Yoiger in Monia ad portum Eskewin in Winta': *Opera*, vi, Dimock, 165. See Bromwich, *Trioedd*, p. 237.

63 *tra Bannawg*. According to Williams, *Canu Llywarch Hen*, pp. 156–7, *Canu Aneirin*, p. 141, *Bannawg* refers to the Grampians in Scotland. Jackson believed that it refers to the hills where Bannock Burn rises; *The Gododdin*, pp. 16, 78–79. See also Bromwich, *Trioedd*, p. 545.

57–9 *Dybu brenin Lloegr . . . yn rheïawg*, Lloyd, *A History*, ii. 532, n. 188 suggests that this is a reference to Henry I's attack in 1114 (*ibid.*, 463–4). One should, however, bear in mind William Rufus's expeditions in 1095 (*ibid.*, 406) and in 1097 (*ibid.*, 408). According to Evans, *Historia*, p. 89, *Historia*, p. 22 refers to the 1097 expedition, and in view of line 58 it is interesting to note that according to *Historia* 22.25 William Rufus took away only one cow in booty. According to *Historia*, p. 29, Henry I made two expeditions against Gruffudd ap Cynan, one in 1114, the other in 1121, *ibid.*, pp. 100, 102, and on each occasion Gruffudd ap Cynan's tactics were to retreat to Snowdonia, to Eryri, and this gives special significance to the *ni yn Eryri* 'we in Eryri' of line 59. Evans as editor of *Historia* does not connect the expedition mentioned here with any particular historical expedition. See *Historia*, pp. cxxxvi and 108.

Modrydaf Cymry, erhy farchawg.
Arwyneb neuadd yn amniferawg,
70   Nerth Rhodri, rhëi rywasgarawg;
Cyn mynd mur ced yn dawedawg
Dy-m-gug, neu'm gorug yn oludawg.
Yfais gan dëyrn o gyrn eurawg
Arfodd faedd feiddiad angas weiniawg;
75   Yn llys Aberffraw, er ffaw ffodiawg,
Bûm o du gwledig yn lleithigawg.
Eilwaith ydd eithum yn negesawg
Goleufer camawn, iawn dywysawg.
Bu fedd eurgylchwy yn fordwyawg,
80   Toresid gormes yn llynghesawg.
Gwedi tonnau gwyrdd gorewynnawg
Dyfforthynt ei seirch meirch rhygyngawg;
A nw neud gweryd yn warweiddiawg:
Gwae a ymdddired wrth fyd bradawg!
85   Ni ŵyr cychwilfeirdd cyhuseidiawg
Tymp pan dreing terwyn torf ddiffreidiawg:
Cwynif, ni byddif ddiebreidiawg,
Delw ydd amgyrwyf bwyf cynheilwawg.
Crist cyflawn annwyd, boed trugarawg
90   Wrth Ruffudd Gwynedd gwyledd fodawg;
Yng ngwlad nef boed ef yn dreftadawg,
N'ad ei enaid hael yn waeleddawg!

Hael a ri a renni yn ei riydd,
Ni chronnai na seirch na meirch gweilydd,
95   Gwladoedd ofynaig, draig Gwyndodydd,
Gŵr a roddai gad cyn dybu ei ddydd.
Gruffudd grym angor, eisor Mechydd,
Marchogai esgar ar elorwydd!
Arbennig cenfaint, ceraint weinydd,
100   Cynreinion ysgwyd, ysgor orwydd.
Yni fu weryd ei obennydd
Ni byddai ddiwyth i lwyth oswydd;

---

70 *Rhodri*, Rhodri Mawr, king of Gwynedd from 844 to 878. His kingdom included Powys and extended as far south as Ceredigion and Ystrad Tywi, but it was under constant attack from the Danes. See Lloyd, *A History*, i. 323–6, *A Dictionary of Welsh Biography*, *s.n.* Rhodri Mawr.

75 *Aberffraw* on the west coast of Anglesey, principal seat of the princes of Gwynedd in early medieval times. See Lloyd, *A History*, i. 232, ii. 682 and n. 151; Ellis, *Welsh Tribal Law and Custom*, pp. 23–4.

80 *llynghesawg*. *Historia* has several references to the use made of ships by Gruffudd ap Cynan. See *ibid.*, pp. 12.7, 21. 14, 23. 25–24. 2.

90 *Gruffudd Gwynedd*, Gruffudd ap Cynan of Gwynedd. Gruffudd's son Owain is known as Owain Gwynedd rather than as Owain ap Gruffudd.

96 *Gwyndodydd*, the people of Gwynedd, Venedotians.

Amug â'u dragon, udd Môn, meinddydd,
Men yd las Trahaearn yng Ngharn Fynydd.
105   I ddau dywysawg (deifniawg ddedwydd)
Brenhinedd Powys a'u Gwenhwysydd,
Gorau gwaith gwyniaith â'i gyweithydd
Pan gedwis ei wyneb heb gywilydd.
Cuddynt cyfnofant cant cyfoedydd,
110   Cyngen gymynid gwyddfid gwrfydd,
Taer terddyn asau talau trefydd,
Torri calchdöed tiredd Trenydd.
Am drefan Dryffwn rhag eiriolydd
Tyrfai rhag llafnau pennau peithwydd,
115   Caith cwynynt, cerddynt gan elfydd,
Cnoynt frain friwgig o lid llawrydd.
Llenwid ddwyreawr ei fawr feysydd,
Delid meirch amliw a biw elfydd,
Gwern gwygid, gwanai bawb yn ei gilydd,
120   Gwaed gwŷr goferai, gwyrai onwydd.
A'r maint a ddyfu ar eu hedrydd
A ddug o'i gadau chweddlau newydd!
Cad rhag Castellmarch, maer ei dyfydd,
A chadau Cynwrig wyrennig wlydd.

---

97 *Mechydd*, one of Llywarch Hen's sons; see Williams, *Canu Llywarch Hen*, pp. 29–30, Bartrum, ed., *Tracts*, p. 86.

104 *Trahaearn*, Trahaearn ap Caradog, ruler of Arwystli and king of Gwynedd for a short time after his victory over Gruffudd ap Cynan in the Battle of Bronyrerw 1075. He was killed in the Battle of Mynydd Carn, 1081, where he fought as an ally of Caradog ap Gruffudd. See Lloyd, *A History*, ii. 378–84; Evans, *Historia*, p. 147; Maund, 'Trahaearn', pp. 468–76; *Dictionary of Welsh Biography*, *s.n.* Trahaearn ap Caradog.
Carn Fynydd, the site of the Battle of Mynydd Carn, 1081. It has not been precisely located although some place in North Pembrokeshire seems likely. See Evans, *Historia*, pp. 77–8 and the comments by D.J. Bowen in *Barn*, no. 215 (Rhagfyr, 1980), p. 373.

105–6 *dau dywysawg – a'u Gwenhwysydd*. Trahaearn ap Caradog, Meilir ap Rhiwallon and Caradog ap Gruffudd's men from Gwent according to G 661. See Evans, *Historia*, p. 14 and n. 74, where it is said that the two princes mentioned here were Meilir and Caradog. Gwennwys can refer to one of the two *costoglwythau* in Powys and it may be that *Gwenhwysydd* refers to them.

123 *Castellmarch*, near Abersoch in south Caernarvonshire: see Thomas, *Enwau Afonydd a Nentydd Cymru*, p. 75. There is a house called 'Castellmarch': see *An Inventory of the Ancient Monuments in Wales and Monmouthshire, Caernarvonshire* iii, 59b–61a, xxx, c/xii, c/xviii, c/xx, c/xxxix and n. 9. For 'Castellmarch' or the fort 'Castell Nant-y-castell' see *ibid.*, p. 39b, and J G Evans, 'Castellmarch', pp. 303–7. According to Evans, *Historia*, p. cxxxvii this may be a reference to the fighting against Cynwrig ap Rhiwallon in 1075, although he remarks in a note (*ibid.*) that *gwyrennig wlydd* is not an apt description of that Cynwrig as he is described in *Historia* (*ibid.*, lines 2–10) and that it is not certain that the two Cynwrigs are identical.

124 *Cynwrig*, Cynwrig ap Rhiwallon. See the references to him in Evans, *Historia*, p. 138, and Lloyd, *A History*, ii. 379–80. *Dictionary of Welsh Biography, s.n.* Cynwrig Hir.

125 I gad gynghywair ym Meirionnydd
    Arglwydd glew gadarn haearn dyfydd,
    Ni noddes mawredd eu merwerydd!
    Yng ngwaith Y Waederw, chwerw chwelidydd.
    Cad Geredigiawn, gyfiawn gywydd,
130 Crynynt wragedd gweddw goddiwedydd;
    Cad yn Iwerddon dirion drefydd,
    Gan a'i canfu ni bu ferydd.
    Cad rhag tâl Prydain, prenial Fechydd,
    Gruffudd a orfu rhag llu gwythrydd;
135 Cad rhag castell Môn, mor ddigerydd,
    Dybu o'i gyffred gwared bedydd.
    Dewisais innau (nid gau ddefnydd)
    Ar emys ei lys a'i luosydd:
    As rhoddwy fy Rhên ran dragywydd
140 Yng ngwerth a roddes ar lles prydydd.
    Ni wddant fanfeirdd ni mawr gynnydd
    Pwy a enillo o'r do ysydd;
    Edewis eurwas, clas gymrëydd,
    Canawon mordai, mynogi rhydd.

125 *ym Meirionnydd*, i.e., the cantref Meirionnydd. This is a reference to the Battle of Gwaed Erw, 1075, according to Evans, *Historia*, cxxxvii. It is certainly not a reference to the Battle of Bronyrerw as Arthur Jones suggests in his edition, *The History*, p. 167 n. 12, for that battle was fought in the vicinity of Clynnog Fawr in Arfon. It should be remembered that *cad* can mean 'army', the meaning adopted in the translation, as well as 'battle'.

128 *Y Waederw.* *Historia*, p. 9 (1.5) mentions a battle in Meirionnydd fought between Gruffudd ap Cynan and Trahaearn ap Caradog in *glynn kyving*, i.e. in 'Narrow Glen', the place called in Welsh *Guaet Erw neu y Tir Guaetlyt*, the Blood Acre or the Bloody Land. Lloyd, *A History*, ii. 380–1 sought to locate the battle in Dyffryn Glyn-cul, but although he found a mill called *keuyng* in that district, his explanation of *glynn kyving* as a place-name is not very convincing.

129 *Cad Geredigiawn* Perhaps a reference to the raids made by the two sons of Gruffudd ap Cynan, Owain and Cadwaladr, into Ceredigion in 1136 and 1137. See Evans, *Historia*, p. cxxxviii, Lloyd, *A History*, ii. 471–3, 475–6 and cf. perhaps Gwalchmai's reference to *Gweith Aberteiui* in H.18.7.

    If it were possible to identify the Mynydd Carn of the battle with the Mynydd Carn in *Gwaith Lewis Glyn Cothi* (ed., Tegid and Gwallter Mechain. 215, the work to which Phillimore called attention in 'The Publication of Welsh Historical Records', as the name of a mountain in Ceredigion, it would then be possible to identify Geredigiawn with the Battle of Mynydd Carn, but it is difficult to do so in view of the remarks by Lloyd, *A History*, ii. 384, n. 88.

133 *Mechydd.* See above on 1.97.

135 *Castell Môn.* Perhaps a reference to the fighting in Anglesey in 1099 for Castell Aberlleiniog, according to Evans, *Historia*, p. cxxxvii. See *ibid.*, 19–20, 85, 87; Lloyd, *A History*, ii. 403–4.

142 *Pwy a enillo o'r do ysydd.* See J.B. Smith, 'Dynastic Succession in Medieval Wales,' pp. 199–232.

145 Dyddwyreo Owain, Eingl ddiduddydd,
     Enillawd llyw ystre lle ei gilydd;
     Gwelant glyw Powys ei bell oesydd
     A hawdd ei ergryd hyd lew dyfydd.
     Cadwaladr gedawl o gynfedydd,
150 Cyntëig ar gan, Calan weinydd.
     Gnawd gwarchan a gân eu hawenydd,
     Yn arfod adwy hwy a orfydd.
     Gruffudd grym wriawr, o'i fawr feuydd
     Ni'm diddoles (nu ni bu gelwydd!)
155 Yni fwyf gynefin â derwin wŷdd
     Ni thorraf â'm câr fy ngherennydd.

     Cerennydd ysydd herwydd Trined,
     I Gristiawn ys iawn ei gyrhaedded:
     Crefydd y Creawdr yng nghyfrifed
160 I Ruffudd, gloywudd a'i cudd tudwed.
     Hyd nas gwnêl pechawd pell eilywed,
     Pedrydawg dëyrn uch cyrn coned,
     Cenif (nis dygif yn ddiabred)
     Marwnad mur tewdor fôr ddylyed.
165 Cedernid rhewynt cyn no'i fyned,
     Ergrynai fy mhwyll ei bell gerdded,
     A dyfo mab Cynan (mawr amgyffred)
     Can Grist geinforawd gwlad ogoned,
     Pan gaffo pen gwŷr (pefr ymddired)
170 Gan englynion foes (ni'm oes neued)
     Yn undawd Drindawd, drwy rybuched,
     Gan lair loyw addef yn nef drefred.

III

THE ELEGY FOR GRUFFUDD AP CYNAN:
IT IS MEILYR BRYDYDD WHO SANG IT

Lord of heaven, so amazing His awesomeness,
Sovereign, Ruler of the world, boundless His praise,
King excellent in His blessings, may we have mercy,
A boon on the part of the Trinity we have included in our
     reckoning.

---

[145] *Owain.* Owain Gwynedd. See Lloyd, *A History*, ii. 487–523. *Dictionary of Welsh Biography, s.n.* Owain Gwynedd.

[149] *Cadwaladr,* one of Gruffudd ap Cynan's sons. See the note on l.129 Gwalchmai refers to him in his ode to Dafydd ab Owain see H 29.19. He died in 1172. On him see Evans, *Historia*, p. 88 (n. on 22.6), Lloyd, *A History*, ii. 471–5. 488–91, 504, 550, *Dictionary of Welsh Biography, s.n.* Cadwaladr (*ob.*1172).

5   Whenever the Lord may come on the appointed day,
     Monarch, arrange a welcome (reception) for the Day of Judgment
     When I may have with the saints a holy abode,
     Since the affliction of certain death will come.
     And the second most dire event (for me) is that the lavish donor
          of wine has died,
10   The light of the kingdom's court, the ferocious one in battle:
     Why are they silent, the bards that do not fashion praise
     To the fiery passionate one whose sea-band was a multitude?
     Songs are not false judgments! Tributes are not fictitious!
     No songster left him with a refusal.
15   Impelled by the Muse I sing a chant of praise
     To a king who gave gifts without apology.
     Gruffudd, the brave ferocious one in his domination
     Genuine now is the woe of his people whose drink was (once) wine.
     A warrior who led a multitude before he languished,
20   A wolf with a multitudinous army, (now he lies) in a piteous
          oak coffin!
     To imperil predators he joined battle,
     Nurturer of princes, rightful monarch of Britain;
     From the lineage of Anarawd was the army-inciter,
     And a descendant of Rhun the Tall, the steely one in battle.
25   Medrawd's peer in the forefront of the army used to make a breach
     Like the honourable Urien and/with his onslaught;
     Unusual (was it) for the chief of hosts,
     Lord of battles, to see about him palisaded halls!
     Before Cynan's son went (entombed) under sand
30   Mead and malt-liquor were had in his hall.
     Because Gruffudd has been buried in a (new) russet grave
     I shall bemoan the ruler of the world on (his) dire day.
     Hurler of spear in battle (was he) before the cataclysm to the host,
     Ferociously did he attack the hordes who were too ready (to test
          him);
35   Let Rome grant him indulgence,
     The champion did not wish to show love to any one.
     On the lord of tenants a blow has fallen,
     Death of the brave one of the nature of a dragon, the protector of
          the weak:
     May his God take cognizance of his ending
40   That he may not be damned because of all his sins.

     From the clash of kings satisfying ravens,
     Whenever a hosting of brave warriors occurred,
     Sovereigns returned enslaved,
     In fives, in fours obediently and with sheathed swords,
45   They were wary, they crept stealthily and cautiously
     Before the one son of Cynan, the unyielding one.
     The awesome brave with a despoiler's hand,

Marvellously his pursuit does not desist.
The champion of furious ferocity, affable yet proud,

50 Though he was called (to be) on his own (unrivalled), he was
        fearless;
Against all kinds he would fight behind his golden shield.
In the forefront of Emrais's army proud in its might,
Destroyer of armies, steely his sword,
'Tis a shame to hear that there is a grinding of the cheek of
        the noble one;

55 In well-known songs he was (made) eminent
From the region of Ysgewin to York harbour.
The king of England came accompanied by hosts,
Though he came he did not return with cattle:
We in Eryri were rich,

60 He did not break into (any) pasture land that contained herds.
Gruffudd of renowned might – he was not hidden –
Defended his men ferociously;
He fought for his right with a thousand knights;
His battling was heard as far as beyond Bannawg!

65 A king furious in battle and ferocious in onset,
Chief of kings with inescapable spears,
Owner of a glorious line of horses from the long-maned stud,
Leader of the Welsh, audacious knight.
Protector of the hall with his host,

70 One of the might of Rhodri, great distributor of wealth;
Before the advocate of generosity became silent (in death)
He repaid me, he made me wealthy.
I drank from golden drinking-horns beside the king
Drinks poured out by the serving hand of the wolf-challenger;

75 At the court of Aberffro, for the fame of the fortunate one,
I sat on the couch beside the ruler.
A second time I went as the emissary
Of the dazzling one in battle, the rightful prince.
The host of the golden shielded one became sea-borne,

80 With his fleet he quashed the enemy.
After (braving) the foam-crested green waves
Ambling steeds bore his armour;
And now he lies prone in the glebe:
Woe to anyone who puts his trust in (this) treacherous world!

85 The pompous vagrant bards know not
The time when the fiery one of the defending host dies:
I will mourn, I will not be restrained,
As I desire let me be an extoller.
Christ perfect in (His) nature, let Him be merciful

90 To Gruffudd of Gwynedd constant in generosity;
In the Kingdom of heaven let him have his patrimony,
Let not his noble soul be wretched.

It was a generous king who used to distribute gifts in his
    sovereignty;
He hoarded neither arms nor unused steeds,
95   The hope of lands, dragon of the Venedotians,
A warrior who gave battle before his death-day came.
Gruffudd of anchor-like steadfastness, Mechydd's peer,
He mounted his enemies on biers!
Foremost of the host, helper of kinsmen,
100   Shield of warriors, defender of the border.
Until the soil became his pillow
He gave no peace to his enemy's people;
The lord of Môn fought with their chiefs mid-day,
Where Trahaearn was slain at Carn Fynydd.
105   On the two princes, (blessed was he as ruler to be)
The kings of Powys and their Gwent-tribe,
He wrought vengeance with his host
When he kept his honour without shame.
His enemies hid with their companions,
110   A notable host was destroyed in battle,
Relentlessly his spears splintered the habitation ramparts,
The armoured one rent the lands of Trenydd.
Around the abode of Tryffwn before the importunate one
The heads of destructive shafts sprang apart before the blades,
115   Prisoners moaned, they drifted along the land,
Carrion-crows gnawed flesh torn by the anger of the generous
    one.
His great fields were filled at the hour of dawn,
Speckled steeds and the world's cattle were caught,
Spears were shattered, each one rushed at the other,
120   The blood of warriors flowed, ash-spears drooped.
And all who returned to their homes
Brought new tidings of his battles!
The battle in front of Castellmarch, great its woe,
And the battles of the humane but steadfast Cynwrig.
125   To the fully equipped army in Merionnydd
The iron arms of the brave strong lord will come,
His might did not accommodate their uproar!
In the Battle of Gwaederw, a fierce demolisher was he, Gruffudd,
The Battle of Ceredigion, well-organized,
130   Widows trembled (in fear) at the end of the day;
The battle in Ireland of the pleasant homesteads
Those who saw it did not deem it devoid of hazard.
The battle facing Britain's headland, a battle with spears like
    Mechydd,
It was Gruffudd who was victorious before the savage host;
135   The battle in front of Môn's castle, so unerring was he,
From his onslaught came the deliverance of Christendom.
I for my part took my choice (no false issue)

From among the war-horses of the yard of his court and his hosts:
May the Lord grant an eternal estate (to him)
140   In exchange for what he gave to benefit (his) poet.
Minor bards who do not make much progress, do not know
Which one of the present generation will win (the succession);
The excellent one, the defender of the country, left
Court descendants of generous nobility.
145   Owain, despoiler of the Angles, will arise,
The defender of the border will win his enemy's place;
The Powys host see his long lifetime (career)
And readily will fear of him come to the brave.
Cadwaladr, the munificent battle-reaper,
150   Speedy rider on a white steed, a benefactor on the Calends.
Recurrent is the song that their (Owain and Cadwaladr's) bard
    sings,
In the battle breach it is they who will overcome.
Gruffudd of the mighty onslaught, of his great possessions
He did not withhold from me a share (now that was no lie!)
155   Until I be habituated to an oak coffin
I shall not break my bond with my friend.

The bond (of friendship) which is according to the Trinity,
It is proper for a Christian to achieve it:
The religious order of the Creator (held) in honour is
160   For Gruffudd, the radiant lord whom the soil covers.
So that sin may not cause him long sorrow,
The perfect sovereign (towering) above his glorious drinking-
    horns,
I shall sing (I shall not do it with restraint)
An elegy for the upholder of might, as brimful as the sea of rights.
165   One of the force of the ice (cold) wind before he departed,
His far-roving confounded my mind,
And may the son of Cynan come – a fine attainment this –
With Christ to the fine journey of the land of glory,
When the chief of men shall have – trust is bright –
170   A welcome from the angels – I do not need anything –
In the unity of the Trinity, through desire,
With the saints a bright home in the heavenly abode.

BIBLIOGRAPHY

ARNOLD, Thomas (ed.) *Henrici Archidiaconi Huntendunensis Historia An-glorum: The History of the English by Henry, Archdeacon of Huntingdon, from A.C. 55 to A.D. 1154, in Eight Books* (London 1879)

ARNOLD, Thomas (ed.) *Symeonis Monachi Opera Omnia* (2 vols, London 1982/5)

ANDERSSON, T.M. 'Kings' Sagas (*Konungasögur*)', in *Old Norse-Icelandic Literature*, edd. Clover & Lindow, pp. 197–238

ANDERSSON, T. & SANDRED, K.I. (edd.) *The Vikings. Proceedings of the Symposium at the Faculty of Arts of Uppsala University June 6–9, 1977* (Uppsala 1978)

AÐALBJARNARSON, Bjarni (ed.) *Snorri Sturluson, Heimskringla* (3 vols, Reykjavík 1979)

BARLOW, Frank *William Rufus* (London 1983)

BARRACLOUGH, Geoffrey (ed.) *The Charters of the Anglo-Norman Earls of Chester, c.1071–1237* (Chester 1988)

BARTRUM, P.C. (ed.) 'Achau Brenhinoedd a Thywysogion Cymru', *Bulletin of the Board of Celtic Studies* 19 (1960–2) 201–25

BARTRUM, P.C. (ed.) *Early Welsh Genealogical Tracts* (Cardiff 1966)

BARTRUM, P.C. 'Further notes on Welsh genealogical manuscripts', *Transactions of the Honourable Society of Cymmrodorion* (1976) 102–18

BARTRUM, P.C. (ed.) 'Pedigrees of the Welsh Tribal Patriarchs', *National Library of Wales Journal* 13 (1963/4) 93–146 *and* 15 (1967/8) 157–66

BARTRUM, P.C. 'Was there a British "Book of Conquests"?', *Bulletin of the Board of Celtic Studies* 23 (1968–70) 16

BARTRUM, P.C. *Welsh Genealogies A.D. 300–1400* (8 vols, Cardiff 1974, and supplement, Cardiff 1980)

BATEY, Colleen E., *et al.* (edd.) *The Viking Age in Caithness, Orkney and the North Atlantic* (Edinburgh 1993)

BAUGH, G.C. (ed.) *The Victoria History of the Counties of England: A History of Shropshire*, III (Oxford 1979)

BELL, A. (ed.) *Geoffrey Gaimer, L'Estoire des Engleis* (Oxford 1960)

BENEDIKTSSON, Jakob (ed.) *Íslendingabók; Landnámabók* (Reykjavík 1968)

BENSON, R.L. & CONSTABLE, G. (edd.) *Renaissance and Renewal in the Twelfth Century* (Oxford 1982)

BERGIN, O.J. 'Bardic Poetry', *Journal of the Ivernian Society* 5 (1912–12) 162–3

187

BERGIN, O.J. 'Varia II', *Ériu* 11 (1930–2) 136–49

BEST, R.I., *et al.* (edd.) *The Book of Leinster, formerly Lebor na Núachong-bála* (6 vols, Dublin 1954–83)

BINCHY, D.A. *Celtic and Anglo-Saxon Kingship* (Oxford 1970)

BINNS, J.W. *Intellectual Culture in Elizabethan and Jacobean England: the Latin Writings of the Age* (Leeds 1990)

BLAKE, E.O. (ed.) *Liber Eliensis* (London 1962)

BOYER, R. (ed.) *Les vikings et leur civilisation: problèmes actuels* (Paris 1976)

BRADLEY, J. (ed.) *Settlement and Society in Early Ireland: Studies presented to F.X. Martin, o.s.a.* (Kilkenny 1988)

BRADNEY, Joseph Alfred (ed.) *Llyfr Baglan, or, the Book of Baglan* (London 1910)

BRAUNMÜLLER, K. & BRØNDSTED, M. (edd.) *Deutsch-nordische Be-gegnungen 9. Arbeitstagung der Standinavisten des deutschen Sprachge-biets 1989 in Svendborg* (Odense 1991)

BREWER, J.S., *et al.* (edd.) *Giraldi Cambrensis Opera* (8 vols, London 1861–91)

BRODERICK, George (ed. & transl.) *Cronica Regum Mannie & Insularum* (Douglas 1979)

BRODERICK, G. 'Irish and Welsh strands in the genealogy of Godred Crovan', *Journal of the Manx Museum* 8 (1980) 32–38

BROMWICH, Rachel (ed. & transl.) *Trioedd Ynys Prydein* (2nd edn, Cardiff 1978)

BYRNE, F.J. (ed. & transl.) 'Clann Ollaman Uaisle Emna', *Studia Hibernica* 4 (1964) 54–94

CARR, A.D. (transl.) 'The Extent of Anglesey, 1352', *Anglesey Antiquarian Society and Field Club Transactions* (1971/2) 158–272

CATON, P.G.F. *Maps of Hourly Mean Wind Speed over the United Kingdom, 1965–73* (1976)

CHARLES, B.G. *Old Norse Relations with Wales* (Cardiff 1934)

CHARLES-EDWARDS, T.M. *Early Irish and Welsh Kinship* (Oxford 1993)

CHARLES-EDWARDS, T.M. 'Some Celtic kinship terms', *Bulletin of the Board of Celtic Studies* 24 (1970–2) 105–22

CHARLES-EDWARDS, T.M. 'The date of the Four Branches of the Mabi-nogi', *Transactions of the Honourable Society of Cymmrodorion* (1970) 263–98

CHESNUTT, M. 'An unsolved problem in Old-Norse Icelandic literary his-tory', *Mediaeval Scandinavia* 1 (1968) 122–34

CHIBNALL, Marjorie (ed. & transl.) *The Ecclesiastical History of Orderic Vitalis* (6 vols, Oxford 1969–80)

CHRISTIE, R.C. (ed.) *Annales Cestrienses* (London 1887)

CLARK, Cecily (ed.) *The Peterborough Chronicle, 1070–1154* (2nd edn, Oxford 1970)

CLARKE, H. (ed.) *Medieval Dublin the Making of a Metropolis* (Blackrock 1990)

CLOVER, C.J. & LINDOW, J. (edd.) *Old Norse-Icelandic Literature: A critical guide* (Ithaca & London 1985)

C[OKAYNE], G.E. (ed.) *Complete Peerage of England, Scotland, Ireland, Great Britain, and United Kingdom, extent, extinct, or dormant* (new edn, 12 vols, London 1910–59)

COLGRAVE, B. 'Bede's miracle stories', in *Bede*, ed. Thompson, pp. 237–66

COX, D.C. 'County government in the early middle ages', in *The Victoria History of the Counties of England: A History of Shropshire*, III, ed. G.C. Baugh (Oxford 1979), pp. 1–32

CRAIGIE, W.A. 'Gaelic words and names in the Icelandic sagas', *Zeitschrift für celtische Philologie* 1 (1896/7) 439–54

CRAWFORD, Barbara E. (ed.) *St Magnus Cathedral and Orkney's Twelfth-century Renaissance* (Aberdeen 1988)

CRONNE, H.A. 'Ranulf de Gernons', *Transactions of the Royal Historical Society*, 4th series, 20 (1937) 103–34

CROUCH, D. 'The slow death of kingship in Glamorgan, 1067–1158', *Morgannwg* 29 (1985) 20–41

CROUCH, D. 'Urban: first bishop of Llandaff, 1107–34', *Journal of Welsh Ecclesiastical History* 6 (1989) 1–15

CUBBON, A.M. & DOLLEY, M. 'The 1972 Kirk Michael viking treasure trove', *Journal of the Manx Museum* 8 (1980) 5–20

CURTIS, E. 'The Fitz Rerys, Welsh lords of Cloghran, Co. Dublin', *County Louth Archaeological Journal* 5 (1921) 13–16

CURTIS, E. 'Muirchertach O'Brien, high king of Ireland, and his Norman son-in-law, Arnulf de Montgomery, *circa* 1100', *Journal of the Royal Society of Antiquaries of Ireland*, 6th series, 11 (1921) 116–24

DARLINGTON, R.R., *et al.* (edd. & transl.) *The Chronicle of John of Worcester* (3 vols, Oxford 1995–)

DAVIES, James Conway *Episcopal Acts and Cognate Documents relating to Welsh Dioceses, 1066–1272* (2 vols, Cardiff 1948)

DAVIES, J. Conway (ed.) *The Welsh Assize Roll 1277–1284* (Cardiff 1940)

DAVIES, R.R. *Conquest, Coexistence and Change: Wales 1063–1415* (Oxford 1987)

DAVIES, R.R. 'Henry I and Wales', in *Studies*, ed. Mayr-Harting & Moore, pp. 133–47

DAVIES, R.R. 'Kings, lords and liberties in the March of Wales, 1066–1272', *Transactions of the Royal Historical Society*, 5th series, 29 (1979) 41–61

DAVIES, R.R. (ed.) *The British Isles 1100–1500: Comparisons, Contrasts and Connections* (Edinburgh 1988)

DAVIES, W. (ed. & transl.) 'Braint Teilo', *Bulletin of the Board of Celtic Studies* 26 (1974–6) 123–37

DAVIES, W. 'Land and power in early medieval Wales', *Past and Present* 81 (1978) 3–23

DAVIES, Wendy *Patterns of Power in Early Wales* (Oxford 1990)

DAVIES, Wendy *Wales in the Early Middle Ages* (Leicester 1982)

DOBBS, M. (ed. & transl.) 'The Ban-Shenchus', *Révue celtique* 47 (1930) 283–339; 48 (1931) 163–234; 49 (1932) 437–89

DOBBS, M. (ed. & transl.) 'The History of the Descendants of Ir', *Revue celtique* 13 (1921) 308–59 *and* 14 (1923) 44–144

DOUGLAS, D.C. 'Rollo of Normandy', *English Historical Review* 57 (1942) 417–36

DUBY, G. 'The culture of the knightly class, audience and patronage', in *Renaissance*, edd. Benson & Constable, pp. 248–62

DUFFY, Seán 'Ireland and the Irish Sea Region, 1014–1318' (unpublished Ph.D. dissertation, Trinity College, Dublin 1993)

DUFFY, S. 'Irishmen and Islesmen in the kingdoms of Dublin and Man, 1052–1171', *Ériu* 43 (1992) 93–133

DUMVILLE, D.N. 'Some aspects of annalistic writing at Canterbury in the eleventh and early twelfth centuries', *Peritia: Journal of the Medieval Academy of Ireland* 2 (1983) 23–57

DUMVILLE, D.N. 'The *œðeling*. A study in Anglo-Saxon constitutional history', *Anglo-Saxon England* 8 (1979) 1–33

EARLE, John & PLUMMER, C. (edd.) *Two of the Saxon Chronicles Parallel with Supplementary Extracts from the others* (2 vols, Oxford 1892/9; rev. imp. by D. Whitelock, 1952)

EDWARDS, J. Goronwy *Calendar of Ancient Correspondence concerning Wales* (Cardiff 1935)

EDWARDS, J.G. 'The Normans and the Welsh March', *Proceedings of the British Academy 42 (1956) 15577*

EINARSSON, Bjarni (ed.) *Ágrip af Nóregskonunga sogum. Fagrskinna – Nóregs konunga tal* (Reykjavík 1984)

ELLIS, Henry (ed.) *Registrum uulgariter nuncupatum 'The Record of Caernarvon'* (London 1838)

ELLIS, T.P. 'Legal references, terms and conceptions in the "Mabinogion" ', *Y Cymmrodor* 39 (1928) 86–148

ELLIS, T.P. *Welsh Tribal Law and Custom in the Middle Ages* (2 vols, Oxford 1926)

EMANUEL, H.D. (ed.) *The Latin Texts of the Welsh Laws* (Cardiff 1967)

EVANS, A.O. 'Nicholas Robinson (1530?–1585)', *Y Cymmrodor* 39 (1928) 149–99

EVANS, D. Simon (ed. & transl.) *A Mediaeval Prince of Wales. The Life of Gruffudd ap Cynan* (Felinfach 1990)

EVANS, D. Simon (ed.) *Historia Gruffud vab Kenan* (Cardiff 1977)

EVANS, J.G. 'Castellmarch', *Archaeologia Cambrensis*, 6th series, 17 (1917) 303–7

Bibliography

EVANS, J.G. & RHYS, J. (edd.) *The Text of the Book of Llan Dâv reproduced from the Gwysaney Manuscript* (Oxford 1893; rev. imp. Aberystwyth 1979)

[FARLEY, Abraham (ed.)] *Domesday Book; seu Liber Censualis Willelmi Primi Regis Anglia* (2 vols, London 1783)

FARRER, William *An Outline Itinerary of King Henry the First* (Oxford 1919)

FAULKES, A. 'Descent from the gods', *Mediaeval Scandinavia* 11 (1978/9) 92–125

FAULKES, Anthony (ed.) *Snorri Sturluson: Edda. Háttatal* (Oxford 1991)

FAULKES, A. & PERKINS, R. (edd.) *Viking Revaluations* (London 1993)

FENTON, A. & PÁLSSON, H. (edd.) *The Northern and Western Isles in the Viking World: Survival, Continuity and Change* (Edinburgh 1984)

FIDJESTØL, B. 'Arnórr Þórðarson: skald of the Orkney jarls', in *The Northern and Western Isles*, edd. Fenton & Pálsson, pp. 239–57

FIDJESTØL, Bjarne *Det norrøne fyrstediktet* (Øvre Ervik 1982)

FIDJESTØL, B. *et al.* (edd.) *Festskrift til Ludvig Holm-Olsen þa hans 70-årsdag den 9. juni 1984* (Øvre Ervik 1984)

FIDJESTØL, B. 'On a new edition of scaldic poetry', in *The Sixth International Saga Conference*, pp. 319–35

FIDJESTØL, B. 'Sogekvæde', in *Deutsch-nordische Begegnungen*, edd. Braunmüller & Brøndsted, pp. 57–76

FIDJESTØL, Bjarne, *et al.* (edd.) *Tekstkritisk teori og praksis. Nordisk symposium i tekstkritikk, Godøysund 19. – 22. mai 1987* (Oslo 1988)

FITZGERALD, B.A. 'The Contacts between Britain and Ireland in the Century preceding the Anglo-Norman Invasion of Ireland' (unpublished M.A. thesis, University of Keele 1966)

FOOTE, P. 'Things in early Norse verse', in *Festskrift til Ludvig Holm-Olsen*, edd. Fidjestøl *et al.*, pp. 74–83

FOOTE, P. 'Wrecks and rhymes', in *The Vikings*, edd. Andersson & Sandred, pp. 57–66

FORD, P.K. 'Llywarch, ancestor of Welsh princes', *Speculum* 45 (1970) 442–50

FRENCH, A. (transl.) 'Meilyr's elegy for Gruffudd ap Cynan', *Études celtiques* 16 (1979) 263–81

GARMONSWAY, G.N. (transl.) *The Anglo-Saxon Chronicle* (3rd edn, London 1972)

GRUFFYDD, R.G. (ed. & transl.) 'A poem in praise of Cuhelyn Fardd from the Black Book of Carmarthen', *Studia Celtica* 10/11 (1975/6) 198–209

GRUFFYDD, R.G. 'Meilyr Awenydd', *Barn* 213 (1980) 313–16

GUÐMUNDSSON, Finnbogi (ed.) *Orkneyinga Saga, Legenda de Sancto Magno, Magnúss Saga Skemmri, Magnúss Saga Lengri, Helga Páttr ok êlfs* (Reykjavík 1965)

HADDAN, A.W. & STUBBS, W. (edd.) *Councils and Ecclesiastical Documents relating to Great Britain and Ireland* (3 vols, Oxford 1869–78)

HAMILTON, N.E.S.A. (ed.) *Willelmi Malmesbiriensis De Gestis Pontificum Anglorum Libri Quinque* (London 1870)

HAMP, E.P. 'Cerenydd', *Bulletin of the Board of Celtic Studies* 24 (1970–2) 683

HARDY, T.D. (ed.) *Rotuli Chartarum in Turri Londonensi asservati, 1199–1216* (London 1837)

HARDY, T.D. (ed.) *Rotuli Litterarum Clausarum in Turri Londonensi asservati* (2 vols, London 1833/4)

HEER, Friedrich *The Medieval Mind* (London 1963)

HELGASON, Jón 'Planer on en ny udgave af skjaldedigtningen', *Acta Philologica Scandinavica* 19 (1950) 130–2

HELGASON, Jón (ed.) *Skjaldevers* (København 1968)

HELGASON, Jón & HOLTSMARK, A. (edd.) *Háttalykill enn forni* (København 1941)

HENNESSY, William M. (ed. & transl.) *The Annals of Loch Cé: a Chronicle of Irish Affairs from A.D. 1014 to A.D. 1590* (2 vols, London 1871)

HOGG, A.H.A. & KING, D.J.C. 'Castles in Wales and the Marches: additions and corrections to lists published in 1963 and 1967', *Archaeologia Cambrensis* 119 (1970) 119–24

HOGG, A.H.A. & KING, D.J.C. 'Early castles in Wales and the Marches: a preliminary list', *Archaeologia Cambrensis* 112 (1963) 77–124

HOWLETT, R. (ed.) *Chronicles of the Reigns of Stephen, Henry II and Richard I* (4 vols, London 1884–9)

HUDSON, B.T. 'The destruction of Gruffudd ap Llywelyn', *Welsh History Review* 15 (1990/1) 331–50

HUGHES, Garfield H. (ed.) *Rhagymadroddion, 1547–1659* (Cardiff 1951)

HUGHES, K. 'The Welsh Latin chronicles', *Proceedings of the British Academy* 59 (1973) 233–58

HUWS, D. 'Llawysgrif Hendregadredd', *National Library of Wales Journal* 22 (1981/2) 1–23

HUWS, D. *Llyfrau Cymraeg 1250–1400* (Aberystwyth 1993)

JACKSON, Kenneth Hurlstone (transl.) *The Gododdin* (Edinburgh 1969)

JAMES, J.W. 'Fresh light on the death of Gruffudd ap Llywelyn', *Bulletin of the Board of Celtic Studies* 30 (1982/3) 147

JAMES, J.W. (ed. & transl.) *Rhigyfarch's Life of St David* (Cardiff 1967)

JAMES, M.R. (ed. & transl.) *Walter Map: De Nugis Curialium, Courtiers' Trifles* (2nd edn, by C.N.L. Brooke & R.A.B. Mynors, Oxford 1983)

JARMAN, A.O.H. (ed.) *Llyfr Du Caerfyrddin* (Cardiff 1982)

JENKINS, D. 'Kings, lords and princes: the nomenclature of authority in thirteenth-century Wales', *Bulletin of the Board of Celtic Studies* 26 (1974–6) 451–62

JENKINS, D. 'Pencerdd a Bardd Teulu', *Ysgrifau Beirniadol* 14 (1988) 19–46

JESCH, J.   'England and *Orkneyinga saga*', in *The Viking Age*, edd. Batey *et al.*, pp. 222–39

JESCH, J.   'History in the "political sagas" ', *Medium Aevum* vol. 62, no. 2 (1993) 210–20

JESCH, J.   'Skaldic verse and viking semantics', in *Viking Revaluations*, edd. Faulkes & Perkins, pp. 160–71

JOHNSON, Charles & CRONNE, H.A. (edd.)   *Regesta Regum Anglo-Normannorum*, II, *1100–1135* (Oxford 1956)

JOLLIFFE, J.E.A.   *Angevin Kingship* (London 1963)

JONES, Arthur (ed. & transl.)   *The History of Gruffydd ap Cynan* (Manchester 1910)

JONES, G.P.   'The Scandinavian settlement in Ystrad Tywi', *Y Cymmrodor* 35 (1925) 117–56

JONES, J. Gwynfor (ed.)   *The History of the Gwydir Family and Memoirs by John Wynn* (Llandysul 1990)

JONES, O., *et al.* (edd.)   *The Myvyrian Archaiology of Wales* (2nd edn, Denbigh 1870)

JONES, Thomas (ed. & transl.)   *Brenhinedd y Saesson, or The Kings of the Saxons: BM Cotton MS. Cleopatra B.v and The Black Book of Basingwerk, NLW MS. 7006* (Cardiff 1971)

JONES, Thomas (transl.)   *Brut y Tywysogion, or the Chronicle of the Princes: Peniarth MS 20 Version* (Cardiff 1952)

JONES, Thomas (ed. & transl.)   *Brut y Tywysogion, or the Chronicle of the Princes: Red Book of Hergest Version* (2nd edn, Cardiff 1973)

JONES, Thomas (ed.)   *Brut y Tywysogion, Peniarth MS 20* (Cardiff 1941)

JÓNSSON, Finnur (ed.)   *Den norsk-islandske skjaldedigtning* (4 vols, København 1912–15)

JÓNSSON, Finnur (ed.)   *Morkinskinna* (København 1932)

KARLSSON, Stefán   'Ættbogi Noregskonunga', in *Sjötíu ritgerðir helgaðar Jakobi Benediktssyni 20. júlí 1977*, edd. Pétursson & Kristjánsson, pp. 677–704

KARRAS, Ruth Mazo   *Slavery and Society in Medieval Scandinavia* (New Haven, CT 1988)

KEYNES, Simon & LAPIDGE, M. (transl.)   *Alfred the Great: Asser's Life of King Alfred and other Contemporary Sources* (Harmondsworth 1983)

KING, David J. Cathcart   *Castellarium Anglicanum: an Index and Bibliography of the Castles in England, Wales and the Islands* (2 vols, New York 1983)

KRAG, C.   'Norge som odel i Harald Hårfagres ætt', *Historisk tidsskrift* (Oslo) 68 (1989) 288–302 [with English summary]

KUHN, Hans   *Das Dróttkvætt* (Heidelberg 1983)

KUHN, Hans   *Kleine Schriften*, I (Berlin 1969)

LAPIDGE, M. (ed. & transl.)   'The Welsh-Latin poetry of Sulien's family', *Studia Celtica* 8/9 (1973/4) 68–106

LEE, Sidney (ed.)   *The Autobiography of Edward, Lord Herbert of Cherbury* (2nd edn, London 1906)

LEHMANN, Winfried P.   *The Development of Germanic Verse Form* (Austin, TX 1956)

LEMARIGNIER, J.-F.   *Recherches sur l'hommage en marche et les frontières féodales* (Paris 1945)

LEWIS, C.P.   'The formation of the honor of Chester, 1066–100', *Journal of the Chester Archaeological Society* 71 (1991) 37–68

LEYSER, K.   'England and the Empire in the early twelfth century', *Transactions of the Royal Historical Society*, 5th series 10 (1960) 61–83

LLOYD, John Edward   *A History of Wales from the Earliest Times to the Edwardian Conquest* (3rd edn, 2 vols, London 1939)

LLOYD, J[ohn] E[dward] *et al.* (edd.)   *The Dictionary of Welsh Biography down to 1940* (London 1959)

LLOYD, J.E.   'Wales and the coming of the Normans (1039–1093)', *Transactions of the Honourable Society of Cymmrodorion* (1899/1900) 122–79

LLOYD-JONES, J.   *Geirfa Barddoniaeth Gynnar Gymraeg* (2 vols, Cardiff 1950–63)

LLOYD-JONES, J.   'The court poets of the Welsh princes', *Proceedings of the British Academy* 34 (1948) 167–97

LLOYD-MORGAN, C.   'Rhai agweddau ar gyfieithu yng Nghymru yn yr oesoedd canol', *Ysgrifau Beirniadol* 13 (1985) 134–45

LOTH, Joseph   *La Métrique galloise de puis les plus anciens textes jusqu'à nos jours* (2 vols, Paris 1900–02)

LOUIS-JENSEN, Jonna   *Kongesagastudier* (København 1977) [with English summary]

LOYN, H.R.   'Wales and England in the tenth century: the context of the Athelstan charters', *Welsh History Review* 10 (1980/1) 283–301

LUARD, H.R. (ed.)   *Annales Monastici* (5 vols, London 1864–9)

LYDON, J.   'Lordship and crown: Llywelyn of Wales and O'Connor of Connacht', in *The British Isles*, ed. R.R. Davies, pp. 48–63

MAC AIRT, Seán (ed. & transl.)   *The Annals of Inisfallen (MS. Rawlinson B.503)* (Dublin 1951)

MAC AIRT, Seán & MAC NIOCAILL, G. (edd. & transl.)   *The Annals of Ulster (to A.D. 1131)*, I (Dublin 1983)

MAGNUSSON, Magnus & PÁLSSON, H. (transl.)   *Laxdæla Saga* (Harmondsworth 1969)

MARSTRANDER, C.   'Lochlann', *Ériu* 5 (1911) 250–1

MARTIN, F.X.   *No Hero in the House: Diarmaid mac Murchada and the Coming of the Normans to Ireland* (Dublin 1977)

MASON, J.F.A.   'Roger de Montgomery and his sons', *Transactions of the Royal Historical Society*, 5th series, 13 (1963) 1–28

MASON, Oliver   *Bartholemew Gazetteer of Britain* (Edinburgh 1977)

Bibliography

Bibliography

MAUND, K.L.   'Cynan ab Iago and the killing of Gruffudd ap Llywelyn', *Cambridge Medieval Celtic Studies* 10 (1985) 57–65

MAUND, K.L.   *Ireland, Wales, and England in the Eleventh Century* (Woodbridge 1991)

MAUND, K.L.   'Trahaearn ap Caradog: legitimate usurper?', *Welsh History Review* 13 (1986/7) 468–76

MAYR-HARTING, Henry & MOORE, R.I. (edd.)   *Studies in Medieval History presented to R.H.C. Davis* (London 1985)

MECHAIN, Tegid & MECHAIN, G. (edd.)   *Gwaith Lewis Glyn Cothi* (Oxford 1837–9)

MEYER, Kuno   *A Primer of Irish Metrics* (Dublin 1909)

MILLER, M.   'The foundation-legend of Gwynedd in the Latin texts', *Bulletin of the Board of Celtic Studies* 27 (1976–8) 515–32

MOODY, T.W., et al. (edd.)   *A New History of Ireland*, IX, *Maps, Genealogies, Lists* (Oxford 1984)

MORGAN, R.   'The territorial divisions of medieval Montgomeryshire', *Montgomery Collections* 70 (1982) 11–32

MORGAN, T.J.   'Dadansoddi'r gogynfeirdd', *Bulletin of the Board of Celtic Studies* 13 (1948–50) 169–74 *and* 15 (1950–2) 1–88

MORRIS, John (gen. ed.)   *Domesday Book* (35 vols in 40, Chichester 1975–86; 3 index vols, 1992)

MORRIS, John   *The Age of Arthur* (London 1973)

MORRIS-JONES, John & PARRY-WILLIAMS, T.H. (edd.)   *Llawysgrif Hendregadredd* (Cardiff 1933)

MUNCH, P.A. (ed.)   *The Chronicle of Man and the Sudreys* (Oslo 1860)

MURPHY, Gerard   *Early Irish Metrics* (Dublin 1961)

NELSON, J.L.   'Inauguration rituals', in *Early medieval Kingship*, edd. Sawyer & Wood, pp. 51–70

NORDAL, Sigurður (ed.)   *Egils Saga Skalla-Grímssonar* (Reykjavík 1933)

NORDAL, S.   'Om Orkneyingasaga', *Aarbøger for nordisk oldkyndighed og historie* 3 raekke, 3 (1913) 31–50

O'BRIEN, M.A. (ed.)   *Corpus Genealogiarum Hiberniae*, I (Dublin 1962; rev. imp., by J.V. Kelleher, 1976)

O'BRIEN, M.A.   'Old Irish personal names', *Celtica* 10 (1973) 216–36

Ó CORRÁIN, D.   '*Caithréim Cellacháin Chaisil*: history or propaganda?', *Ériu* 25 (1974) 1–69

Ó CORRÁIN, D.   'High-kings, vikings and other kings', *Irish Historical Studies* 21 (1977/8) 283–323

Ó CORRÁIN, D.   'Irish regnal succession: a re-appraisal', *Studia Hibernica* 11 (1971) 7–39

Ó CUÍV, B. (ed. & transl.)   'A poem in praise of Raghnall, king of Man', *Éigse* 8 (1955–7) 283–301

Ó CUÍV, B.   'Personal names as an indicator of relations between native Irish and settlers in the Viking period', in *Settlement*, ed. Bradley, pp. 79–88

Ó MAOLAGÁIN, P. 'Uí Chremthainn and Fir Fernmaighe', *County Louth Archaeological Journal* 11 (1945–8) 157–63

Ó RIAIN, Pádraig (ed.) *Corpus Genealogiarum Sanctorum Hiberniae* (Dublin 1985)

OWEN, H. & BLAKEWAY, J.B. *A History of Shrewsbury* (2 vols, London 1825)

PÁLSSON, Hermann & EDWARDS, P. (transl.) *Egil's Saga* (Harmondsworth 1976)

PÁLSSON, Hermann & EDWARDS, P. (transl.) *Orkneyinga Saga: The History of the Earls of Orkney* (Harmondsworth 1978)

PÁLSSON, Hermann & EDWARDS, P. (transl.) *The Book of Settlements: Landnámabók* (Winnipeg 1972)

PARRY, T. 'Statud Gruffudd ap Cynan', *Bulletin of the Board of Celtic Studies* 5 (1929–31) 25–33

PÉTURSSON, E.G. & KRISTJÁNSSON, J. (edd.) *Sjötíu Ritgerðir Helgaðar Jakobi Benediktssyni 20. Júlí 1977* (Reyjavík 1977)

PHILLIMORE, E.G.B. (ed.) 'Pedigrees from Jesus College MS. 20', *Y Cymmrodor* 8 (1887) 83–92

PHILLIMORE, E.[G.B.] (ed.) 'The *Annales Cambriæ* and Old-Welsh genealogies from *Harleian MS.* 3859', *Y Cymmrodor* 9 (1888) 141–83

PHILLIMORE, E.[G.B.] 'The publication of Welsh historical records', *Y Cymmrodor* 11 (1890/1) 133–75

PIERCE, T. Jones *Medieval Welsh Society* (Cardiff 1972)

POOLE, R.G. (ed. & transl.) *Viking Poems on War and Peace. A Study in Skaldic Narrative* (Toronto 1991)

POUNDS, N.J.G. *The Medieval Castle in England and Wales: a Social and Political History* (Cambridge 1990)

POWER, R. 'Magnus Barelegs' expeditions to the west', *Scottish Historical Review* 65 (1986) 107–32

PRYCE, H. 'Church and society in Wales, 1150–1250: an Irish perspective', in *The British Isles*, ed. R.R. Davies, pp. 27–47

PRYCE, H. 'The prologues to the Welsh lawbooks', *Bulletin of the Board of Celtic Studies* 33 (1986) 151–87

REES, Una (ed. & transl.) *The Cartulary of Haughmond Abbey* (Cardiff 1985)

RHYS, J. (ed.) *The Red Book of Hergest* (Oxford 1887)

RICHARDS, Melville (ed.) *Breudwyt Ronabwy* (Cardiff 1948)

RICHTER, M. 'The political and institutional background to national consciousness in medieval Wales', *Historical Studies* [Proceedings of the Irish Conference of Historians] 11 (1978) 37–55

ROBERTSON, J.C. (ed.) *Materials for the History of Thomas Becket* (7 vols, London 1875–85)

RODERICK, A.J. 'Marriage and politics in Wales, 1066–1282', *Welsh History Review* 4 (1968/9) 3–20

RODERICK, A.J. 'The feudal relationship between the English crown and the Welsh princes', *History*, new series, 37 (1952) 201–12

ROYAL COMMISSION ON ANCIENT AND HISTORICAL MONUMENTS IN WALES AND MONMOUTHSHIRE *An Inventory of the Ancient Monuments in Anglesey* (London 1937)

ROYAL COMMISSION ON ANCIENT AND HISTORICAL MONUMENTS IN WALES AND MONMOUTHSHIRE *An Inventory of the Ancient Monuments in Caernarvonshire* (3 vols, London 1956–64)

ROYAL COMMISSION ON ANCIENT AND HISTORICAL MONUMENTS IN WALES AND MONMOUTHSHIRE *An Inventory of the Ancient Monuments in Glamorgan*, iii (1A): *Medieval Secular Monuments: The Early Castles from the Norman Conquest to 1217* (London 1991)

RYAN, J. 'Pre-Norman Dublin', in *Medieval Dublin*, ed. Clarke, pp. 110–27 (reprinted from *Journal of the Royal Society of Antiquaries of Ireland* 79 [1949] 64–83)

RYMER, Thomas (ed.) *Foedera, Conventiones, Litterae etc.* (4 vols, London 1816–69)

SAWYER, P.H. 'Harald Fairhair and the British Isles', in *Les Vikings et leur civilisation*, ed. R. Boyer, pp. 105–9

SAWYER, P.H. & WOOD, I. (edd.) *Early medieval kingship* (Leeds 1977)

SEEBOHN, Frederic *The Tribal System in Wales* (2nd edn, London 1904)

SIMMS, Katharine *From Kings to Warlords: the changing political structure of Gaelic Ireland in the later middle ages* (Woodbridge 1987)

SMITH, J.B. 'Castell Gwyddgrug', *Bulletin of the Board of Celtic Studies* 26 (1974–6) 74–7

SMITH, J.B. 'Dynastic succession in medieval Wales', *Bulletin of the Board of Celtic Studies* 33 (1986) 199–232

SMITH, J. Beverley *Llywelyn ap Gruffudd, Tywysog Cymn* (Cardiff 1986)

SMITH, J.B. 'The "Cronica de Wallia" and the dynasty of Dinefwr', *Bulletin of the Board of Celtic Studies* 20 (1962–4) 261–82

SMITH, J.B. 'The lordship of Glamorgan', *Morgannwg* 2 (1958) 9–37

SMITH, J.B. 'The succession to Welsh princely inheritance: the evidence reconsidered', in *The British Isles*, ed. R.R. Davies, pp. 64–81

SMYTH, Alfred P. *Scandinavian Kings in the British Isles 850–880* (Oxford 1977)

SMYTH, Alfred P. *Scandinavian York and Dublin: the History and Archaeology of Two Related Viking Kingdoms* (2 vols, Dublin 1975/9)

SOUTHERN, R.W. (ed. & transl.) *The life of St. Anselm, Archbishop of Canterbury, by Eadmer* (Oxford 1972)

STACPOOLE, G.C. 'Gormflaith and the Northment of Dublin', *Dublin Historical Record* 20 (1964/5) 4–18

STEPHENSON, David *The Governance of Gwynedd* (Cardiff 1984)

STOKES, W. 'On the Gaelic names in the Landnamabok and runic inscriptions', *Revue celtique* 3 (1877) 186–91

STOKES, W. (ed. & transl.) 'The Annals of Tigernach', *Revue celtique* 16 (1895) 374–419; 17 (1896) 6–33, 119–263, 337–420; 18 (1897) 9–59, 150–97, 267–303

STORM, Gustav (ed.) *Monumenta Historica Norvegiæ. Latinske kildeskrifter til Norges historie i middelalderen* (Oslo 1880)

STUBBS, William (ed.) *The Historical Works of Gervase of Canterbury. The Chronicle of the Reigns of Stephen, Henry II and Richard I, by Gervase, the Monk of Canterbury* (2 vols, London 1879/80)

STUBBS, William (ed.) *Radulfi de Diceto Decani Lundoniensis Opera Historica: the Historical Works of Master Ralph de Diceto, Dean of London* (2 vols, London 1876)

STUBBS, W. (ed.) *Chronica Magistri Rogeri de Houedene* (4 vols, London 1867–71)

STUBBS, William (ed.) *Willelmi Malmesbiriensis Monachi De Gestis Regum Anglorum Libri Quinque* (2 vols, London 1887/9)

SVEINSSON, Einar Ól. (ed.) *Laxdæla Saga, Halldúrs Pættir Snorrasonar, Stúfs Páttr* (Reykjavík 1934)

SVEINSSON, Einar Ól. *Sagnaritun Oddaverja* (Reykjavík 1937) [with English summary]

SZARMACH, Paul E. & OGGINS, V.D. (edd.) *Sources of Anglo-Saxon Culture* (Kalamazoo MI 1986)

THOMAS, R.J. *Enwau Afonydd a Nentydd Cymru* (Cardiff 1938)

THOMPSON, A.H. (ed.) *Bede: His Life, Times and Writings* (Oxford 1935)

THORNTON, D.E. (ed.) 'A neglected genealogy of Llywelyn ap Gruffudd', *Cambridge Medieval Celtic Studies* 23 (1992) 9–23

THORNTON, David E. 'Power, Politics, and Status: Aspects of Genealogy in Mediaeval Ireland and Wales' (unpublished Ph.D. dissertation, University of Cambridge 1991)

THORPE, Benjamin (ed.) *Florentii Wigorniensis Monachi Chronicon ex Chronicis* (2 vols, London 1848/9)

THORPE, Lewis (transl.) *Gerald of Wales, The Journey through Wales, The Description of Wales* (Harmondsworth 1978)

TÓMASSON, Sverrir *Formálar íslenskra sagnaritara á miðöldum* (Reykjavík 1988) [with English summary]

TRILLMICH, Werner & BUCHNER, R. (edd. & transl.) *Quellen des 9. bis 11. Jahrhunderts zur Geschichte der Hamburgischen Kirche und des Reiches* (Darmstadt 1978)

TURVILLE-PETRE, E.O.G. *Haraldr the Hard-Ruler and his Poets* (London 1968)

TURVILLE-PETRE, E.O.G. *Origins of Icelandic Literature* (Oxford 1953)

TURVILLE-PETRE, J. 'The genealogist and history: Ari to Snorri', *Saga-Book of the Viking Society* 20 (1978/9) 7–23

U.S. NAVAL OCEANOGRAPHIC OFFICE *Oceanographic Atlas of the North Atlantic Ocean, Section 1, Tides and Currents* (NSTL Station 1965)

VAN HAMEL, A.G. 'Norse history in the *Hanes Gruffudd ap Cynan*', *Revue celtique* 42 (1925) 336–44

VON SEE, K. 'Skaldenstrophe und Sagaprosa', *Mediaeval Scandinavia* 10 (1977) 58–82

WADE-EVANS, A.W. (ed. & transl.) *Vitae Sanctorum Britanniae et Genealogiae* (Cardiff 1944)

WAINWRIGHT, F.T. 'Ingimund's invasion', *English Historical Review* 63 (1948) 145–69

WHALEY, Diana *Heimskringla. An Introduction* (London 1991)

WHALEY, D. 'Nicknames and narratives in the sagas', *Arkiv för nordisk filologi* 108 (1993) 122–46

WHALEY, D. 'The kings' sagas', in *Viking Revaluations*, edd. Anthony Faulkes & R. Perkins (London 1993), pp. 43–64

WHITELOCK, Dorothy, *et al.* (transl.) *The Anglo-Saxon Chronicle: a Revised Translation* (London 1961; rev. imp., 1965)

WILIAM, A.I.Rh. (ed.) *Llyfr Iorwerth* (Cardiff 1960)

WILIAM, D.W. 'Dafydd Benfras a'i ddisgynyddion', *Anglesey Antiquarian Society and Field Club Transactions* (1980) 33–5

WILLIAMS, Ifor & BROMWICH, R. (edd. & transl.) *Armes Prydein; the prophecy of Britain, from the Book of Tuliesin* (Dublin 1972)

WILLIAMS, Ifor (ed.) *Canu Aneirin* (Cardiff 1938)

WILLIAMS, Ifor (ed.) *Canu Llywarch Hen* (Cardiff 1935)

WILLIAMS, Ifor (ed.) *Canu Taliesin* (Cardiff 1960)

WILLIAMS, Ifor (ed.) *Pedeir Keinc y Mabinogi* (Cardiff 1930)

WILLIAMS, Ifor & WILLIAMS, J.E.C. (edd. & transl.) *The Poems of Taliesin* (Dublin 1968)

WILLIAMS, J.E.C. 'Arant: Ffriw', *Bulletin of the Board of Celtic Studies* 24 (1970–2) 44–5

WILLIAMS (ab Ithel), John (ed.) *Annales Cambriæ* (London 1860)

WILLIAMS, Glanmor *Bywyd ac Amserau'r Esgob Richard Davies* (Cardiff 1953)

WILLIAMS, R. (ed.) 'Life of Griffith ap Cynan', *Archaeologia Cambrensis*, 3rd series, 12 (1866) 30–45 *and* 112–31

WILLIAMS, S.J. & POWELL, J.E. (edd.) *Cyfreithian Hywel Dda yn ôl Llyfr Blegywryd* (2nd edn, Cardiff 1961)

WOOD, C.T. *The French Apparages and the Capetian Monarchy 1224–1378* (Cambridge, MA 1966)

WORMALD, P. 'Celtic and AngloSaxon kingship: some further thoughts', in *Sources of Anglo-Saxon Culture*, edd. P. Szarmach & V.D. Oggins (Kalamazoo, MI 1986), pp. 151–83

INDEX